Corporations and Sustainability

The South Asian Perspective

Corporations and Sustainability

THE SOUTH ASIAN PERSPECTIVE

EDITED BY P.D. JOSE

Routledge
Taylor & Francis Group
LONDON AND NEW YORK

First published 2016 by Greenleaf Publishing Limited

Published 2017 by Routledge
2 Park Square, Milton Park, Abingdon, Oxon OX14 4RN
711 Third Avenue, New York, NY 10017, USA

Routledge is an imprint of the Taylor & Francis Group, an informa business

Cover by LaliAbril.com.

British Library Cataloguing in Publication Data:
A catalogue record for this book is available from the British Library.

ISBN-13: 978-1-78353-084-7 [hbk]

Contents

Introduction: Corporations and sustainability in South Asia

P.D. Jose
IIM Bangalore, India

We have seen rapid and often dramatic changes in the institutional and economic contexts of firms operating in South Asian economies over the last few decades. The most significant drivers of this change have been the economic liberalization attempts of national governments in the region resulting in relatively easier and quicker flows of information, labour and capital between these economies and the rest of the world. In many South Asian economies, these policy reforms have focused on export-led growth, particularly in industries such as manufactured goods and outsourced services, in which these countries are perceived to have a comparative advantage.

The somewhat frenetic pace of industrialization without a supporting infrastructure has caused severe environmental degradation in many areas, making effective environmental management an issue of urgent national priority. Further, even where a comprehensive legislative framework exists, the quantum of national-level losses associated with poor environmental performance is staggering. In the Indian case alone, the environmental cost of degradation has been estimated to be as high as 10% of the country's GDP.

This has led to an intense debate on the issue of economic growth and industrial greening at national levels. While industrial sustainability is well understood in developed-country contexts, greening or sustainability may differ in terms of approaches as well as outcomes in emerging economies. Available evidence indicates that economic growth, driven by economic liberalization and rapid industrialization, may lead to adverse environmental impacts unless managed appropriately. As a result, global environmental and social concerns are increasingly driving governmental and corporate decision-making processes for firms operating in South Asia. Issues such as climate change, destruction of global commons, poverty alleviation and labour rights have become important inputs in the decision-making of firms active in South Asian markets.

In response to these challenges, firms have begun to re-evaluate and redesign their strategies, structures and processes as well as to incorporate sustainability principles into their corporate strategies. Despite these attempts, several barriers continue to hamper the sustainability initiatives of firms operating in emerging economies. These include prevailing market conditions, the absence of institutional incentives, the lack of appropriate infrastructural support, and poor access to cleaner technologies and financial resources for small and medium-sized enterprises. Globalization and climate change are affecting businesses across the continent but the pressures for profit challenge the broader goals of attaining economic growth in a sustainable way. South Asia is currently a particular case in point. With its rapidly growing economies, South Asia, and India in particular, is set to influence the health and prospects of the global economy in the next few decades. But with this promise comes great responsibility and challenges. The projected rapid growth is also likely to be accompanied by increasing pressures on the environment and society. Unless carefully managed, the South Asian growth story could also turn out to be a sustainability problem that will significantly impact the quality of that growth. This book brings together research and insights from leading scholars on how key industries in the region are currently performing in terms of delivering on these important goals.

In Chapter 1, "Changing the climate in Indian Aviation", Karamanos *et al.* discuss India's commitment to addressing climate change while safeguarding the aviation industry's potential to grow. With a growing aviation market that already represents around 1.5% of India's GDP, India is expected to become the world's third-largest aviation market by 2020. Against this development, Karamanos *et al.* introduce the climate change mitigation initiatives already undertaken by the Indian government and aviation institutions, before examining the latest developments regarding aviation carbon footprints on a global scale. Having estimated the carbon footprint of various emission sources in the years 2011–13, the authors predict the long-term evolution of CO_2 emissions and argue that, as part of a proactive approach to reducing/monitoring Indian aviation emissions, existing carbon emission control policies need to be consistently implemented and new initiatives introduced where necessary.

Chapter 2, "Implementing environmental management accounting (EMA): A case study from India" by Debnath, presents findings from a study conducted in an Indian manufacturing unit's implementation of material flow cost accounting (MFCA). The author points out that such practical and contextual aspects of EMA implementation have so far remained limited, supporting the view that contributions from the developing world towards newer EMA methodologies are largely peripheral and prescriptive. However, in order to highlight the knowledge contributions made by developing countries, this chapter analyses the implications of cost accounting practices that are currently being followed in India and whether new-age EMA tools can be implemented in the Indian context, given the systemic and contextual challenges that might prove impediments to its successful adoption.

Chapter 3, "Corporate sustainability initiatives reporting: A study of India's most valuable companies", analyses the sustainability initiatives of India's most valuable companies. With significant variance in reporting across the multiple variables related to sustainability, Jose and Saraf investigate what types of information are currently made publicly available across different industry sectors and highlight areas for improvement. The highest reported variables were related to corporate governance, followed by those related to CSR initiatives and measures to improve operational efficiency. Information on sustainability issues related to the supply chain is, however, less commonly disclosed. By presenting the striking sectoral differences, the study sheds light on some interesting trends in what information is made publicly available by the country's top 100 companies.

Chapter 4, "Voluntary green ratings in the construction industry: Exploring the underlying agendas", charts the progress of India's construction industry in fostering sustainable growth and adopting green standards. Due to the increasing demands created by India's exceptional economic growth, the projected carbon footprint of this industry is considerable. Such projections have necessitated an urgent need for adoption of environment assessment tools by the Indian construction industry. Shabari Shaily critically examines the motivations for large and small private-sector developments, as well as governmental institutions, to foster sustainable growth. With empirical evidence presented regarding strategic policy formulation for green building practices, this chapter illustrates the progress made by the construction industry but also highlights the challenges that remain.

The impacts of globalization and climate change in a South Asian context are examined in Chapter 5, "Coping with globalization and climate change: Lessons learned from pro-poor business in South Asia", with an emphasis on opportunities for and risks of doing pro-poor business under an integrated economic scenario. Domestic stakeholders initiate and support the proposed strategies to integrate economic activities, address poverty, and accelerate green growth, partly because of the non-climate benefits such as energy security, reduced local pollution levels and inclusive growth. Venkatachalam Anbumozhi explores the factors that have driven private companies to reinvent business strategies in order to do pro-poor business and adopt green corporate practices. Doing pro-poor green business will, Anbumozhi writes, give South Asian countries a competitive advantage among globally integrated economies. However, an affirmative public–private partnership (PPP) agenda is needed to transform value chain activities for the benefits of society.

Chapter 6, "The dyestuff industry in Gujarat", examines the initiatives undertaken within the Indian dyestuff industry—specifically focusing on the state of Gujarat, which accounts for nearly 80% of the country's dyestuff production—to manage long-term environmental damages and move towards more environmentally friendly processes. As increasing environmental concerns have exerted enormous pressure on the dyestuff industry to adopt greener measures, leading companies have felt the need to innovate and shift focus towards cleaner technologies and greener products. Pangotra and Shukla explore whether Common Effluent

Treatment Plans (CETPs) are indeed a viable solution for managing water pollution or if further problems arise for small-scale industries. The authors call for governmental regulatory enforcements so that the industry can continue to function and grow, while at the same time ensuring that the environment and local community remain unharmed.

Chapter 7, "An approach for assessing the multi-stakeholder perspective: A case study in steel plants", emphasizes the continuing importance of organization–stakeholder relationships in organizational studies. Rajesh Kumar Singh and A.K. Dikshit note a lack of clarity on the linkage between proactive sustainability management practices by the firms and their understanding of the needs and expectations of the stakeholders. The authors investigate various aspects of the importance of stakeholder relationships. With results from an empirical study conducted at a typical integrated steel plant in central-eastern India, the authors examine the views and perceptions of the stakeholders and the organization in the context of the sustainability performance of an organization. Suggestions are made as to how the organization–stakeholder relationships can be improved through developing stakeholder-specific strategies, strengthening communication and categorizing stakeholders.

As media and government attention in relation to environmental sustainability has predominantly focused on the realm of large businesses, the environmental impact of many small and medium-sized enterprises (SMEs), to whom large engineering corporations outsource their activities, have largely remained overlooked. Although a large body of research is available on green SMEs in developed economies, so far there have been fewer studies in the context of developing economics. A phenomenal 7.3 million manufacturing SMEs support the Indian engineering industry. In Chapter 8, "Greening engineering SMEs in India", Nulkar calls attention to the significant environmental burden that is passed to these smaller enterprises, which in turn pose huge challenges to regulatory bodies. The study discusses the findings from research on environmental performance of SMEs in India and offers recommendations for reducing their environmental impacts.

Considering operations of oil and gas companies, which have contributed immensely to India's growth, there is an increasing need for research into CSR initiatives in order to measure damages caused by these companies to the environment and other stakeholders. Chapter 9, "Rethinking CSR: The case of the oil and gas sector in India", highlights the implications of the recently revised section 135 of the Companies Act, pertaining to CSR, and stresses the need for CSR practices within the oil and gas sector. Using secondary data from seven major oil and gas companies in India, the authors identify the various social and environmental interventions undertaken by these firms and provide a framework for further researching the CSR impact of Indian oil and gas companies. Further suggestions are made to ensure the future success of the CSR activities and community development programmes undertaken by these companies.

One of the policy prescriptions advanced in international forums to address the issue of climate change is to implement mitigation strategies that prevent the adverse impacts of conventional fossil fuels. In Chapter 10, "Intellectual property and business enablers for transfer of Carbon Capture and Storage Technologies in South Asia", Damodaran presents the clear implications that such a move has for a coal-dependent country such as India, where 67% of the country's electricity production depends on coal-fired power plants. The chapter focuses on the Intellectual Property Rights (IPRs) related to Carbon Capture and Storage Technologies (CCS), an attractive solution in overcoming the CO_2 problems of coal. Damodaran argues that, despite policy concerns, sound technology transfer regimes can provide viable solutions to issues arising from IPRs. With enabling business models and global financing systems, CCS could be a commercial reality and useful way forwards for India as a coal- and oil-dependent country.

While South Asia is widely expected to be the growth engine for the world economy in the coming decades, as highlighted by the chapters in this collection, the sustainability challenges facing countries in the region are also large. For one, there is a renewed focus in countries such as India to reap the benefits of a low-cost economy by initiatives such as "make-in-India". While this can give a boost to the Indian economy, if left unmanaged it can also turn India into the environmental sink of Asia. In the case of the services sector too, while country-level advantages are often highlighted, environmental and social impacts of the sector are often unexplored or understated. As stated in the following chapters, there is an urgent need to place South Asia on a sustainable growth trajectory. In turn, that calls for revisiting prevailing development paradigms, restructuring and/or strengthening current policy regimes and recasting existing business models.

1

Changing the Climate in Indian Aviation*

Panagiotis Karamanos
European Union–India Civil Aviation Cooperation Project, India

Lalit Gupta
Directorate General of Civil Aviation (DGCA), India

Indranil Chakraborty
Aircraft Engineering Directorate, DGCA, India

Michael O'Connor
Athens International Airport, Greece

Rohit Thakur
Aircraft Engineering Directorate, DGCA, India

India's growing aviation market handled 190 million passengers during fiscal year 2014/2015; aviation represents around 1.5% of India's GDP. India's aviation industry significantly contributes to the development of the country, but inevitably also leads to environmental challenges, especially regarding climate change. The country's aviation stakeholders have taken a number of important steps to address their contribution to climate change. In 2015 India submitted the Action Plan on Reducing Carbon Emissions from Civil

* This chapter was written within the framework of the European Union–India Civil Aviation Cooperation Project. The authors would like to express their thanks to Ms Francesca Renzi, Mr Richard Koppmair and Mr Tsitsiridis Rampampadas for their valuable support.

Aviation to the International Civil Aviation Organisation (ICAO). The Directorate General of Civil Aviation (DGCA) has issued a detailed Civil Aviation Requirement addressing emission issues and is delivering regular environmental training sessions, Indian airlines operate modern aircraft fleets, three airports are participating in the prestigious *Airport Carbon Accreditation*, while several initiatives are contributing to improved traffic management. A key element of Indian policy is the carbon footprint of aviation, as it provides the opportunity to understand the sources and magnitude of CO_2 emissions, identify areas for intervention, make comparisons, formulate emission reduction policies, and assess progress. Even though Indian aviation emissions are not as high as in other countries, as part of a proactive approach it is beneficial to ensure that the existing policies are consistently implemented and where necessary new initiatives are introduced. In this context, the development of annual carbon footprints, provision of information and delivery of workshops, international leadership, airport infrastructure and airline operational improvements, air navigation services upgrades, and identification of funding mechanisms, underscore India's commitment to address the challenge of aviation and climate change in a comprehensive and effective manner while safeguarding the industry's potential to grow.

1.1 Introduction

India represents a growing aviation market with more than 100 airports that during fiscal year 2014/2015 handled 190 million passengers and 1.6 million aircraft movements (Figures 1.1 and 1.2). The major scheduled passenger airlines operate more than 400 aircraft. Aviation represents around 1.5% of India's GDP and supports 9 million jobs, while the country ranks ninth in the global civil aviation market. It is expected that domestic and international passenger traffic will continue to grow at rates of 12% and 8% respectively and that India will become the third-largest aviation market in the world by 2020 (MOCA, 2012, 2011; AAI, 2013, 2012; CAPA India, 2012, 2011).

Figure 1.1 **Passenger evolution in India**

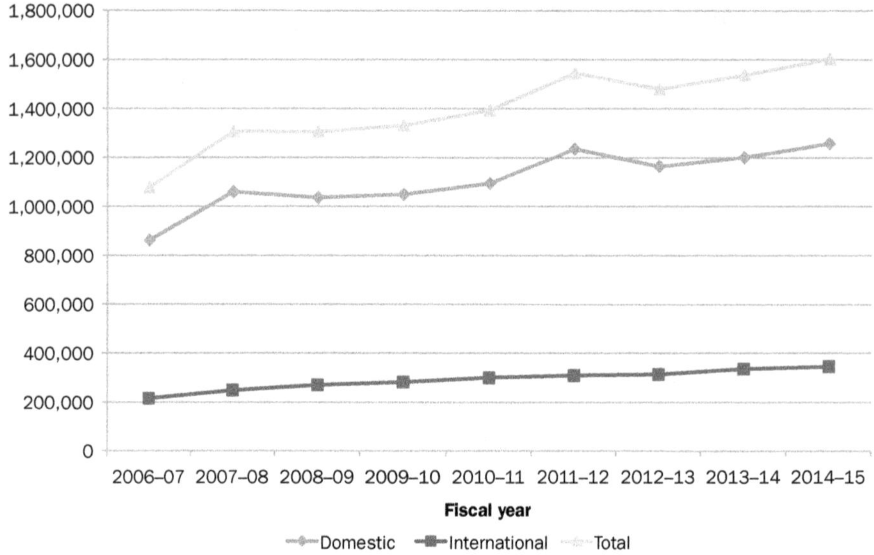

Figure 1.2 **Aircraft movements in India**

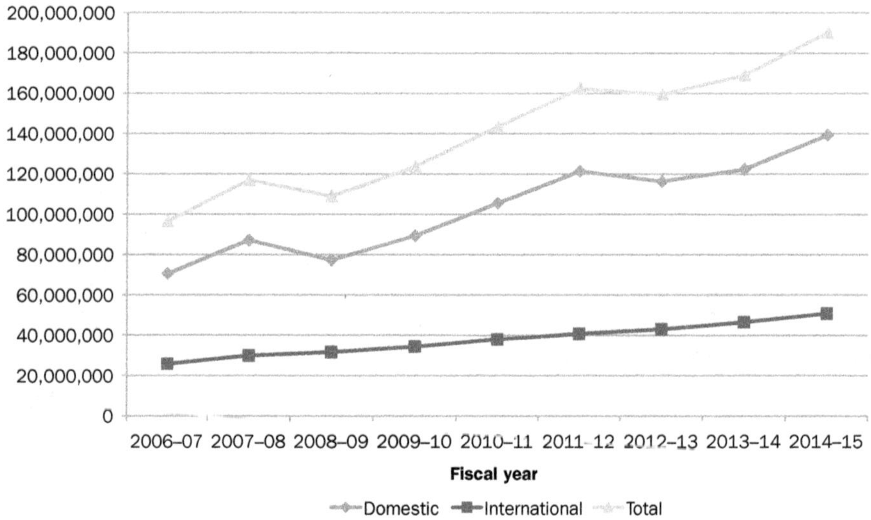

India's aviation industry significantly contributes to the development of the country, but inevitably also leads to environmental challenges, especially regarding climate change. In order to formulate an effective policy to address the challenge of climate change, an important requirement is to determine the sources and level of aviation's CO_2 emissions, identify trends and make predictions about future growth. This is especially important for fast-growing industries, such as Indian aviation.

At the same time, the country's aviation stakeholders have taken a number of important steps to address their contribution to climate change. In 2015 India submitted the Action Plan on Reducing Carbon Emissions from Civil Aviation to ICAO. The DGCA has issued a detailed Civil Aviation Requirement addressing emission issues and is delivering regular environmental training sessions, Indian airlines operate modern aircraft fleets, three airports are participating in the prestigious *Airport Carbon Accreditation*, while several initiatives are contributing to improved traffic management.

Section 2 introduces the climate change initiatives by the government, airlines, airports and other institutions. Section 3 examines the latest developments regarding global aviation carbon footprints, while Section 4 presents the methodology of this report. Section 5 presents the results of various carbon footprint calculations for Indian aviation. Section 6 discusses the results of the carbon footprint and examines a number of environmental policies for Indian aviation while Section 7 provides brief concluding comments.

1.2 Indian climate change initiatives

India has been active in addressing the climate change challenge. India ratified the Kyoto Protocol, has been involved in the international negotiations to develop a successor to this protocol, formulated a National Action Plan on Climate Change (2008), introduced eight National Missions (e.g. enhanced energy efficiency, strategic knowledge for climate change), established the Indian Network for Climate Change Assessment, formulated state climate change plans, and developed several Clean Development Mechanism projects.

Regarding aviation and climate change, in a breakthrough development in late 2013, the International Civil Aviation Organization (ICAO) agreed to develop by 2016 a global market-based system for international aviation emissions (to be implemented from 2020) and to establish a CO_2 emissions standard. As of early 2016, ICAO was pursuing the development of a carbon offsetting scheme as its market-based mechanism.

Until recently Indian airlines flying to European Union (EU) countries were to participate in the EU's Emissions Trading Scheme (ETS). India took a leadership role in opposing the EU ETS (e.g. organizing state meetings, refusing to provide data) with many other countries (e.g. US, Russia, China), but in the meantime supported the work of ICAO. The ICAO agreement signalled an end to the EU's initiative to include foreign airlines in their ETS. This was further corroborated by the EU's decision in 2014 to restrict the ETS only to intra-European flights.

Within this framework, a number of initiatives are also being implemented in the Indian aviation sector.

1.2.1 Government initiatives

In 2015 India submitted the Action Plan on Reducing Carbon Emissions from Civil Aviation to ICAO. The Action Plan includes details about the ongoing measures to reduce emissions as well as the expected initiatives. By mid-2015, the DGCA had issued four Circulars addressing the use of aircraft power supply, fuel efficiency, data reporting, etc. However, in August 2015 these Circulars were superseded by Civil Aviation Requirement (CAR) Series B, Part I on Climate Change Initiatives and Local Air Quality Monitoring in Civil Aviation. According to this important CAR, airlines and airports shall submit fuel and electricity consumption data on a regular basis, develop their own carbon footprint, develop technical and operational measures, report about progress of initiatives, etc. The DGCA also undertook the first-ever detailed carbon footprint of Indian aviation for 2011, as discussed later in this report. Furthermore, a number of training sessions and workshops on climate change have been delivered to industry representatives both in India and abroad.

1.2.2 Airline initiatives

Indian airlines play an important role regarding emissions reductions. They operate modern, fuel-efficient aircraft (e.g. Boeing 787 Dreamliner, Airbus 320/B737 NG with sharklets/winglets) resulting in significant fuel savings. At the same time, they have been changing the mode of operations to reduce their emissions as well. Table 1.1 presents some indicative airline initiatives.

Table 1.1 **Indicative emissions reduction initiatives by Indian airlines**

Air India	Use of Pratt & Whitney's EcoPower engine wash to clean the aircraft engine fuel path and the turbine blades to improve aerodynamic characteristics is expected to reduce fuel consumption on an average by 1.2% (ICAO, 2011, p. 87).
Blue Dart	Blue Dart uses single engine taxi procedures and has provided awareness sessions and training for planning and executing constant descent profiles.
IndiGo	IndiGo has opted for the installation of sharklets on new aircraft, which can increase fuel efficiency by 3–4%.
Jet Airways	Jet Airways has established a programme to continuously monitor and reduce the weight of various catering, cabin and galley items, which has contributed to fuel savings. It has also developed an Integrated Emissions Management System (IEMS) for monitoring and optimization of aviation fuel usage.
SpiceJet	Fuel management improvements regarding extra fuel carried on flights have led to an estimated 0.5% emissions reduction per flight. Additional benefits are realized through systematic implementation of single-engine taxi procedures during arrivals.

1.2.3 Airport initiatives

As of 2013, several Indian airports have obtained LEED certifications (Leadership in Energy and Environment Design), use energy-efficient systems, operate environmentally friendly vehicles, etc. Further, three Indian airports are participating in *Airport Carbon Accreditation* (Box 1.1).

Box 1.1 **Airport carbon accreditation in India**

airport carbon accreditation

MAPPING I REDUCTION I OPTIMISATION I NEUTRALITY

Airport Carbon Accreditation was developed and launched by Airports Council International (ACI)-Europe in 2009. As of late 2014, *Airport Carbon Accreditation* had expanded to all ACI regions, thus achieving global status. It is the only institutionally endorsed carbon management certification standard for airports. The programme consists of four different levels of accreditation:

1. **Mapping** Development and verification of a carbon footprint
2. **Reduction** Establishment of carbon management plan and emission reduction target
3. **Optimization** Engagement of third parties in emission reductions
4. **Neutrality** Offsetting of the airport operator's emissions*

As of early 2016 its membership includes 151 airports accounting for more than 31% of global passenger traffic, such as London, Paris, Montreal, Frankfurt, Sydney, Madrid, Seattle, Amsterdam, Rome, Abu Dhabi, Athens, Zurich, Hong Kong, Milan, Seoul (Incheon), Brussels and Manchester. Twenty airports have been accredited as carbon-neutral.

As of early 2016, **Bangalore, Mumbai** and **New Delhi** airports have been accredited at the *Optimization* level. These airports have established carbon footprints and have taken additional measures, such as adoption of green design principles and energy efficiency initiatives. The table below shows the number of airports at each level, indicating the significant achievement of the Indian airports that are participating at a high accreditation level.

Participation in airport carbon accreditation

	Mapping	Reduction	Optimization	Neutrality
Airports	45	58	28	20

* Scope 1 and 2 emissions

1.2.4 Air navigation services initiatives

India has launched the Future India Air Navigation System (FIANS) initiative, which is based on projects in the fields of communication, navigation and surveillance. Indicative projects include implementation of Performance Based Navigation (PBN), use of Automatic Dependent Surveillance-Broadcast (ADS-B), harmonization with international systems, human resources development and training, etc. A PBN roadmap has been developed and several projects have already been launched. For example, PBN implementation at some airports has already reduced flight distance (MOCA, 2012)

In 2011, the Indian Ocean Strategic Partnership to Reduce Emissions (INSPIRE) was launched. This project represents a partnership between the Airports Authority of India (AAI), Airservices Australia, Dubai Airports, airlines, and many other organizations, which are "dedicated to improve the efficiency and sustainability of aviation". Relevant initiatives include the development of operational procedures, technologies and best practices, establishment of performance indicators, development of systematic processes, and communication initiatives. A number of test flights have been conducted, while the project partners have established recommended procedures, practices and services that are environmentally beneficial (Inspire Green, 2013).

1.2.5 Biofuel initiatives

Biofuels have been identified as one of the major vehicles for reducing CO_2 emissions from aviation and other forms of transport. Biofuels have additional advantages, such as the possibility of local production from a number of different feedstocks (e.g. jatropha), as well as reduction of fuel price volatility and reliance on fossil fuels.

Starting with Virgin Atlantic in early 2008, more than 20 test flights have been flown to date. In 2011, seven different carriers performed commercial flights using up to 50% biofuel. While the safety and feasibility of this fuel type has been demonstrated, what remains is building up capacity and becoming cost competitive with aviation turbine fuel (ATF). For biofuels to become a viable alternative, they need to capture a minimum of 1% of the aviation fuel market (ATAG, 2011a). IATA has estimated that if by 2020 a 6% mix of biofuels is used, CO_2 emissions could be reduced by 5%. IATA has set a target of 10% blending by 2017.

In India, there have been some encouraging developments regarding biofuels and aviation based on cooperation between Indian companies, public institutions, and foreign entities (e.g. Indian Oil Corporation, Airbus, Indian Institute of Technology, Pratt & Whitney Canada, McGill University). These efforts have focused on design and research issues mainly regarding camelina and jatropha For example, the Hydroprocessing Lab of the Indian Institute of Petroleum has developed aviation jet fuel from jatropha for engine testing that meets international specifications, while a pilot plant is in operation that can produce 20 litres/day (Kondaiah, 2014; Sinha, 2014). Both Jet Airways and Air India have plans to use biofuel on a domestic demonstration flight.

However, significant challenges remain, such as lack of technology adoption and feedstock supplies, while in order to promote the use of biofuels in aviation an innovative and cooperative framework is required among all stakeholders (Ray, 2013).

In conclusion, India and its aviation industry have taken a number of important steps to address aviation's contribution to climate change.

1.3 Global aviation carbon footprints

In 2013, global passenger airline operations emitted approximately 705,000,000 tonnes of CO_2, representing around 2–3% of global anthropogenic CO_2 emissions (Figure 1.3). Within the industry, aircraft emissions represent approximately 95–98% of emissions, while the remaining 2–5% are related to airport activities (ATAG, 2014, p. 6; IPCC, 2007; ACI-Europe and WSP, 2011; Southgate, 2013, p. 46)

Figure 1.3 **Distribution of global CO_2 emissions**

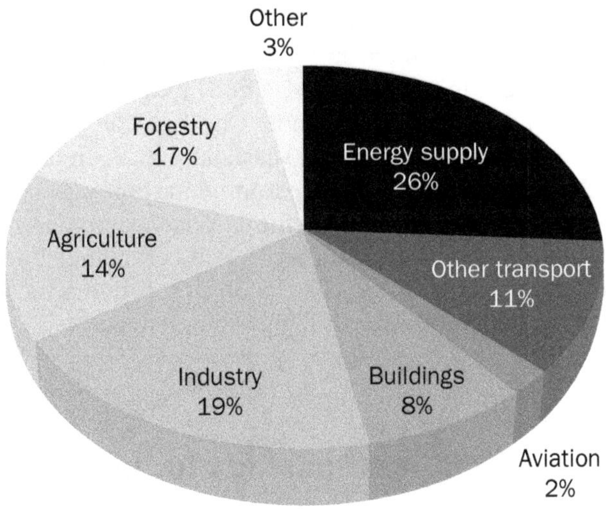

The most comprehensive information on emissions from domestic and international (i.e. bunker fuel emissions) scheduled passenger flights was published in 2013 by D. Southgate (2013), providing detailed data on a per country, airline, and airport basis. The methodology is based on analysis of datasets of aircraft operations, average fuel consumption, distance and emissions calculations, etc. According to Southgate (2013), global emissions from aviation bunker fuels in 2012 ranged between 360,000,000 and 470,000,000 tonnes of CO_2. Emissions from international flights in the Asia-Pacific region were responsible for 106,000,000 tonnes of CO_2.

Table 1.2 **2012 aviation CO_2 emissions of selected countries (thousand tonnes)**

Source: Southgate, 2013

	USA	China	UK	Germany	Australia	Brazil	Thailand	S. Korea	Indonesia
Domestic	96.956	36.806	1.487	1.796	7.044	9.796	1.464	1.247	5.637
International	47.871	13.899	24.654	18.729	9.489	5.929	8.207	8.305	3.064
Total	**144.827**	**50.705**	**26.141**	**20.525**	**16.533**	**15.725**	**9.671**	**9.552**	**8.701**

Table 1.2 shows the estimated 2012 domestic and international aviation CO_2 emissions of a number of countries. The USA is by far the main CO_2 emitter, followed by China (with a very significant domestic sector) and the UK (with a very significant international sector).

With respect to the situation in India, in 2013 emissions of Indian scheduled passenger airline operations to/from domestic destinations were estimated at 6,365,000 tonnes of CO_2. The CO_2 emissions related to bunker fuels from Indian and foreign airlines to international destinations from India reached 6,472,000 tonnes.

It is worth mentioning that a detailed carbon footprint of Indian aviation was developed for the first time for 2011 operations, and annually thereafter. The Director General of Civil Aviation of India and the Secretary General of ICAO presented the 2011 carbon footprint in 2012 in New Delhi. The carbon footprint, which was developed in cooperation with the EU-India Civil Aviation Cooperation Project, was widely distributed in the general and specialized aviation press and was presented at ICAO's Committee of Aviation Environmental Protection (CAEP/9) where it obtained significant recognition from the aviation community. According to Southgate (2013, p. 5) "there is a surprising lack of consolidated aviation carbon footprint reports at the country level...The notable exception is India and its leadership in aviation carbon footprinting is highly commended."

1.4 Carbon footprint methodology for India

1.4.1 Stakeholders

The development of the carbon footprint of the Indian aviation sector requires the contribution from various entities regarding policy developments, data collection, reviews, development of databases and other initiatives. The following stakeholders were mainly involved with these tasks (Figure 1.2):

Directorate General of Civil Aviation (DGCA): Nodal point for issuing the relevant circular, communicating requests to airlines and airports, collecting/presenting data, and undertaking analysis.

EU-India Civil Aviation Cooperation Project (ICCA): Provision of resources, advice, and analysis to produce the carbon footprint.

Airlines/airports: Submission of information and data regarding their operations.

Others: Provision of additional information regarding fuel consumption, emission levels, etc. by institutions such as the Ministry of Environment and Forests (MOEF), the Ministry of Petroleum and Natural Gas (MOPNG), and the International Energy Agency.

Figure 1.4 **Main stakeholders of the carbon footprint of Indian aviation**

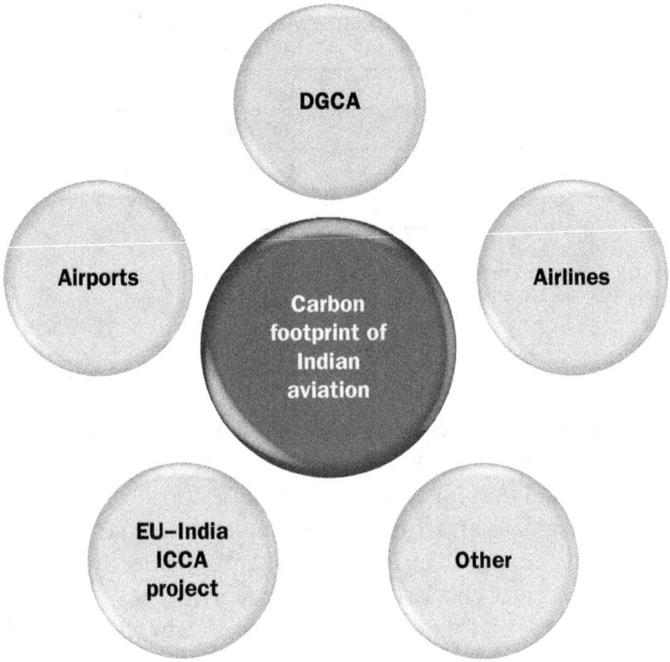

1.4.2 Data collection

The methodology for the development of the carbon footprint follows the Tier 1 approach of the Intergovernmental Panel on Climate Change (i.e. aggregate ATF quantities from airlines and other sources). Information from Indian airlines and airports is based on the form contained in the DGCA's Circular 2 of 2013 on *Climate Change Initiatives in Civil Aviation*. This form focuses on ATF from scheduled airlines as well as electricity and fuel consumption from operations (e.g. vehicles, generators) of large airports (i.e. airports with more that 50,000 annual aircraft movements). Information on ATF uplift of foreign airlines was based on MOPNG aggregate statistics.

In 2013, the Indian aviation industry consisted of six main scheduled passenger airlines, which were responsible for the transportation of more than 77,000,000 passengers and cargo. From March–June 2014, the six scheduled passenger airlines and the four joint venture airports submitted the above data (Table 1.3). Additional fuel data were collected from the MOPNG.

Table 1.3 **Main aviation data sources**

Scheduled passenger airlines	Joint venture airports
Air India Group*	Bangalore
GoAir	Delhi
IndiGo	Hyderabad
Jet Airways	Mumbai
JetLite	
SpiceJet	

* Includes Air India, Air India Express and Alliance Air.

1.4.3 Calculations and reliability

This section describes how CO_2 emissions were calculated for each emission source as well as the level of data reliability.

Aviation Turbine Fuel (ATF): For airlines, ATF is in most cases initially reported in the aircraft technical logs and then transferred to a corporate database. Various departments, such as Finance, Quality Control and Engineering undertake comparisons and quality control checks (e.g. through fuel invoices). On some occasions external verifiers or other institutions (e.g. IATA) certify that the methodology used for data collection is in accordance with international guidelines. Given that fuel has historically been one of the most significant cost and operational inputs for airlines, there is a reliable system of tracking consumption overtime. Therefore, reliability of ATF data is considered high.

The MOPNG (Petroleum Planning and Analysis Cell) provided ATF uplift information in India broken down into categories, such as foreign airlines, Indian airlines, and other consumption.[1] As this refers to aggregate statistics, there is some level of data uncertainty.

Electricity: The joint venture airports implement adequate data collection and verification processes, given the clear boundaries of operation and availability of electricity invoices. Electricity consumption data for the whole airport as well as consumption by the airport operating company only were collected. As a result, it was possible to estimate the aggregate electricity consumed by third parties (e.g. airlines, handlers, etc.) operating at the airport. The reliability of electricity data is considered high.

Other fuels: In the case of petrol, diesel, CNG and LPG, which are used for vehicles, generators, etc., the data sources are mainly related to invoices from refuelling stations. Where possible, quality control is undertaken (e.g. Finance Department through invoices). Potential sources of error may be related to mistakes in data entry, incorrect charging of fuel type, omissions, etc. In general, the joint venture

1 "Other" refers to general aviation, resellers, etc.

airports have a well-developed system for data collection and analysis, which in some cases is also verified by external institutions (e.g. Bureau Veritas).

Table 1.4 presents the various fuel types, the emission factors, and the relevant references. Where necessary, airports and airlines provided additional data and clarifications on data collection procedures, validity, calculations, etc. Furthermore, regarding quality control it was possible to compare the carbon footprint data and indicators of this study with data from different sources (e.g. MOPNG), alternative indicators (e.g. emissions per passenger), past carbon footprint data, as well as other studies that have addressed Indian emissions. All data have been entered in a database. Overall, the data collection and analysis process allows for a reliable analysis of the carbon footprint of Indian aviation.

Table 1.4 **Emissions factors information**

Fuel type	Emission factor	Reference
ATF	3.157 tonnes of CO_2/tonne	ICAO (2011), Guidance Material for the Development of State Action Plans, p. 19
Petrol	3.15 tonnes of CO_2/tonne	DEFRA (2013) GHG Conversion Factor Repository
Diesel	3.16 tonnes of CO_2/tonne	
CNG	2.70 tonnes of CO_2/tonne	
LPG	1.49 tonnes of CO_2/m^3	
Electricity NEWNE*	0.82 tonnes of CO_2/MWh	Ministry of Power (2014), Central Electricity Authority, CO_2 Baseline Database for the Indian Power Sector, Table S-1
Electricity South*	0.85 tonnes of CO_2/MWh	

* Two emission factors are available depending on the location of service provision (NEWNE: Integrated North Eastern Western and North-Western regional grids and South: Southern Grid).

1.5 Indian aviation carbon footprint for 2013

This section provides detailed information regarding the carbon footprint of Indian scheduled passenger airlines for 2013 and makes comparisons with earlier data.[2] Figure 1.5 delineates the breakdown of CO_2 emissions.

The emissions of Indian scheduled passenger airlines to/from domestic destinations for 2013 were 6,365,000 tonnes of CO_2, a 5.8% reduction compared to 2011, but somewhat higher than the 2012 emissions.

The emissions of Indian scheduled passenger airlines to/from international destinations for 2013 were 5,585,000 tonnes of CO_2, a 6.1% reduction compared to 2011, but somewhat higher than the 2012 emissions.

2 Numbers in this report are rounded.

In total, the carbon footprint of Indian scheduled passenger airlines to/from domestic and international destinations for 2013 was 11,950,000 tonnes of CO_2, a 5.9% reduction compared to 2011, but higher than the 2012 emissions.

The emissions of foreign scheduled airlines to international destinations from India for 2013 were 3,680,000 tonnes of CO_2, a 1.6% increase compared to 2011, but lower than the 2012 emissions.[3]

Consequently, the total emissions of Indian scheduled passenger airlines to/from domestic and international destinations as well as of foreign scheduled airlines to international destinations from India for 2013 reached 15,630,000 tonnes of CO_2, a 4.3% reduction compared to 2011, and at the same time somewhat higher than the 2012 emissions.

Figure 1.5 **Indian aviation CO_2 emissions**

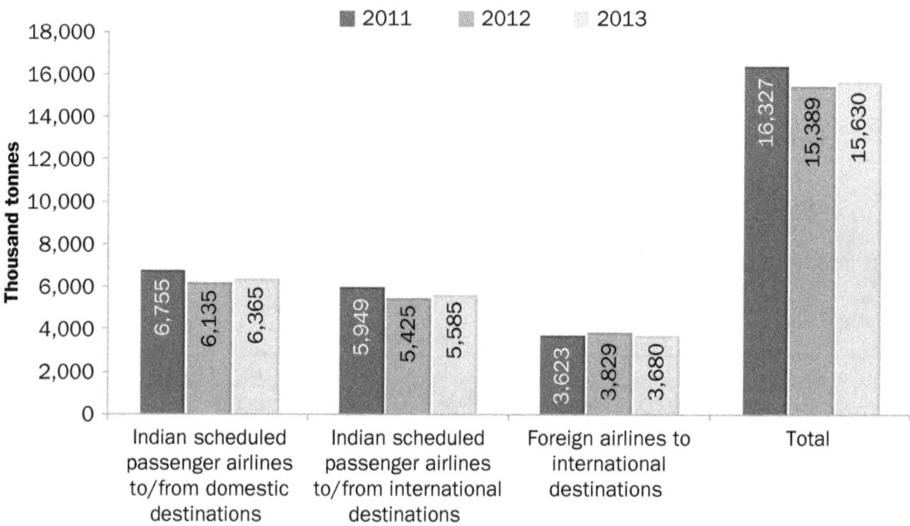

3 Based on ATF uplift data from India obtained from the MOPNG. Only emissions of foreign airlines "to" international destinations are included (and not "from") in order to be consistent with International Energy Agency guidance on international bunkers and to avoid double counting. Airlines that did not uplift fuel in India are also excluded due to lack of data. It should be expected that the emissions of foreign airlines "from" international destinations would be roughly at the same level as emissions "to" international destinations.

In accordance with international standards, international aviation bunkers (i.e. emissions from fuel use for international civil aviation) should be reported separately. Emissions of Indian scheduled passenger airlines as well as foreign scheduled airlines to international destinations from India for 2013 reached 6,472,000 tonnes of CO_2, a 1.9% reduction compared to 2011 (IPCC, 1996; ICAO, 2011). Figure 1.6 depicts the 2013 CO_2 emissions by destination and airline category.[4]

Figure 1.6 **2013 CO_2 emissions by destination and airline**

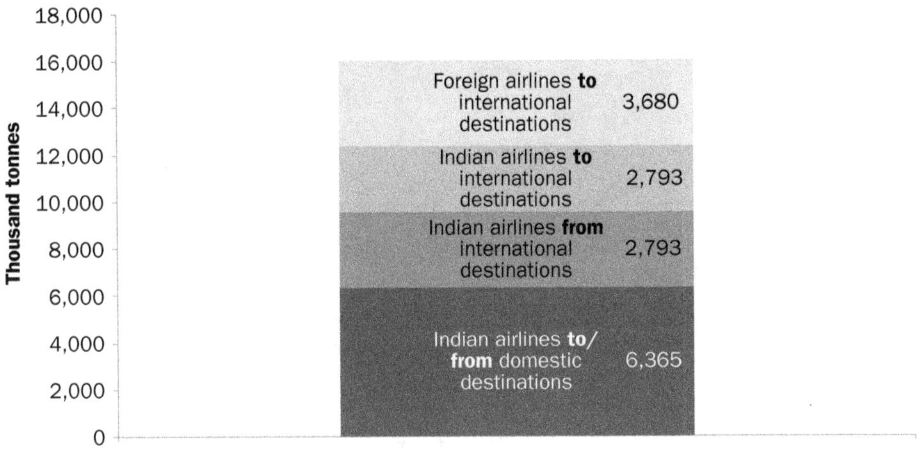

Figure 1.7 compares the 2011, 2012, and 2013 CO_2 emissions by destination and airline category on a percentage basis, suggesting that the contribution of each of the three categories remained relatively stable over the last three years.

4 For validation purposes, the emissions from international flights from India and for domestic flights were compared with the outcomes of the *Aviation Carbon Footprint—Global Scheduled International Passenger Flights* and *Global Scheduled Domestic Flights* studies for 2012. The estimates from these studies differ by 9.8% and 2.2% respectively compared to the emissions estimated in this chapter. Given the different methodologies used, this outcome provides further evidence about the validity of the results.

Figure 1.7 **2011–2013 CO_2 emissions by destination and airline**

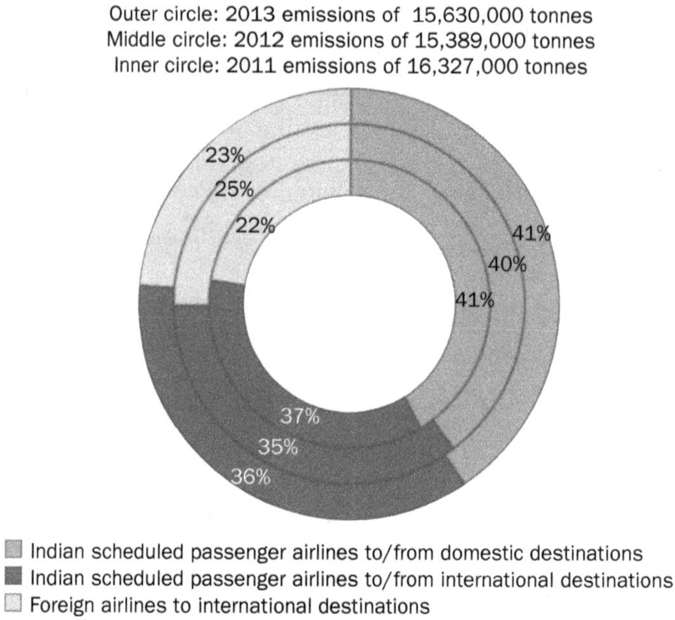

It is also important to predict the long-term evolution of CO_2 emissions. This task incorporates some inherent difficulties since predictions for the growing and changing Indian market are difficult to make. However, such a forecast can set the baseline for Indian aviation's future emissions in the absence of any reduction measures. The MOPNG (no date) predicts an annual growth rate of ATF fuel consumption of 9% (2014–2016) and 8% (2017–2020). For the period 2021–2050, this report uses a 7% growth rate.

Figure 1.8 suggests that the baseline emissions of Indian scheduled passenger airlines from domestic and international operations in 2020 are estimated at approximately 11,000,000 and 10,000,000 CO_2 tonnes respectively. Emissions of foreign scheduled airlines to international destinations emissions are estimated at 6,500,000 tonnes.

Figure 1.8 **Projected growth in CO_2 emissions**

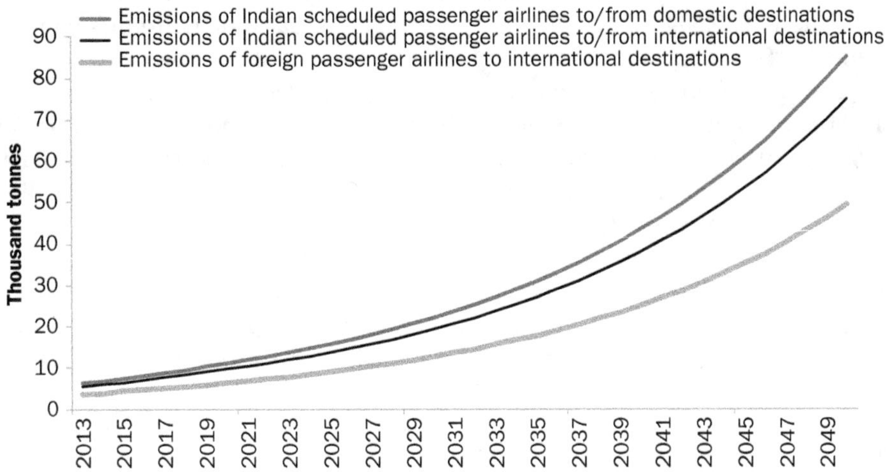

The internationally accepted efficiency indicator for carbon emissions is kg CO_2 per RTK. The average for Indian airlines in 2013 was estimated at 0.96 compared to 0.99 in 2012 and 1.06 in 2011. This is a significant improvement of 9.9% over a two-year period (Figure 1.9).[5] Although this number remains above the 2011 global average of 0.95, it shows a declining trend (Steele, 2012).[6]

Figure 1.9 **Indian scheduled passenger airlines efficiency indicator (CO_2 emissions/RTK)**

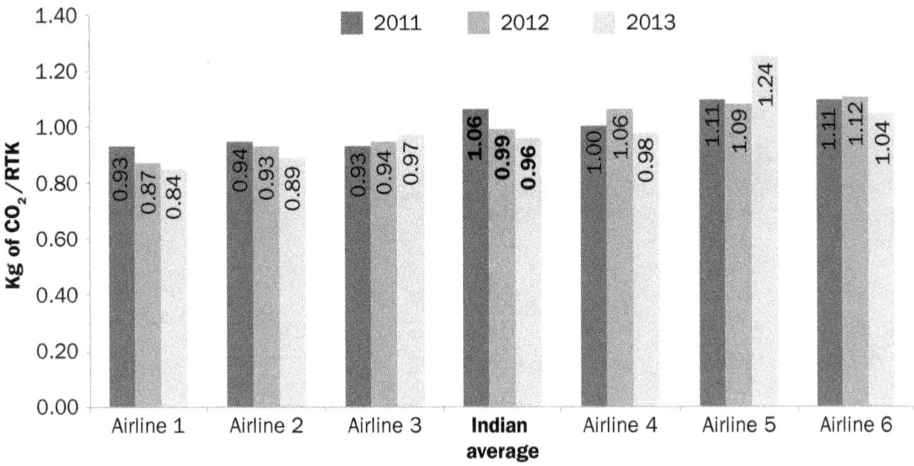

5 RTK = Distance × Payload where: Distance means the actual distance flown by the aircraft; Payload means the total mass of revenue-based freight, mail and passengers carried. Names of airlines and airports are not presented for confidentiality reasons.

6 Calculations based on the 2011 average global fuel consumption of 37.49 litres/100 RTK. The global CO_2/RTK for 2012 or 2013 is not yet available.

Approximately 95–98% of aviation's emissions are emitted from aircraft while the remaining originate from airport-related activities. Applying this assumption (i.e. 5%) to the 15,630,000 tonnes of CO_2, it is estimated that Indian airports emitted around 780,000 tonnes of CO_2. This number is consistent with data provided by four joint venture airports, which was then extrapolated for all Indian airports.

It should be noted that while several airports achieved significant reductions in energy consumption, their corresponding emissions increased in 2013 partially due to an increase in the electricity emission factors (kg CO_2 per kWh) by the Ministry of Power, consequently reducing the overall efficiency of the airports.

Figure 1.10 presents the CO_2 emissions (in kg per passenger) for the four joint venture airports. These emissions are related to sources that are owned or controlled by these airports as well to electricity consumption for their operations (excluding third parties). At two airports, emissions declined; at one airport remained stable; and at one they increased.

Figure 1.10 **Joint venture airport CO_2 emissions**

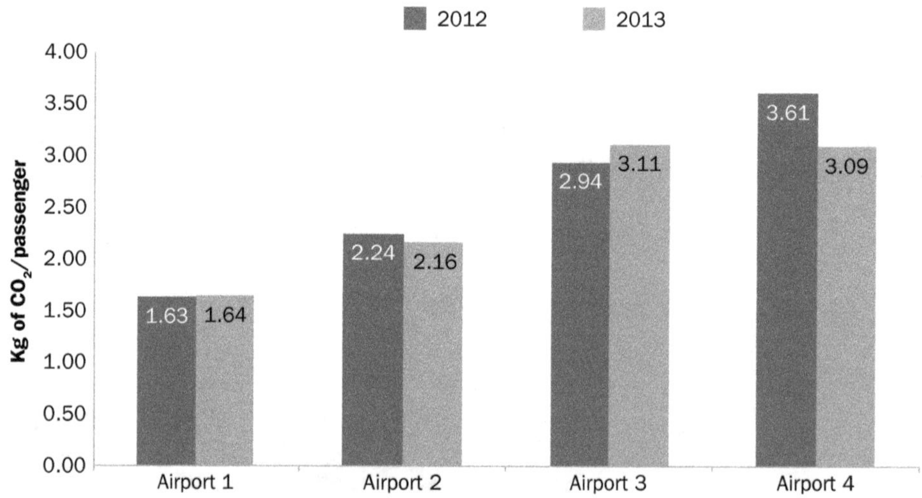

1.6 Discussion

One of the most important and encouraging observations from the carbon footprint analysis is that the average Indian airline efficiency indicator of kg of CO_2/RTK has been declining. However, this change is not uniform. Some airlines show a reduction while others an increase. The declining trend is attributed to a number of factors, such as the discontinuation of Kingfisher's operations (which was quite inefficient regarding emissions per RTK), as well as the improved efficiency of some

Indian airlines, due to higher load factors and use of newer more fuel-efficient aircraft (e.g. Air India's 787, SpiceJet's Q400). At the same time the efficiency level of airlines that fly public service obligations routes or for other reasons are obliged to operate with lower load factors, is expected to be lower. As some Indian airlines are still above the global average there is room for improved efficiency.

In general, the emissions of Indian airlines follow the aircraft movement trends. On the contrary, the emissions of foreign airlines to international destinations in 2013 declined despite the increase in aircraft movements compared to 2012. This outcome may be attributed to change of fleets (e.g. Lufthansa using the fuel-efficient 747-8), route changes, and efficiency improvements.

Overall, in 2013 global airline operations were responsible for the emission of 705,000,000 tonnes of CO_2, representing approximately 2–3% of global anthropogenic emissions. In comparison, emissions of Indian scheduled passenger airline operations to/from domestic/international destinations as well as of foreign airlines to international destinations (i.e. 15,630,000 tonnes of CO_2) represented less than 1% of India's anthropogenic emissions (ATAG, 2014, p. 6).

Regarding airports, although they make a small contribution to CO_2 emissions compared to aircraft operations, they represent a focal point for climate change interventions, such as aircraft taxi times and power provision. The changes in emissions at the four joint venture airports can be attributed to efficiency improvements and construction works, as well as passenger number fluctuations. Electricity consumption is the main source of airport emissions. Comparisons between airports are complex as differences are not only relevant to variations in efficiencies, but also to infrastructure characteristics (e.g. size/condition of buildings, area, number of runways, etc.).

Given the significant expected growth of Indian aviation, inevitably CO_2 emissions are likely to increase. In order to minimize the rate of increase, maximize the effectiveness of climate change policies, and sustain the growth of the industry, India is moving forward by adopting a number of important policies.

1.6.1 Development of annual carbon footprint

It is important to continue with the development of annual carbon footprints to establish trends, monitor progress, and identify areas of potential intervention. The annual update is especially important given the evolving nature of the Indian aviation industry (e.g. high growth, new entrants), which influences the level of emissions. The existing policies provide for the development of annual carbon footprints both at the national level as well as at the airport and airline levels.

1.6.2 Information and workshops

The carbon footprints could also be publicized both within the Indian aviation industry (e.g. airlines, airports, DGCA website), internationally (e.g. ICAO, IATA,

ACI), as well as with the general and specialized aviation press, in order to showcase the meaningful efforts of India regarding aviation and climate change. Furthermore, workshops for Indian airlines and airport operators will promote increased awareness concerning aviation's role in climate change, improve data collection procedures, identify areas for efficiency interventions and encourage collaboration amongst aviation's stakeholders.

1.6.3 Leadership in international climate change initiatives

In 2013, the 38th ICAO Assembly agreed on Resolution 17/2, "Consolidated statement of continuing ICAO policies and practices related to environmental protection—Climate change". ICAO shall develop global market-based measures for international aviation emissions to be approved at the next Assembly in 2016 and implemented from 2020. As of early 2016, deliberations on the exact nature of the concept are in progress.

Over the past few years, India has taken a leadership role in working through ICAO. It should continue to cooperate with its stakeholders, while ensuring that the specific conditions of India (e.g. growth of aviation market, level of development) are taken into consideration in order to meet both its developmental and environmental protection aspirations. Furthermore, India should pursue the initiatives described in the 2015 Action Plan.

1.6.4 Airport infrastructure improvements

Since airports represent a nodal point of aviation activities, such as airline flights, passenger/public access, and third-party operations (e.g. ground handling, catering, fuelling), they can and must play a central role in emission reductions as pressure concerning the climate change issue increases.

The main contributor to airport emissions is electricity consumption. Consequently, measures related to the improvement of energy efficiency, such as implementation of green building codes, use of energy-efficient cooling/heating and lighting systems, provision of fixed electric ground power for aircraft, and introduction of renewable energy projects (e.g. solar energy for terminal buildings), can lead to significant environmental benefits and cost savings. For example, Athens International Airport in Greece operates one of the largest photovoltaic installations at an airport in the world (8 MW). Additional measures are related to equipment/vehicle fleet modernization, improvement of public transport access, and awareness campaigns as well as participation in offsetting programmes.

Airports can also contribute to the reduction of aircraft emissions through more efficient use and planning of airport infrastructure. Close cooperation between airports, airlines and the public authorities is always necessary to achieve improvements in this field. For example, ACI has issued the *Guidance Manual: Airport Greenhouse Gas Emissions Management* that can be of use to Indian airports.

1.6.5 Airline operations improvements

For airlines, emphasis should be given to operational efficiency through improved flight planning, aircraft weight reduction, single-engine taxi procedures, minimal use of Auxiliary Power Units, etc. which can lead to emissions reductions and cost savings. Airlines have the additional opportunity to work with IATA's *Green Teams* to obtain advice from aviation experts as well as with airports. For example, Delhi International Airport has been working effectively with the AAI and airlines on collaborative decision-making. IATA suggests that with operational measures, CO_2 emissions reductions in the range of 3% are feasible by 2020 (IATA, 2009). Airlines can also participate in carbon offsetting initiatives, such as IATA's relevant programme and collaborate with other aviation stakeholders on promoting the adoption of biofuels.

1.6.6 Continuation of air navigation services efficiency improvements

Air Navigation Services (ANS) efficiency improvements represent an important opportunity for CO_2 emissions reduction, but also for increased capacity and improved safety. IATA suggests that air traffic management (ATM) improvements can lead to a 4% reduction in CO_2 emissions by 2020 (IATA, 2009). In Australia, new ATM procedures for the Sydney–Melbourne route are expected to reduce CO_2 emissions by 40,000 tonnes per year (Australian Government, 2009; Airservices, 2012). NavCanada initiatives in this field are expected to achieve reductions of more than eight million tonnes of greenhouse gases during the 2009–2016 period (ICAO, 2011, p. 79). India will continue to aggressively pursue ANS improvements, such as PBN and CDA development, the INSPIRE project, the GPS-aided Geo Augmented Navigation (GAGAN), etc. As part of its 12th five-year plan (2012–2017), AAI has allocated around 800 million US dollars for ANS-related projects (MOCA, 2011, p. 53).

1.6.7 Funding mechanisms for greenhouse reduction projects

Information about funding opportunities for projects to reduce greenhouse gas emissions or the impact of climate change is essential. Given the evolving nature of sources of funding, the aviation industry should review on a regular basis the availability of funding and pursue the relevant opportunities (ICAO, 2011, p. 204). Table 1.5 presents some indicative funding sources for aviation.

Table 1.5 **Indicative potential funding sources for aviation**

UN Framework Convention, Finance Portal:	www.unfccc.int/pls/apex/f?p=116:1:2970383912626217
World Bank:	www.worldbank.org/en/topic/climatefinance/projects
Global Environment Facility:	www.thegef.org/gef/
Heinrich Böll Foundation:	www.climatefundsupdate.org/
Other:	www.climateinvestmentfunds.org/cif/governance

1.7 Conclusions

India is committed to addressing the challenge of climate change in the aviation industry and has implemented a number of initiatives to this end, which have been recognized by the international community. Within this context, the development of annual carbon footprints, provision of information and delivery of workshops, international leadership, airport infrastructure and airline operational improvements, air navigation services upgrades, and identification of funding mechanisms, underscore India's commitment to address the challenge of aviation and climate change in a comprehensive and effective manner while safeguarding the industry's potential to grow.

Bibliography

AAI (Airports Authority of India). (2013). About AAI. Retrieved from www.aai.aero.

AAI (Airports Authority of India). (2012). Traffic summary. Retrieved from www.aai.aero/traffic_news/mar2k14annex1.pdf.

ACI-Europe and WSP. (2011). *Airport Carbon Accreditation Annual Report 2010–2011.* Brussels: ACI-Europe.

Airservices. (2012). New approach to air traffic management sees positive results. Retrieved from www.newsroom.airservicesaustralia.com/releases/new-approach-to-air-traffic-management-sees-positive-results.

ATAG (Air Transport Action Group) (2014). *Aviation Benefits Beyond Borders.* Geneva: ATAG.

ATAG (Air Transport Action Group) (2013). *Facts and Figures.* Geneva: ATAG.

ATAG (Air Transport Action Group) (2011a). *Beginners Guide to Aviation Biofuels* (2nd ed.). Geneva: ATAG.

ATAG (Air Transport Action Group) (2011b). *Powering the Future of Flight.* Geneva: ATAG.

Australian Government (2009). National Aviation Policy White Paper. Canberra: Australian Government.

CAPA (Centre for Asia Pacific Aviation) India (2012). *Aviation Outlook 2012/2013.* New Delhi: CAPA India.

CAPA (Centre for Asia Pacific Aviation) India (2011). *Managing Change in Civil Aviation in India.* New Delhi: CAPA India.

IATA (International Air Transport Association) (2009). *A Global Approach to Reducing Aviation Emissions.* Montreal: IATA.

ICAO (International Civil Aviation Organization). (2011). *Guidance Material for the Development of States' Action Plans.* Montreal: ICAO.

IPCC (Intergovernmental Panel on Climate Change) (2007). *Fourth Assessment Report.* Geneva: IPCC.

IPCC (Intergovernmental Panel on Climate Change) (1996). *Guidelines for National Greenhouse Gas Inventories: Understanding the Common Reporting Framework.* Geneva: IPCC.

Inspire Green (2013). *Work Program.* Retrieved from www.inspire-green.com.

Kondaiah, B. (2014). Drop in renewable fuels for aviation: Challenges and opportunities. Paper presented at the Australia–India Strategic Research Scheme Workshop on "Bio-Jet-Fuel, A Key to Future Green and Sustainable Aviation", India.

Lane J. (2012). Aviation biofuels: Which airlines are doing what with whom? Retrieved from www.biofuelsdigest.com.

MOCA (Ministry of Civil Aviation) (2012). *India: The Emerging Aviation Hub.* New Delhi: MOCA.

MOCA (Ministry of Civil Aviation) (2011). *Report of Working Group on Civil Aviation for Formulation of Twelfth Five Year Plan (2012–2017).* New Delhi: MOCA.

Oxford Economics. (2011). *Economic Benefits from Air Transport in India.* Oxford: Oxford Economics.

Petroleum Planning and Analysis Cell (no date). Demand Projection XII and XIII Plan. Retrieved from www.ppac.org.in/content/7_1_ForecastandAnalysis.aspx.

Ray, A. (2013). Bio-jet fuel: Recent advances. India Oil and Gas Review Summit, Mumbai.

Sharma, R. (2012, August 3). India seeks to conduct flight trials using biofuels. *Dow Jones Newswires.*

Southgate, D. (2013). Global scheduled international passenger flights: 2012. Retrieved from www.electricvehicleaustralia.com/2013/08/27/carbon-footprint-of-scheduled-domestic-passenger-flights-2012.

Sinha, A.K. (2014). Bio-jet fuel conversion process and standardization. Paper presented at the Australia–India

Steele, P. (2012). Air Transport Action Group, aviation and environment. Paper presented at the 68th IATA AGM Meeting, Beijing.

Strategic Research Scheme Workshop on "Bio-Jet-Fuel, A Key to Future Green and Sustainable Aviation", India.

Winrock International (2010). *Biofuels and the Aviation Industry.* 7th International Biofuels Conference, New Delhi.

2

Implementing environmental management accounting (EMA)

A case study from India

Somnath Debnath*

Birla Institute of Technology, India

Within methodological developments of environmental management accounting (EMA), waste accounting and material flow cost accounting (MFCA) have been experimented with in industrial organizations around the world. However, literature from developing countries has contributed prescriptive and empirical studies, but limited on-the-ground kind of experiments that can uncover practical and contextual aspects of implementing EMA in these countries. This chapter is based on the findings of a case study conducted in an Indian manufacturing unit to implement EMA. The study has used MFCA technique to analyse the flow of energy, materials, resources and also evolved cost of waste and emissions. The chapter also analyses the implications of cost accounting practices being followed in India and its suitability to support implementation of new age EMA tools, not to mention the discovery of systemic and contextual challenges that might prove impediments to its successful adoption.

* The author would like to thank Mr S.K. Pande, Factory Manager of the FPP, Mumbai (India), for giving his support to the study.

Within the last decade, environmental management accounting (EMA) has grown into an independent field of research. EMA supports organizations in generating information on environmental aspects through accounting artifacts that are redesigned to incorporate and support environmentally conscious decision-making. As conventional accounting constructs are yet to live up to the challenges of environmental and social accounting (Gray and Babbington, 2001), EMA has created its own space, thanks to the efforts of academia and industry practitioners from around the world (IFAC, 2005). These contributions have helped EMA to develop methods and techniques that could analyse environmental costs, improve decision-making processes, and help firms in sharing ecological responsibilities. EMA has developed UNDSD methodology (UNDSD, 2001) and material flow cost accounting (MFCA) as innovations of accounting-based constructs and embraced environmental life-cycle costing (E-LCC) as an improvised life-cycle technique (IFAC, 2005). Implementation experiences of these methodologies in different organizations in different countries have contributed towards better understanding of success factors and contextual barriers in adopting EMA.

Recent review on the methodological developments of EMA and associated case studies suggests that implementation of newer methodologies has mostly been contributed by and experimented with in developed countries like Australia, Austria, Germany, Japan, etc. (Debnath *et al.*, 2011). On the contrary, the review of literature on environmental accounting from the developing countries reveals contributions towards understanding the developments in disclosure practices of organizations (Huang and Kung, 2010; Lee, 2011; Lodhia, 2003; Singh and Joshi, 2009), country-specific environmental insights (Setthasakko, 2010; Xiaomei, 2004) and empirical studies on environmental practices of firms (Lee *et al.*, 2005; Scavone, 2005). However, very few studies have covered experimentations to advance EMA methodologies. This supports the view that the contributions from the developing world towards newer EMA methodologies are largely peripheral and prescriptive, which also contributes to the opinion that developing countries are environmental laggards in adopting environmentally conscious thinking as part of business activities (Pulver, 2007). This chapter is an attempt to fill the void in literature and contribute to the knowledge base of EMA with its contextual findings.

The chapter covers a field study conducted in a manufacturing unit of Mother Dairy Fruit & Vegetable Project Pvt. Ltd, India, and examines the feasibility of implementing EMA in Indian environment. Also, the prevailing cost accounting practices are examined to understand contextual challenges. The learning from these processes supported the contention that Indian policy-makers should initiate policy level changes to allow organizations to adopt and experiment with new environmental accounting methodologies. Accordingly, the remainder of the chapter has been arranged in the following manner: the next section provides a literature review on EMA methodologies and its implementation in firms. The third section discusses the contemporary state of research in environment management and management accounting practices in India. The fourth section covers the research process and case study. Thereafter, findings from the case study are presented, followed by analyses of contextual challenges. The final section summarizes the chapter and offers suggestions for future research.

2.1 Literature review

The literature review analyses accounting-based EMA methodologies and synthesizes experiential learning from case studies reported in the literature.

2.1.1 EMA methodologies

USEPA (1995) was the first agency to promulgate environmental cost accounting (ECA) and its deployment within firms to generate environmentally sensitive cost information. This was followed by waste accounting methodology, developed under the aegis of UNDSD (2001). The waste accounting methodology was the first accounting inspired methodology to use environmental cost drivers for identification and classification of environmentally sensitive accounting data from the ledgers. The method was simple to implement and successfully piloted around the world. The waste accounting method generated post-operative statement(s) to reflect environmentally sensitive incomes and expenditures of a firm. However, such (re)statements of expenditures remained within the traditional boundary of financial accounting and did not incorporate environmental contingencies (Jasch, 2003; Jasch, 2006). The reformed presentation is expected to support firms in understanding the expenditures incurred on waste and its treatment and prevention activities. Other than that it could generate information to integrate environmental perspectives as part of decision-making activities (Nikolaou, 2007; Schaltegger *et al.*, 2012).

Simultaneously, MFCA was developed by IMU (Institute für Management und Umwelt, Germany)—a technique to evaluate cost of waste based on process costing. While process costing in traditional format allocates cost of all the ingredients to the finished product and follows the economic principle to transfer costs between by-products, joint, or co-products, MFCA differs on the apportionment of costs by switching it on the basis of output quantities (including wastes), thereby treating waste akin to the joint products. This would result in waste value that is based on the costs of material and resource being turned away from the production value chain. Following the principle of mass-balance, MFCA developed an alternative interpretation of waste that could associate economic importance to it (Onishi *et al.*, 2009). Experiments conducted with MFCA within Japanese industries reported improved yields and process efficiencies that resulted in reduced levels of waste (Nakajima, 2011). This helped EMA to grow as a management technique to analyse internal processes of the organization and reduce environmental impacts by improving material yields and resource efficiencies (Nakajima, 2009). However, MFCA did not alter the cost structure or incorporate costs that are contingent and outside the boundaries of the firm. In that sense, the transactional boundary of MFCA remained firm within the economic realm of business.

Life-cycle costing (LCC) is another methodology that has been improvised by researchers in the last two decades. Though life-cycle methodologies are not new and have been in practice for some time, it remained confined (mostly) to the construction industry, due to the involvement of substantial public funds and longer life of assets (Korpi and Ala-Risku, 2008). LCC studies the feasibility of projects by including the end-of-life expenditures of the project. The life-cycle costs might include estimated abatement costs to handle environmental damages, while the end-of-life costs could include demolition, site restoration, and pollution costs, or taxes that might be levied in future. While it can be argued that this is not a traditional cost accounting methodology, but more of a decision-making approach (Steen, 2005), it brought environmental considerations and life-cycle thinking within the future costs as part of decision-making exercise (Geissdoerfer *et al.*, 2009), broadening the notion of transactional ownership within the accounting boundaries.

Full cost accounting (FCA) is another technique that can be used to record the full range of costs associated with the organizational activities (IFAC, 2005). FCA aims to incorporate *all* costs that transpire within and across an organization and could be traced to develop cost objects, and goes beyond what is recognized in books by following generally acceptable accounting standards (GAAP). In spite of some successful attempts by companies like Ontario Power Generation, BSO/Origin, and PowerGen, setting up such a framework has proved to be time-consuming, tedious and inconsistent due to the methodological challenges. Multiple methods to monetize environmental impacts would show variation in costs, by a factor of 1 to 12,000 per unit of product, even when less than 10% of flows are targeted (Antheaume, 2004). FCA can be considered as an ideological shift towards "inclusive accounting", yet to be developed into a practical accounting tool. Also, the study of FCA within the framework of EMA is still missing from the literature.

In addition to these methodologies, scholars have also devised other accounting and non-accounting-based methods that have been experimented and tested throughout the last decade (Gray and Laughlin, 2012). However, it has been difficult to find widespread diffusion of these methods other than the ones already covered (Debnath *et al.*, 2011), including the ones that are in incubation and would need further support to evolve, e.g. ABC methodology (Tsai *et al.*, 2010) and total cost approach (TCA)-based techniques. Still this supports the view that EMA offers a fertile ground for experimentation of methodological improvements to help organizations assess adverse impacts of their decisions.

2.1.2 Implementation experience of EMA methodologies

A number of case studies reported in the literature have covered the implementation experience of these methodologies and contribute to the understanding of the practical aspects of its adoption. Using the case study of Swedish pulp and paper company SCA Laakirchen, Jasch (2003) could detail the techniques of material flow balance and input–output analysis. In this study, by using suitable environmental cost drivers overhead analysis was tested to analyse costs associated with waste treatment activities. Stasiškienė and Juškaitė (2007) used UNDSD methodology to investigate waste generation processes in cardboard manufacturing units and demonstrated improvement in the flow of information by linking production information with the generation of waste, thereby supporting the adoption of clean manufacturing technology.

Viere *et al.* (2007) could use the case study of Neumann Gruppe Vietnam Ltd to demonstrate the efficiency of supply chain in coffee bean processing by implementing life-cycle accounting (LCA) with materials and energy flow analysis (MEFA). Similarly, a UNIDO-sponsored case study from Honduras offered insights of using TEST (transfer of proven practices of environmentally sound practices) and EMA as baseline techniques to calculate environmental costs and savings due to the cleaner technologies. The study proposed the use of guesstimate (rule of thumb) to compute environmental sensitive costs and supplement incomplete information, which might need substantial time to perfect (Jasch *et al.*, 2010). Similar experimentation of MFCA implementation is also reported within Japanese industries and is discussed next.

2.1.2.1 MFCA and learning from Japanese experience

MFCA was popularized in Japan by the combined efforts of the Ministry of Economy, Trade and Industry (METI) and the Ministry of Environment (MOE) (Kitada *et al.*, 2009). MFCA uses the principle of mass-balance and derives process waste by computing the difference between equivalent weights of output and input materials within a given process. The waste thus arrives, gets converted into monetary value on the same principle as that of the final product and generates stage-wise physical quantities of waste to form part of "waste value stream". Value of the waste is derived as the sum of all direct and indirect costs (including overheads or system costs) discarded from production stream within the permissible boundary of materials ownership and costs (IFAC, 2005).

MFCA modified the traditional outlook of waste by valuing it at par with the finished products and apportioning all costs that are traditionally borne by the finished products (Kokubu and Nashioka, 2005). Kokubu and Nakajima (2004) experimented with MFCA implementation in Tanabe Seiyaku Co by using a case study method and traced material flow quantities at operational levels, and wastes as negative products. The organization used MFCA as an extension of existing SAP R/3 ERP system and the cost data were simulated to generate quantified waste value from different processes. Nakajima (2009) revisited case studies on MFCA experiments that were carried out in four of the major Japanese organizations as pilot studies by METI in the previous decade. To offer insights that MFCA support was crucial to witness improvements in resource productivity and material yields.

Nakajima (2009) attributed the success to the visibility of losses within the material chain and valuation of wastes that this technique provides, which is not available in the traditional cost accounting methods.

Kitada *et al.* (2009) reviewed previous case studies of MFCA implementations in large Japanese organizations and contrasted the case findings from implementation of MFCA in SMEs. Similarly to the other studies, the authors felt that this method had helped in uncovering those aspects of wastes that were ignored earlier. In the case study of Nihon Denki Kagaku Co. Ltd, the company identified the process deficiencies and improvised the processes to generate lower waste and better quality levels. This study verified that SMEs are characterized by relatively weak negotiating position and fewer management resources, which can become constraints for successful implementations. Still, effective MFCA can help SMEs to improve resource productivities in shorter time-frame. Kokubu and Kitada (2010) reasoned that since MFCA helps management to look at operations in a way that is different to the traditional costing approach, management might need to adopt non-traditional thinking to gain its full advantage. Based on the adoption of MFCA in three organizations and the concepts from responsibility accounting, the authors illustrated different approaches within MFCA which might present conflicting situations to the decision-makers, if environmental decisions are directed compared against the economic benefits.

These case studies supported the ability of MFCA to improve organizational understanding of EMA and the role of environmental accounting practices in organizational decision-making. The studies also examined the practical utility and operational aspects of MFCA implementation, although mostly within the manufacturing industry. ISO (2010) standardized MFCA as ISO 14051 and introduced Quality Center (QC) as a unit of production, service or warehouse, within which material flows are to be studied. The new ISO standard can be considered a step closer to connect sustainability with quality and manufacturing functions (ibid.).

2.2 Prevailing cost accounting practices in India

In India, Companies Act 1956 acts as central legislation to cover all the regulatory aspects of private and public companies (from company formation to winding up). Companies Act and its subsequent amendments, as well as accounting standards issued by the Institute of Chartered Accountants of India (ICAI)—the apex body for defining accounting standards in India—do not mention any provisions for organizations to issue statements or prepare, maintain and report accounts on environmental performances. This is also the case with Security and Exchange Control Board of India (SEBI), the watchdog of market regulations in India, which does not have any norm/regulation for listed organizations to report environmental performance. Accordingly, Indian organizations are under no legal obligation to account and report environmental performance in any form, and environmental disclosures made by Indian companies, if any, are entirely voluntary in nature (Singh and Joshi, 2009).

From the perspective of cost accounting, section 209(1)(d) of the Companies act mandates the adoption and maintenance of cost accounting records by companies involved in production, processing, manufacturing and mining activities. Companies within these industry sectors are supposed to maintain records of utilization of materials, labour and other items of costs in specific formats and as prescribed by law. Section 233B of the same act empowers the Central Government to issue audit notifications to such class of companies (as per Companies Cost Audit Report Rules, 2011). To uphold the framework of cost accounting in Indian companies, the Indian Parliament passed the Cost and Works Accountants Act, 1959. This act has created "The Institute of Cost Accountants of India" as the apex body to promote cost and management accounting practice in the country. The Institute has issued generally accepted cost accounting practices (GACAP) and 14 other cost accounting standards for organizations to follow (CASBICWAI.org, 2011). GACAP promulgates the use of GAAP as the default method of accounting and inventory valuation (p. 21, ch. 7) (Cost Accounting Standards Board of ICWAI, 2011).

So far as the research of corporate environmental accounting practices in India is concerned, research studies have contributed to understanding the voluntary disclosure practices of Indian organizations (Malarvizhi and Yadav, 2008/2009; Singh and Joshi, 2009), comparison of environmental and financial performances (Singh, 2004), proactiveness of environmental strategies within Indian organizations (Sangle, 2010), etc. Some of the articles also studied the prevailing environmental laws and legal jurisprudence within the backdrop of current emphasis on industrial developments (Perez, 2002; Sidhu, 2011). The contrasting practice of voluntary environmental reporting and statutory nature of cost accounting practice limits the scope of Indian organizations to experiment with new ideas in cost accounting. Besides, the trend of research in EMA is nowhere close to that of the developed countries. This chapter is an attempt to cover this considerable gap with the hope of generating more of such contributions in future.

2.3 Research design

The research design is a map of research topology that helps researchers to navigate through the process, duly supported by scientific thinking and deliverance, and to meet the objectives of the study (Lee and Lings, 2008). The main objective of this chapter is to experiment with implementation of EMA in an Indian organization and answer the following research questions:

1. What are the challenges to successful adoption of MFCA in India?
2. What kind of experimentation would help EMA to expand its scope?
3. What are the future implications of the present case study?

2.3.1 Research method

The statutory nature of cost accounting practices in India does not allow the researchers to understand the overlap of MIS and accounting practices in organizations from a distance. Also, empiricism would not contribute to understanding the issues that challenge the feasibility of implementing new cost accounting methodology. As a result, study on the ground was necessitated. In management accounting, field research has its own place and importance. Young (1999) established that field research is playing important roles in contemporary research and more so in manufacturing. Additionally, case-based methods allow extended study of problem areas in real time, which is vital to understand the subject. In order to retain objectivity, findings from the case are abstracted in this chapter to build the logic that could be supported through the data collected. Also, the generalizability of the research is maintained by confining the study within the area of interest (Lee and Lings, 2008), i.e. to implement EMA using MFCA and uncover contextual challenges, instead of delving into the current accounting practices of the organization. The traceability and verifiability of data was maintained by cross-referencing it with the organizational records from the SAP R/3 ERP system.

2.3.2 Research boundary

The research boundary covers discussions on the project site, manufacturing environment and operational details.

2.3.2.1 The project site

The study was carried out in one of the manufacturing units (FPP hereinafter) of Mother Dairy Fruit & Vegetable Project Pvt. Ltd, located within the western suburbs of Mumbai, India. The organization is in the business of supply and marketing of farm and agriculture produce (motherdairy.com, 2011). FPP manufactures pulps and concentrates of tropical fruits and is a certified ISO 9001:2004 and HACCP (hazard analysis and critical control points) certified production unit. This study was a collaborative initiative to lay the foundations for future implementation of environmental management system (EMS). The first part of the study included an onsite study of six to eight days (between February and April 2011) to understand its operational structure. Questions related to seasonality of the industry, processes, data recording procedures of FPP, etc. were covered through semi-structured and unstructured interviews conducted with the departmental contacts. Subsequently, operational data was gathered throughout the year. Between May and July 2011, processing of mangoes (also called mango processing season) was carried out and the activities from this season have formed the basis of this chapter. Since the organization was not keen on sharing financial data, a mix of arbitrary and market rates have been used as financial proxies to translate physical data into financial equivalents.

2.3.2.2 The manufacturing environment

FPP specializes in manufacturing pulps and concentrates of tropical fruits, e.g. mango, guava, banana, papaya, pomegranate, etc. The pulps and concentrates are natural extracts of these fruits, hermitically packed and sealed in aseptic bags of standard pack sizes of 1 kg (in sample bags), 20 kg (in corrugated boxes), and 200–250 kg (in steel drums). The products are of standard specifications and sold in international and local markets. This fully automatic plant is manned by a permanent staff of around 40 employees. Based on the production schedules, contract workers are hired during the processing season to support production activities. During full load, the plant operated in two shifts of eight hours each followed by another half shift for cleaning.

2.3.2.3 Operational details

The study mapped the processes of FPP and collected data of stocks and flow of materials in following sequence:

1. Create block diagram to describe entire process flow (gate-to-gate),
2. Collect/collate stage-wise materials and resource usage, and
3. Derive environmental impacts at every stage based on the principle of mass-balance.

The outline of the complete manufacturing environment (gate-to-gate cycle) is detailed in the block diagram (Figure 2.1). Inputs to thc process boxes show stage-wise consumption of physical quantities of materials, water, and energy, while the discards are shown as outflows from the processing blocks to waste, which travels to the dump yard (materials) or ETP (waste-water). The arrows joining two boxes (processes) represent movement of outputs to the next process.

Figure 2.1 **Operational layout of the project site**

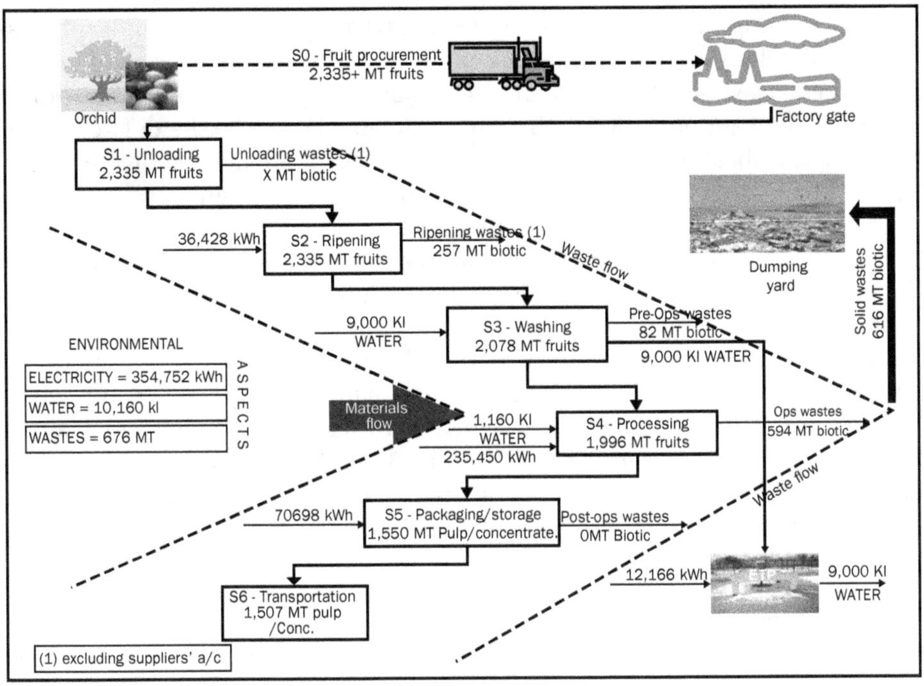

FPP manufactures fruit pulps and concentrates through the sequence of physical operations labelled in the block diagram as procurement (S0), unloading (S1), ripening (S2), washing and sorting/grading (S3), processing (S4), packing and warehousing (S5). The finished products are used by the industrial manufacturers (S6) as raw ingredients in a variety of food items, e.g. fruit drinks, ice creams, chocolates, flavours, etc. (motherdairy.com, 2011). Based on customer orders and dispatch schedules, finished goods are transported (S6) to customer.

2.4 Results

Due the similarity of MFCA to traditional cost accounting methodologies and its suitability to process industries, this chapter has used MFCA as the EMA technique to analyse the collected data. To evaluate material value chain, manufacturing processes (S2 to S5) are synthesized into four MFCA stages (Stage I to IV). By following stage-wise computation of outputs, the study was able to track the movements of materials, consumption of energy, water, other resources, and flow of waste. For the purpose of this study, waste generated during procurement (S0) and unloading

(S1) is considered as out-of-boundary, as the fruit procurement followed "receipt weight" policy. Fruits purchased on the basis of "receipt weight" transferred the ownership of wastes during transportation of raw fruit to the producers/suppliers account. Similarly, due to the time lag associated with the transportation (S6) of finished goods, waste on account of storage and transportation of finished products has been kept out of MFCA boundary (Table 2.1). Due to the differences in technical specifications (e.g. brix, pH, acidity, concentration, etc.), different categories of finished products from the same fruit (say, mango) are not comparable to one another. In order to achieve comparability, finished products are measured in equivalent quantities of raw fruits (equivalent tonnage or eMT). The output of the analysis is as per Table 2.1. For easy identification, the waste stream is displayed in bold type.

However, as emissions produced during the production activities cannot be derived using MFCA, as MFCA is incapable of handling waste outside of mass-balance, information on emission is generated by using independent greenhouse gas (GHG) accounting frameworks (WRI and WBCSD, 2004). Even though emission accounting is a subject of study in itself, the use of GHG accounting framework is limited in this study to cover the quantification of emissions from direct and indirect energy use and is computed in Table 2.2.

Table 2.1 **Material flow cost analysis of fruit pulp manufacturing**

Mango processing season (2-3 months)	Cum. qty.	Units[1]	Avg. rate (INR/unit)	Value (INR/ unit)
Stage I—Ripening (covering S2)				
Input (from procurement after unloading)	2335	MT	50,000	116,750,000
Electricity consumption for ripening	36,428	kWh	5	182,140
Total			50,078	116,932,140
Less: driage (moisture loss)	**257**	MT	50,078	**12,870,047**
Less: ripening waste	**82**	MT	50,078	**4,092,625**
Ready for production (to stage II)	1,996	MT	50,078	99,969,468
Waste at stage I (to stage IV)	**339**	MT		**16,962,672**
Stage II—Processing (covering S3–S4)				
Fruits issued to production	1,996	MT	50,578	99,955,698
Production costs:				
Electricity consumption for processing	235,450	kWh	4.1	965,345
Furnace oil (for boiler)	18.7	kl	43,000	804,100
Briquette consumption (for boiler)	145.57	MT	2,800	407,596

➜

1 Abbreviated units: eMT, equivalent metric tons of inputs (raw fruits); FG, finished goods; INR, Indian rupees; kl, kilolitre; kWh, kilowatt-hour; MT, metric ton.

Mango processing season (2-3 months)	Cum. qty.	Units[1]	Avg. rate (INR/unit)	Value (INR/ unit)
Water (for boiler)	1,160	kl	50	58,000
Consumption of auxiliary materials		INR/MT	350	698,749
Labour		INR/MT	200	399,285
Theoretical finished goods	1,996	eMT	51,748	103,302,460
Less: Production waste (to stage IV)	**594**	MT	51,748	**30,729,335**
Finished goods to packing (to Stage III)	1,403	eMT	51,748	72,573,125
Stage III–Packing (covering S5)				
Packing Costs	1,403	INR/eMT of FG	4,000	5,610,376
Support costs		INR/MT	300	420,778
Overall cost of production			56,047	78,603,634
Stage IV–Waste Treatment (covering S2–S5)				
a) Waste-water	9,000	kl	50	450,000
Electricity consumption (for ETP)	12,166	kWh	4.1	49,881
Cost of ETP treated water	**9,000**	kl	55.54	**499,881**
b) Transport charges for waste disposal	676	MT	3	2,028
Waste stream from Stage I and II	**933**	MT	51,141	**47,694,035**
Cum. waste stream value (a+b)	**933 + 9,000**	MT (solid) kl (water)		**48,193,916**
Fruit yield (%) (on weight basis)				60%
Cum. value of waste stream as % of total cost (in financial terms)				38%

Table 2.2 **Emissions due to energy consumption quantified as per GHG accounting framework**

Energy source (scope)	Fuel cons. (from MFCA study)	Eq. energy (in MJ)	Emission factors (based on fuel types)	Total emission ($eTCO_2$)
Electricity (scope 2)	354,742 kWh*	1, 277,071.2	0.98 ($eTCO_2$/MWh)**	347.647
Furnace oil (scope 1)	18.7 kl	744.34	77.649 ($eTCO_2$/TJ)***	57.797
Briquette (scope 1)	145.57 MT	551.27	1.87 ($eTCO_2$/TJ)***	1.031
Total for period		1,279,338.81		406.740

* Energy consumption includes 70,698 kWh towards production post care.

** Abbreviated units: $eTCO_2$, GHG in eq. tons of CO_2; MWh, 1,000 kWh. Selected emission factor is as per Central Electricity Authority (2011).

*** TJ, terajoule (10^{12} J). Selected emission factors are as per UNFCCC Project Reference # 1497 (Fresenius Kabi India Private Limited, 2009).

2.5 Discussions

In this chapter, the objectives of the study were to understand challenges for adoption of MFCA in India and search for specific ways to broaden the coverage of EMA. Also, the study aimed to find its future relevance. These points are discussed in this section.

2.5.1 MFCA and the waste flows

In comparison to traditional cost accounting methods, MFCA calculates the output stream on the basis of mass-balance, and apportions materials and system costs to the wastes (IFAC, 2005). Accordingly, waste streams are loaded with disposal and other directly allocable service costs. In this exercise (Table 2.1), the energy consumption of ETP is allocated to the waste-water stream. MFCA computation shows that during mango season (between May and June 2011), the plant was able to achieve 60% yield (ratio of output over input quantity) while the value of "waste stream" worked out to be around 38% of total costs (in financial terms). EMA brings out the layered nature of costs of waste that is comprised of: (a) the materials, (b) manufacturing and overheads, and (c) disposal costs. On the other hand, Table 2 reflects that 406 $eTCO_2$ was generated in this period due to energy use. The less tangible cost of emissions was arrived at by using voluntary market rates for emission credits in a voluntary market of USD 4.5/tCO_2e (INR 225 at exchange rate of INR 50 per USD) for Indian projects (Ecosystem Marketplace, 2011, p. 27), while preventive expenditures included the cost of disposal and running ETP. The information from Tables 2.1 and 2.2 can be combined to generate the waste profile that could theoretically improve the flow of information on waste (Table 2.3) and help the management with decision-making to lower it further. The incomparability of costs evidences that traditional accounting frameworks are yet to consider cost of waste holistically.

Table 2.3 **Waste profile as per EMA**

Costs (in INR)	Traditional accounting	As per EMA	Deviation
Material waste	16,950,000	46,600,000	(+) 175%
Non-performing operations	-	1,141,888	*Not comparable*
Preventive expenditures	452,028	452,028	-
R&D expenditure	-	-	-
Others	-	-	-
Less tangible costs (emissions)	-	91,516	*Not comparable*
Total	17,402,028	48,285,432	(+) 177%

2.5.2 Challenges to adoption of EMA

The application of MFCA generated the value of the waste stream that could offer information on stage-wide losses (in physical and monetary terms). This would help to develop a modified cost matrix of products. However, certain contextual challenges remained unaddressed in this process and are explored hereafter. First of all, organizations in India (within specific industry sectors) are supposed to maintain cost accounting records by following prevailing regulations of GACAP. As mentioned earlier, GACAP promulgates GAAP as the default base of cost accounting practices (p. 21, ch. 7) (Cost Accounting Standards Board of ICWAI, 2011a). GACAP supports transfer of costs of normal scrap, defectives, and rejects to the saleable finished units. Also, in the case of abnormal losses, material costs are to be treated as loss after giving credit to the realizable value, if any (principle 11 of the same GACAP, p. 24 and standard 5.4 of Cost Accounting Standards, CAS-6, p. 6) (Cost Accounting Standards Board of ICWAI, 2011b). As a result, even if waste is considered as a joint product (per MFCA), the associated costs cannot exceed its realizable value within the cost accounting records (principle 5 of Joint costs, p. 43 of GACAP). In essence, MFCA contradicts established valuation norms of products (costs and net realizable value, whichever is less) and limits its scope to that of a simulation tool.

The present case also raises an interesting issue that can be attributed to the type of industry selected for the study. Engineering industries normally look forward to 5Rs (reduce, reuse, recycle, remanufacturing, and reverse logistics) to reduce wastes and improve material productivity. A number of articles have used flow cost accounting and other methods in considering the effects of recycle or reuse of waste materials from manufacturing processes (Heubach *et al.*, 2002; Kakkuri-Knuuttila, *et al.*, 2008; Kasai, 1999). However, in fruit pulp manufacturing, fruit wastes, e.g. peel, waste pulp and stones, cannot be reused or consumed through any of the previous waste treatment policies. As a result, yield or material efficiency of processes could be normalized at a theoretical upper limit. This limitation would hold true for the entire food processing industry, where discards and wastes cannot be brought back within the production chain. Further, as part of the existing MIS, FPP management kept track of operational efficiencies (fruit yields). As a result, EMA was unable to deliver a substantial contribution other than to improve computational accuracy through valuation of waste. Additionally, the information generated by EMA is dependent on basic operational data and this makes it a reactive tool to support end-of-the-pipe analysis. The historical nature of information does not help the organizations to cover the issues of environmental impacts in totality (e.g. emissions that are not considered). For EMA to become an instrument of strategic importance, it needs to cover all types of environmental aspects within the organizational boundary, including emissions (Nakajima, 2011).

2.5.3 Generalizations and further scope

This chapter has used a Sankey diagram to map water, energy and materials flow using STAN2 software (downloaded from www.iwr.tuwien.ac.at/resources/downloads/stan.html, courtesy Institute for Water Quality, Resource and Waste Management, Vienna). These flows are designed in separate layers, so as to maintain mass balance (see appendix) within each layer. However, there are immediate challenges to accommodate emission flows in a Sankey diagram, due to the non-equivalency of GHG within mass balance. For EMA to become an effective tool that can help management in environmental sensitive decision-making, it needs to bridge emissions with waste flows. Considering the fact that global warming has become one of the critical areas of ecological restitution, EMA needs to expand its link and cover GHG accounting (Nakajima, 2011).

Within the standard accounting and environment management texts, financial liabilities associated with polluting the environment or adding GHG inventory beyond permissible limits is still being debated. As corporate accounting practices and current level of research on EMA are yet to embrace the financial obligations associated with environmental liabilities beyond organizational boundaries (Jasch, 2006), this study perceives accounting of GHG inventory (WBCSD and WRI, 2004) in physical units only, while market value is used only as a numéraire (Table 2.2). The coverage of GHG accounting within a single construct will strengthen EMA to emerge as the umbrella framework of environmental accounting and help organizations with ease of adoption (Table 2.3) and has been further explored in Debnath (2014).

As part of the future research, by accepting the upper limit of efficiency in any process and inevitability of waste generation, EMA can be advanced to understand the behaviour of non-linear flow of materials and energy, where supply chain or networked manufacturing scenarios can contribute towards designing waste-to-cradle flows. On the accounting front, EMA could be trialled with simultaneous use of other traditional costing methodologies like standard costing or activity-based costing (ABC) etc., and support methodological advancements in this field. MFCA and EMA have high specificity towards manufacturing industries. While MFCA has limitations in its applicability beyond industries that do not follow mass-balance, for EMA would have to evolve beyond manufacturing industries by developing methods and techniques that could be applied, it would need transition to a construct that is not based on internal control of waste but how externalities and its knowledge could be incorporated as part of organizational decision-making.

2.6 Conclusions

In this study, EMA was examined for implementation in an Indian organization. From methodological perspectives, no significant challenge was observed that could impede the adoption of MFCA in Indian organizations. However, the statutory nature of prevailing cost accounting practices in India is an environmental challenge for industries to adopt EMA or experiment with any other technique of cost accounting that has not been statutorily prescribed. Interestingly, adoption of MFCA in Japan was successful due to the support of governmental agencies (Nakajima, 2009). This supports the view that the policy-makers of India can develop policies and strategies to encourage experimentations by the Indian organizations and pave the way for its successful diffusion. Since MFCA helps management by analysing operations in a way that is different to that of the traditional approach, management might need to adopt non-traditional thinking to gain its full advantage. Moreover, it may present conflicting situations to the decision-makers where environmental decisions might have to be weighed against the economic benefits (Kokubu and Kitada, 2010).

Although the methodological developments within EMA are positioned to satisfy the information needs of management, it has not challenged the accounting practices to change significantly. As seen from the literature survey, EMA methodologies are yet to break free from the economic considerations and assimilate the hidden costs associated with waste streams that are being borne by the society (Jasch, 2006). The new methods picked up the expenses recorded by conventional accounting practices and moved these from one presentation layer to another, without challenging the prevailing economic nature of costs. Within the Indian context, it is interesting to note that GACAP defines pollution costs as all real and future remediation expenses that can be measured and linked to the act of pollution abetment. However, the provisions for future remediation costs or liabilities to compensate social obligation or future legislation is "best kept out of general purpose of cost statements", as per Cost Accounting Standard-14, p. 4 (Cost Accounting Standards Board of ICWAI, 2012), until such payouts become certain. But, if remediation cost cannot be recorded in accounting artifacts, how would it become part of emissions cost? This limits EMA to the computational methodologies that lose temporality of information as part of computational procedures.

To hold organizations liable towards their share of environmental aspects, EMA needs to break away from the economic perspective of waste and evolve as an umbrella framework to provide information on the externalities that the disposed waste produces. The argument around the "inclusive" role of accounting started with the very notion that accounting theories have to play an important role in helping the management understand externalities beyond "organizational" considerations (Gray and Babbington, 2001) and bring these within the decision-making arena. However, such a level of inclusiveness is yet to find its place within the purview of EMA. This chapter has covered its implementation in India with the hope that this would contribute to broadening the coverage of EMA and help accounting functions evolve beyond reporting to support the organizational quest of sustainability.

References

Antheaume, N. (2004). Valuing external costs—from theory to practice: Implications for full cost environmental accounting, *European Accounting Review,* 13(3): 443-464. doi:10.1080/0963818042000216802

CASBICWAI.org (2011). Cost accounting standard board (CASB). Retrieved from www.casbicwai.org/CASB/casb-about.asp.

Central Electricity Authority. (2011). CO_2 Baseline Database for the Indian Power Sector. User Guide (Ver 6.0). Retrieved from www.cea.nic.in on 15 May 2012.

Cost Accounting Standards Board of ICWAI. (2011a). Generally accepted cost accounting principles (GACAP) (India: The Institute of Costs and Works Accountants of India. Retrieved from www.casbicwai.org/CASB/casb-resources.asp.

Cost Accounting Standards Board of ICWAI. (2011b). Guidance note on cost accounting standards on material cost (CAS-6) (India: The Institute of Costs and Works Accountants of India). Retrieved from www.casbicwai.org/CASB/casb-resources.asp.

Cost Accounting Standards Board of ICWAI. (2012). Guidance note on cost accounting standards on pollution control cost (CAS-14) (India: The Institute of Costs and Works Accountants of India). Retrieved from www.casbicwai.org/CASB/casb-resources.asp.

Debnath, S. (2014). Expanding environmental management accounting: an experimental construct to integrate material wastes and emission flows. *Int. J. Business Information Systems,* 16(2):119-133.

Debnath, S., Bose, S.K., and Dhalla, R.S. (2011). Environmental management accounting: An overview of its methodological development. *International Journal of Business Insights and Transformation,* 5(1): 44-57.

Ecosystem Marketplace and Bloomberg New Energy Finance (2011). Back to the future: State of the voluntary carbon markets 2011. Retrieved from www.forest-trends.org/documents/files/doc_2829.pdf.

Fresenius Kabi India Private Limited. (2009). Boiler fuel conversion from RFO to biomass based briquettes at Fresenius Kabi India Private Limited, Ranjangaon (M.S.), India. Retrieved from www.cdm.unfccc.int/Projects/DB/DNV-CUK1199787528.27/view.

Gray, R., and Babbington, J. (2001). *Accounting for the Environment* (2nd ed.). London: Sage Publications.

Gray, R., and Laughlin, R. (2012). It was 20 years ago today: Sgt Pepper, *Accounting, Auditing and Accountability Journal,* green accounting and the Blue Meanies. *Accounting, Auditing and Accountability Journal,* 25(2): 228-255.

Greenham, T. (2010). Green accounting: a conceptual framework. *International Journal of Green Economics,* 4(4): 333-345.

Heubach, D., Jürgens, G., Döring, E., and Loew, T. (2002). Flow-cost accounting: Environmental and economical analysis of material recycling loops in industry. Aalborg: 3rd Euro Environment Conference on Business and Sustainable Performance.

Huang, C.-L., and Kung, F.-H. (2010). Drivers of environmental disclosure and stakeholder expectation: Evidence from Taiwan. *Journal of Business Ethics,* 96: 435-451. doi:10.1007/s10551-010-0476-3

IFAC (International Federation of Accountants) (2005). *International Guidance Document: Environmental Management Accounting.* New York: International Federation of Accountants.

ISO (International Organization for Standardization. (2010). *Environmental Management: Material Flow Cost Accounting—General Framework—Draft International Standard ISO/DIS 14051* Geneva: International Organization for Standardization.

Jasch, C. (2003). The use of environmental management accounting (EMA) for identifying environmental costs. *Journal of Cleaner Production*, 11: 667-676. doi:10.1016/S0959-6526(02)00107-5

Jasch, C. (2006). Environmental management accounting (EMA) as the next step in the evolution of management accounting. *Journal of Cleaner Production*, 14(14): 1,190-1,193. doi:10.1016/j.jclepro.2005.08.006

Jasch, C., Ayres, D., and Bernaudat, L. (2010). Environmental management accounting (EMA): Case studies in Honduras: An integrated UNIDO project. *Issues in Social and Environmental Accounting*, 4(2): 89-103.

Kakkuri-Knuuttila, M.-L., Lukka, K., and Kuorikoski, J. (2008). Straddling between paradigms: A naturalistic philosophical case study on interpretive research in management accounting. *Accounting, Organizations and Society*, 33: 267-291. doi:10.1016/j.aos.2006.12.003

Kasai, J. (1999). Life cycle assessment, evaluation method for sustainable development. *Journal of Society of Automotive Engineers Review*, 20: 387-393.

Kitada, H., Okada, H., and Kokubu, K. (2009). Material flow cost accounting at Japanese medium size company. *8th Australasian Conference on Social and Environment Accounting Research*. Christchurch, New Zealand: CSEAR 2009.

Kokubu, K., and Kitada, H. (2010). Conflicts and solutions between material flow cost accounting and conventional management thinking. *6th Asia-Pacific Interdisciplinary Perspectives on Accounting Research (APIRA)*, Sydney: University of Sydney: www.apira2010.econ.usyd.edu.au/conference_proceedings/.

Kokubu, K., and Nakajima, M. (2004). Material flow cost accounting in Japan: A new trend of environmental management accounting practices. *Fourth Asia Pacific Interdisciplinary Research in Accounting Conference*: 1-16, Singapore, July 2004.

Kokubu, K., and Nashioka, E. (2005). Environmental management accounting practices in Japan. In P.M. Rikhardsson, M. Bennett, J.J. Bouma, and S. Schaltegger (Eds.), *Implementing Environmental Management Accounting* (pp. 321-342). Dordrecht: Springer.

Korpi, E., and Ala-Risku, T. (2008). Life cycle costing: A review of published case studies. *Managerial Auditing Journal*, 23(3): 240-261.

Lee, B.-W., Jung, S.-T., and Kim, J.-H. (2005). Environmental accounting guidelines and corporate cases in Korea: Implications for developing countries. In P.M. Rikhardsson, M. Bennett, J.J. Bouma and S. Schaltegger (Eds.), *Implementing Environmental Management Accounting* (pp. 239-255). Dordrecht: Springer.

Lee, K.-H. (2011) Motivations, barriers, and incentives for adopting environmental management (cost) accounting and related guidelines: A study of the republic of Korea. *Corporate Social Responsibility and Environmental Management*, 18: 39-49. doi:10.1002/csr.239

Lee, N., and Lings, I. (2008). *Doing Business Research: A Guide to Theory and Practice*. New Delhi, India: Sage Publications India Pvt. Ltd.

Malarvizhi, P., and Yadav, S. (2008/2009). Corporate environmental disclosures on the internet: An empirical analysis of Indian companies. *Issues in Social and Environmental Accounting*, 2(2): 211-232.

Motherdairy.com (2011) About us. Retrieved from: www.motherdairy.com/MotherDairyPages/ourcompany.aspx.

Nakajima, M. (2009). Evolution of material flow cost accounting (MFCA): Characteristics on development of MFCA companies and significance and relevance of MFCA. *Kansai University Review of Business and Commerce*, 11: 27-46.

Nakajima, M. (2011). Environmental management accounting for cleaner production: Systematization of material flow cost accounting (MFCA) into corporate management system. *Kansai University Review of Business and Commerce*, 13: 17-39.

Nikolaou, I. (2007). Environmental accounting as a tool of qualitative improvement of banks services: The case of Greece. *International Journal of Financial Services Management*, 2(1/2): 133-143.

Onishi, Y., Kokubu, K. and Nakajima, M. (2009). Introducing material flow cost accounting into a pharmaceutical company: An analysis of environmental management accounting practice in Japan. In: S. Schaltegger, M. Bennett, R.L. Burritt and C. Jasch, (Eds.) *Environmental Management Accounting for Cleaner Production, Eco-Efficiency in Industry and Science* (pp. 395-409). New York: Springer.

Perez, O. (2002). Reflections on an environmental struggle: P&O, Dahanu, and the regulation of multinationals. *Georgetown International Environmental Law Review*, 15(1): 1-27.

Pulver, S. (2007). Introduction: Developing-country firms as agents of environmental sustainability? *Studies in Comparative International Development*, 42: 191-207. doi:10.1007/s12116-007-9011-7

Sangle, S. (2010). Empirical analysis of determinants of adoption of proactive environmental strategies in India. *Business Strategy and the Environment*, 19: 51-63. doi:10.1002/bse.651

Scavone, G.M. (2005). Environmental management accounting: Current practice and future trends in Argentina. In P.M. Rikhardsson, M. Bennett, J.J. Bouma, and S. Schaltegger (Eds.). *Implementing Environmental Management Accounting* (pp. 257-277). Dordrecht: Springer.

Schaltegger, S., Viere, T., and Zvezdov, D. (2012). Paying attention to environmental pay-offs: The case of an Indonesian textile manufacturer. *International Journal of Global Environmental Issues*, 12(1): 56-75.

Setthasakko, W. (2010). Barriers to the development of environmental management accounting: An exploratory study of pulp and paper companies in Thailand. *EuroMed Journal of Business*, 5(3): 315-331. doi:10.1108/14502191011080836

Sidhu, B. (2011). The Niyamgiri hills bauxite project: Balancing resource extraction and environment protection. *Environmental Policy and Law*, 41(3): 166-171.

Singh, G., and Joshi, M. (2009). Environment management and disclosure practices of Indian companies, *International Journal of Business Research*, 9(2): 116-128.

Stasiškien , Ž., and Juškait , R. (2007). Optimization of the cardboard manufacturing process in accordance with environmental and economic factors. *Environmental Research, Engineering and Management*, 2(40): 70-79.

Steen, B. (2005). Environmental costs and benefits in life cycle costing. *Management of Environmental Quality*, 16(2): 107-118.

Tsai, W.-H., Lin, T.W. and Chou, W.-C. (2010). Integrating activity-based costing and environmental cost accounting systems: A case study. *International Journal of Business and Systems Research*, 4(2): 186-208.

UNDSD (2001). *Environmental Management Accounting Procedures and Principles.* New York: United Nations.

USEPA (1995). *An Introduction to Environmental Accounting As a Business Tool: Key Concepts and Terms.* Washington, DC: USEPA.

Viere, T., Schaltegger, S., and von Enden, J. (2007). Supply chain information in environmental management accounting: The case of a Vietnamese coffee exporter. *Issues in Social and Environmental Accounting*, 1(2): 296-310.

WBCSD and WRI (2004). *The Greenhouse Gas Protocol: A Corporate Accounting and Reporting Standard.* Geneva: WBCSD; Washington, DC: WRI.

Xiaomei, L. (2004). Theory and practice of environmental management accounting: Experience of implementation in China. *International Journal of Technology Management and Sustainable Development*, 3(1): 47-57. doi:10.1386/ijtm.3.1.47/0

Young, S.M. (1999). Field research methods in management accounting. *Accounting Horizons*, 13: 76-84.

Appendix

Sankey Diagram of materials, water, and energy flow

a) Materials flow:

Material, water and energy flow of fruit processing plant

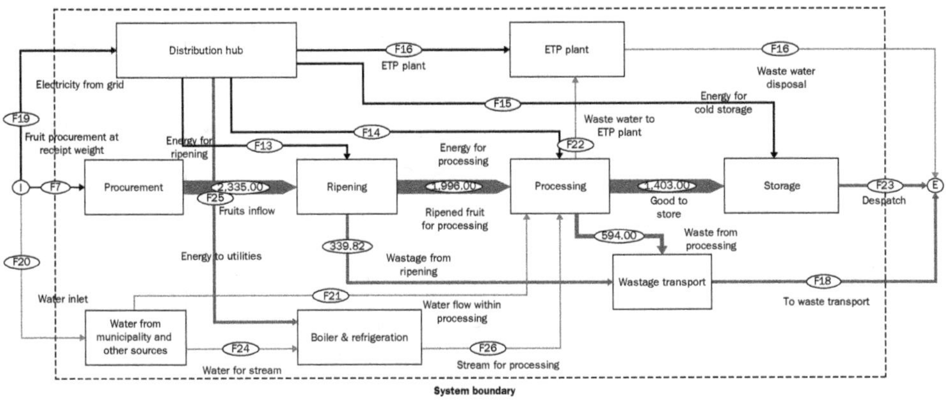

b) Energy flow:

Material, water and energy flow of fruit processing plant

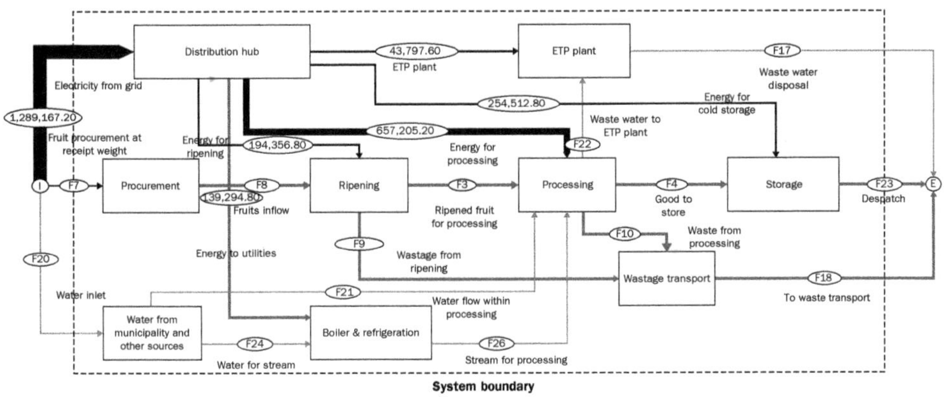

c) Water flow:

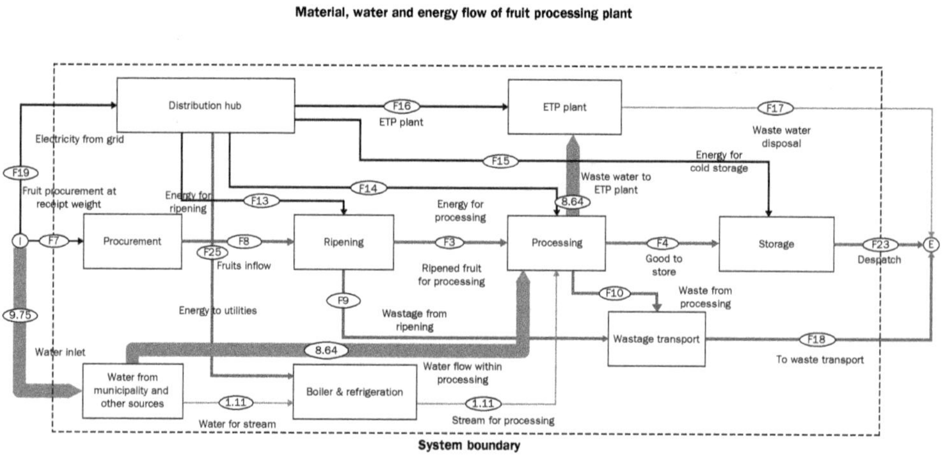

Notes:

a) For water, the unit of measurement has been converted to kilograms from litres and for electricity to megajoules (MJ) from kilowatt-hours (kWh) using standard conversion factors in these diagrams.

Sankey Diagrams are drawn using STAN2 software (courtesy Institute for Water Quality, Resource and Waste Management, Vienna, downloaded from www.iwr.tuwien.ac.at/resources/downloads/stan.html).

3

Corporate sustainability initiatives reporting

A study of India's most valuable companies*

P.D. Jose
IIM Bangalore, India

Saurabh Saraf
Consultant, Biopolus

This study analyses the sustainability initiatives of India's top 100 companies across multiple variables related to sustainability. The study reveals significant variance in reporting across sectors as well as on the variables reported. The highest reported variables were related to corporate governance, followed by those related to CSR initiatives and measures to improve operational efficiency. Most initiatives in the area of CSR focused on four areas—education, healthcare, community livelihood, and infrastructure development. Operations-related measures included resource conservation (energy, water, paper) and waste management (emissions, solid waste, water). Less than 20% of the companies that were surveyed currently disclose information on sustainability issues related to the supply chain. The sectoral differences in reporting were also striking. The cement, metals and mining, electric utilities, and information technology sectors outperformed the other sectors on most indicators. The realty, telecom and TV, pharmaceuticals, and banking and finance sectors had not disclosed as

* This study was sponsored by the National Stock Exchange of India. The authors gratefully acknowledge the research support provided by Green Evangelists. An earlier version of this study for the year 2009 received support from the Ministry of Environment and Forests.

much as the others did. The study also highlights areas for improvement. Voluntary sustainability reporting was still limited. Disclosures on CSR finances and donations were also nearly non-existent.

3.1 Introduction

This research study analyses the sustainability initiatives of India's most valuable companies as disclosed on their websites, including the annual reports, sustainability reports, policies, and various codes. The objectives of this study are to investigate what type of information related to sustainability and business operations companies are currently being disclosed and to map the type of information according to the industry type and sector.

3.2 Methodology

In the present study, specific sustainability initiatives taken up by the companies under study as disclosed on their websites and in their annual reports, sustainability reports, policies, codes and so on were considered for analysis. In general, Corporate Sustainability Initiatives (CSIs) were defined as including:

- Any voluntary action taken by the company to ensure reduced impact of their operations on the environment or the society beyond legal compliance;
- Those initiatives that are embedded in the core or mainstream business or are carried out by an extended arm of the corporate; and
- All initiatives that indicate that the company in general is concerned about the social and environmental aspects along with the economic aspects explicit in its strategic behaviour or planning.

The research findings regarding the Corporate Sustainability Initiatives (CSIs) incorporated by the sample companies are reported in three sections—organization and management; operations and core business Practices; and Corporate Social Responsibility (CSR). These sections are briefly described in Box 3.1.

3.2.1 Sample selection and data collection

In order to review the kind and extent of initiatives undertaken by the prominent companies of India to address the issues outlined earlier, the present study was carried out on a focus group of the 100 most valuable private sector companies, as rated by *Business Today* 500 (*BT* 500) in 2010. To manage and analyse the data, these companies were classified into 15 different sectors as shown in Figure 3.1 and Table 3.1.

Box 3.1 **Research findings related to CSIs**

Organization and management	This section describes organizational structures within the company able to execute the Corporate Sustainability Initiatives and various ways to manage it such as policies, codes of conducts, audits and certifications, communications and adherence to (inter)national voluntary sustainability principles and codes of conduct.
Operations and core business practices	The findings with regard to greening and ethically advancing their operations and reducing their negative environmental impacts are included in this section
Corporate social responsibility	Initiatives to improve the lives of the people in the surrounding communities and society at large are highlighted in this section. These initiatives do not directly impact core business practices of a company as such; however, these can be a part of public relations, CSR commitments, or investments in particular market segments which can be tapped in the future.

Figure 3.1 **Sector-wise distribution of top 100 companies in the study sample**

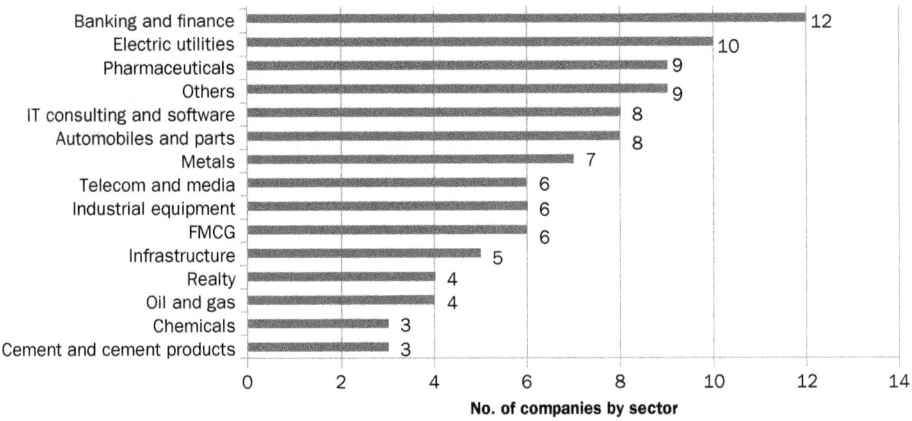

3.2.2 Data collection and analysis

For the present report, data on the sustainability initiatives undertaken by these companies was collected from their respective websites and/or from the information provided in their annual reports or CSR/sustainability reports. The period of data collection was July to September 2011. The latest reports provided on their websites were referred to for both the sectors in order to collect information on their sustainability initiatives.

Based on the information available, an initial list of different parameters was prepared, covering almost all the aspects of economic, social and environmental responsibility initiatives that an organization could undertake in order to operate in a sustainable manner. After further analysis, this list was refined to include a total of 24 variables categorized into about 162 sub-variables. Overall, these

Table 3.1 **Sector-wise classification of companies**

Sector	Company
Automobiles and parts	· Bajaj Auto · Hero Honda Motors · Bosch · Exide Industries · Mahindra & Mahindra · Maruti Suzuki · Ashok Leyland · Tata Motors
Banking and finance	· Axis Bank · HDFC Bank · ICICI Bank · Indusind Bank · Kotak Mahindra Bank · Yes Bank · Infrastructure Development Finance Co. · Reliance Capital · Shriram Transport Finance · SKS Microfinance · Housing Development Finance Corpn. · Bajaj Holdings & Invst.
Cement and cement products	· ACC · Ambuja Cements · Ultratech Cement
Chemicals	· United Phosphorus · Tata Chemicals · Jain Irrigation Systems
Electric utilities	· Adani Power · GMR Infrastructure · Jaiprakash Power Ventures · JSW Energy · Lanco Infratech · Reliance Infrastructure · Reliance Natural Resources · Reliance Power · Tata Power · Torrent Power
FMCG	· ITC · Nestle India · Colgate-Palmolive (India) · Dabur India · Godrej Consumer Products · Hindustan Unilever
Industrial equipment	· ABB · Crompton Greaves · Siemens · Suzlon Energy · Thermax · Cummins India
Infrastructure	· Jaiprakash Associates · Larsen & Toubro · Mundra Port & Special Economic Zone · IRB Infrastructure Developers · Jaypee Infratech
IT consulting and software	· HCL Technologies · Infosys · Mahindra Satyam · Mphasis · Oracle Financial Services Software · Tata Consultancy Services · Tech Mahindra · Wipro
Metals	· Hindalco Industries · Sterlite Industries · Jindal Steel & Power · JSW Steel · Sesa Goa · Tata Steel · Hindustan Zinc
Oil and gas	· Cairn India · Essar Oil · Reliance Industries · Castrol India
Others	· United Spirits · Adani Enterprises · Pantaloon Retail (India) · Aditya Birla Nuvo · Asian Paints · Indian Hotels Co. · Titan Industries · Grasim Industries · Jaybharat Textiles & Real Estate
Pharmaceuticals	· Cadila Healthcare · Cipla · Divis Laboratories · Dr Reddy's Laboratories · GlaxoSmithKline Pharmaceuticals · Lupin · Piramal Healthcare · Ranbaxy Laboratories · Sun Pharmaceutical Industries
Realty	· DB Realty · DLF · Housing Development & Infrastructure · Unitech
Telecom and TV	· Sun Tv Network · Zee Entertainment Enterprises · Bharti Airtel · Idea Cellular · Reliance Communications · Tata Communications

24 variables fall into the three sections that were described in Box 3.1 (as shown in Table 3.2). The data was then analysed overall as well as sector-wise. In some cases, the sub-variables were also analysed for all 100 companies. The charts and trends arising from this data analysis led to interesting insights, which have been showcased throughout the report. Figure 3.2 illustrates the various steps of this study.

Table 3.2 **Section-wise classification of 24 variables**

Organization and management	Operations and core business practices	Corporate social responsibility
· Organizational structure	· Green operations	· CSR finances
· Policies	· Climate change	· Donations and sponsorship
· Internal codes of conduct	· Research and development	· Disaster relief
· Voluntary sustainability principles and codes of conduct	· Greening supply chain	· Education
· Certifications and audits	· Renewable energy	· Healthcare
· Communication with employees and stakeholders	· Health & safety	· Infrastructure development
· Awards	· Workplace	· Cultural conservation
		· Community livelihood
		· Environment conservation
		· Other CSR initiatives

Figure 3.2 **Methodology adopted for the study**

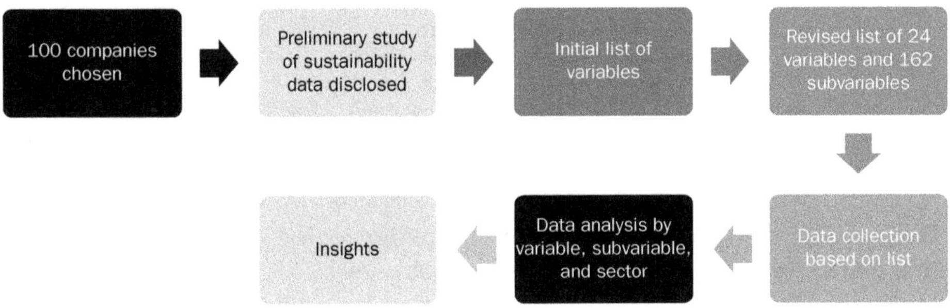

3.3 Overall findings

An analysis of the reported Corporate Sustainability Initiatives (CSIs) for the top 100 companies revealed that more than 90% of these companies had developed codes of conduct as well as internal policies (Figure 3.3). This indicates a strong emphasis at the top with respect to governance. After governance, the most reported initiatives were CSR-related (community livelihood, healthcare, education, and so on), operational efficiency-driven (green operations, including energy and resource conservation), or communication-centred initiatives.

Figure 3.3 **Reported CSIs for top 100 companies categorized according to 24 variables**

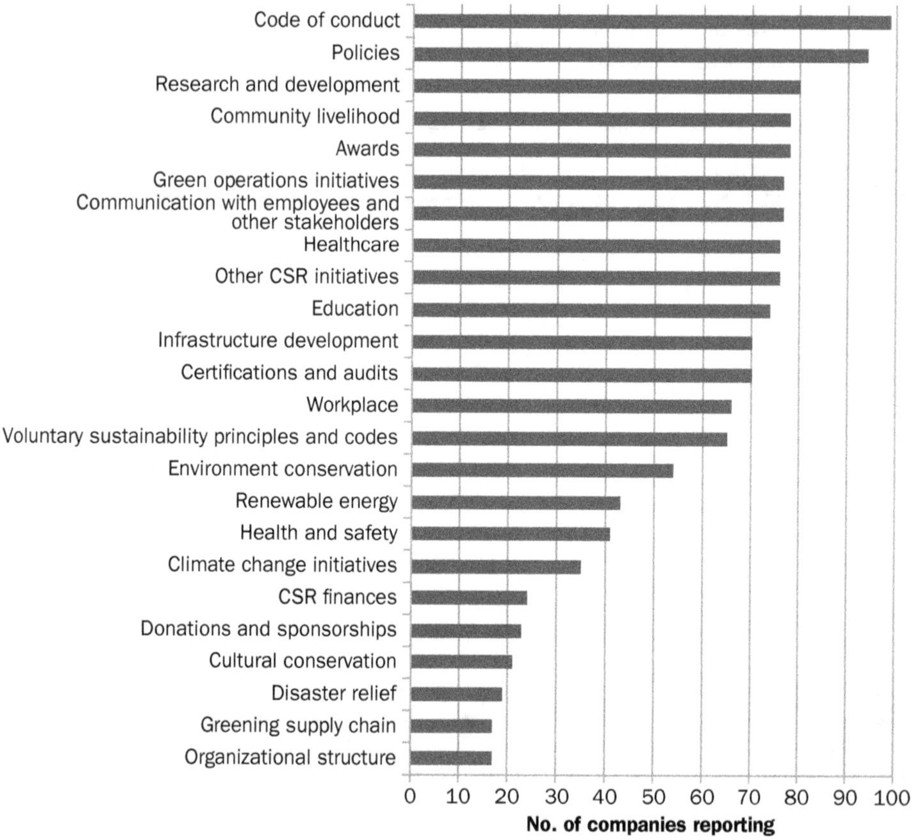

An analysis of the CSIs that were most reported by the top 25 and bottom 25 companies revealed that the difference lay not in which CSIs were reported (in fact, the same or similar CSIs were the most reported for both groups) but **the extent of data reported**. The top 25 companies were more likely to report on a greater number of CSIs than the bottom 25. More than 80% of the companies reported all the top 12 CSIs for the top 25 companies (Figure 3.4), whereas only 60% of companies reported all the top 11 CSIs in the bottom group (Figure 3.5). Figure 3.6 and Table 3.3 present the most reported data by top 5 sectors, which covers 47% of the companies.

Figure 3.4 **Top 12 reported CSIs for top 25 companies**

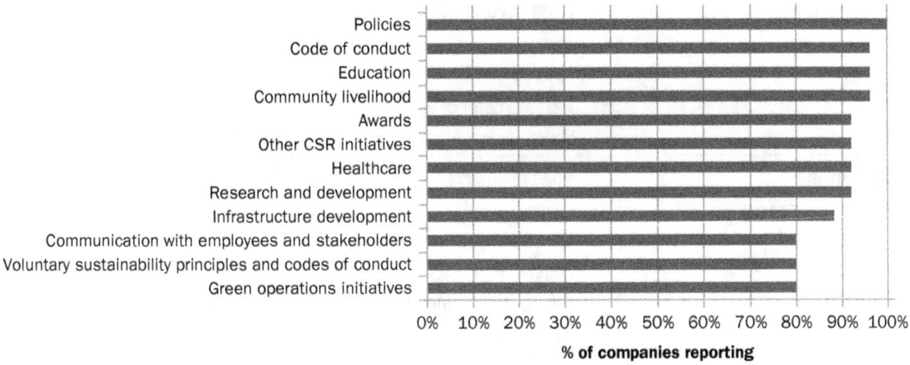

Figure 3.5 **Top 11 reported CSIs for bottom 25 companies**

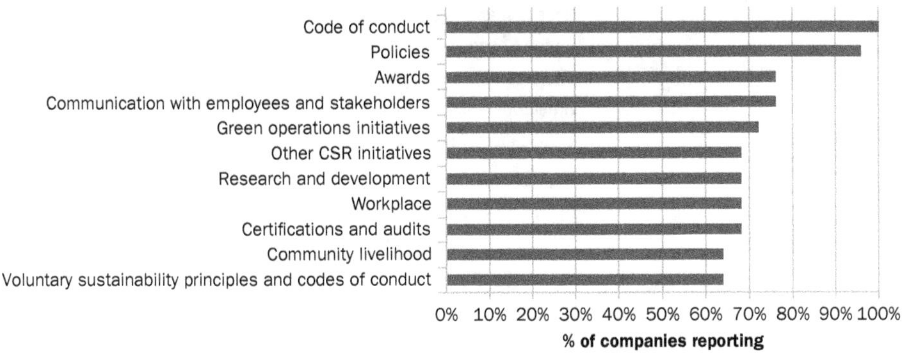

Figure 3.6 **Most reported data by top five sectors (covering 47% of the companies)**

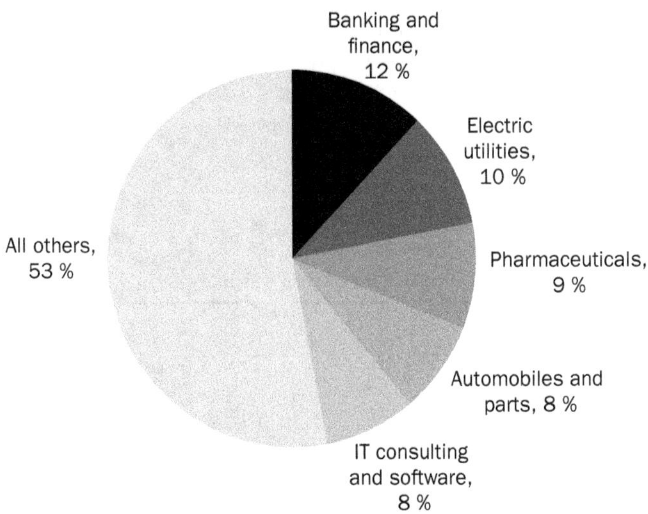

Table 3.3 **Sector-wise distribution of most reported CSIs**

Banking and finance	· Code of conduct · Awards · Policies · Research and development · Voluntary sustainability principles and codes of conduct
Electric utilities	· Code of conduct · Policies · Communication with employees and stakeholders · Education · Voluntary sustainability principles and codes of conduct · Healthcare · Community livelihood · Green operations initiatives
Pharmaceuticals	· Policies · Research and development · Code of conduct · Healthcare · Green operations initiatives · Certifications and audits
Automobiles and parts	· Code of conduct · Other CSR initiatives · Policies · Research and development · Healthcare · Awards · Community livelihood
IT consulting and software	· Code of conduct · Policies · Community livelihood · Workplace · Other CSR initiatives · Research and development · Awards · Green operations initiatives · Certifications and audits · Education · Communication with employees and stakeholders

3.4 Organization and management

In order for companies to become more sustainable entities, they need to incorporate sustainability principles through goals and objectives, vision, mission, strategies, management practices, and operations. Companies can apply different methods to achieve this, such as changing their organizational structure, updating their policies and codes of conduct, having their practices verified and certified, and communicating any changes in management, operations and progress towards more sustainable business practices to their employees and customers.

The various CSIs that fall under this category are listed in Table 3.4.

Table 3.4 **Organization and management CSIs**

CSI	Description
Organizational structure	Special structural arrangements to address Corporate Sustainability Initiatives: · Environment department, CSR department, R&D department for sustainable issues, and health & safety department
Policies	Policies related to sustainability used by the company: · CSR, environment, health & safety, HIV/AIDS, human resources, quality, and any other policies related to corporate governance
Internal codes of conduct	Sustainability-related concepts that are included in a company's codes of conduct: · Compliance with laws, diversity, environment, equal opportunities, differently abled people, gender, non-discrimination, harassment, health & safety, society, whistle-blowing
Voluntary sustainability principles and codes of conduct	Adherence to voluntary principles and codes of conduct related to sustainability, developed by external organizations and adopted by the company: · Global Reporting Initiative (GRI), United Nations Global Compact (GC), Carbon Disclosure Project and Millennium Development Goals (MDGs), and sector-specific initiatives
Certifications and audits	Verification and certification of current systems and practices to identify progress towards sustainable business practices: · AA1000, ISO 14000 and 9000 series, OHSAS 18000, quality certification, SA8000, and Six Sigma
Communication with employees and stakeholders	Communication with employees about sustainability and with consumers about products and services (safe usage, life-cycle, etc.)
Awards	Awards received for CSR, energy conservation, environment conservation, green building, quality, R&D, resource conservation, safety, sustainability, water conservation, and so on

3.4.1 Organizational structure

In this study, the focus was on the existence of departments such as environment departments, CSR departments, safety departments, or centres within a company that focus on these respective areas. Many companies have either separate departments or a consolidated Health, Safety, and Environment (HSE) department with a manager or an employee to look after the functioning of environmental measures, safety, and the implementation of CSI.

- **CSR department**: The CSR department would be responsible for implementing the CSR initiatives of the company.
- **Environment department**: The aim of this department would be to focus on the environmental management of the operations of the company and regularly monitor the efficiency of the manufacturing processes to ensure compliance with environmental standards.
- **Safety department:** This department would be responsible for maintaining the safety of the employees as well as the factories. The responsibilities could include training manpower, conducting audits and mock drills, framing policies, conducting health check-ups, and taking up other initiatives that improve safety.

Figure 3.7 presents the percentage of companies in each sector that report specific departments in charge of CSR, health & safety, and/or environment.

3.4.2 Policies

Policies are issued by companies for their employees on various issues; the employees are required to comply with these policies. In this study, we looked at the policies for environment protection, CSR, HSE, HIV/AIDS prevention, Total Productivity Management, and any other sustainability-related policy. Figure 3.8 presents the percentage of companies in each sector that reported internal policies. Figure 3.9 presents the number of companies reporting various types of internal policies.

Figure 3.7 **Sector-wise percentage of companies reporting departments for CSR, health & safety and/or environment**

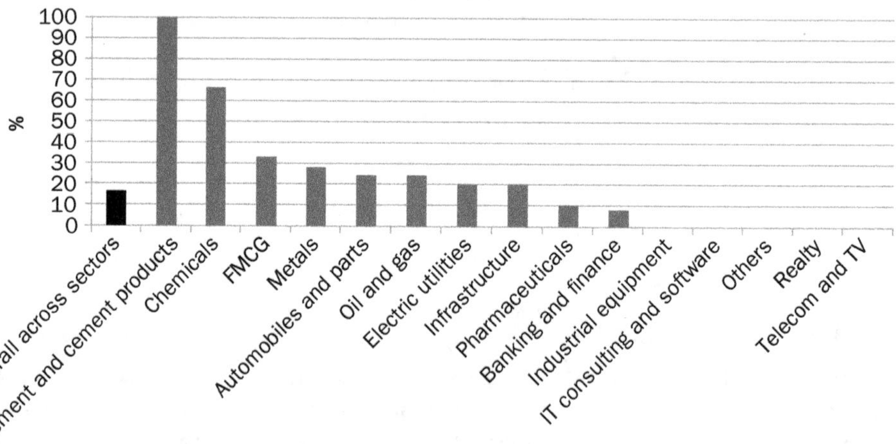

Figure 3.8 **Sector-wise percentage of companies disclosing internal policies**

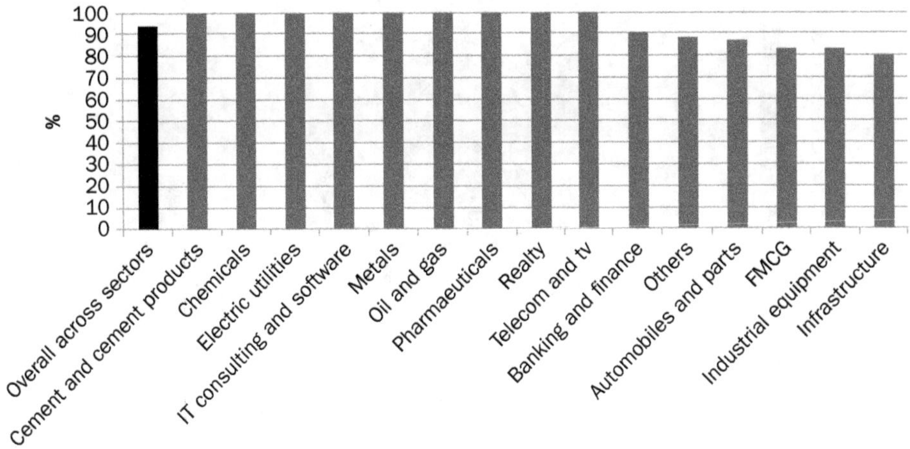

3.4.3 Internal codes of conduct

A vast majority of the top 100 companies have either formulated their own codes of conduct or have disclosed elements that usually form codes of conduct. Figure 3.10 presents the data pertaining to the percentage of companies in each sector with a code of conduct. Figure 3.11 shows the number of companies that disclosed various elements of a code of conduct.

Figure 3.9 **Number of companies reporting different types of internal policies**

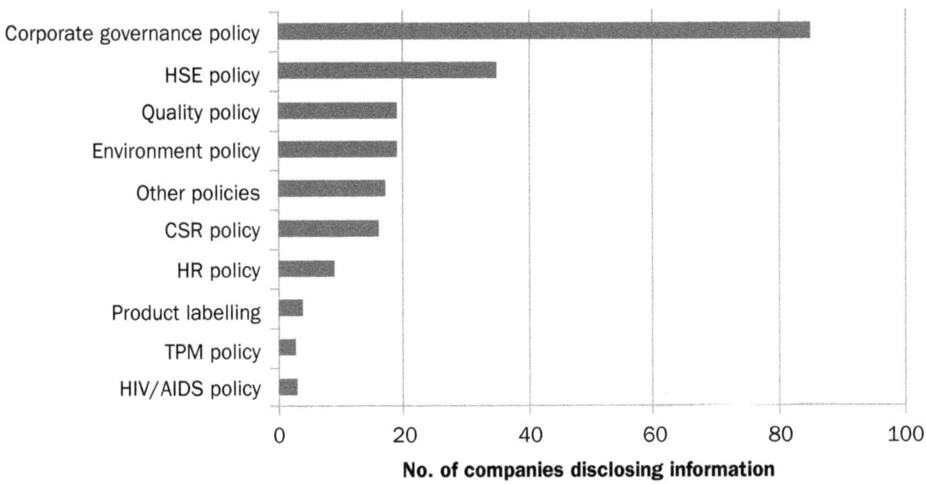

Figure 3.10 **Sector-wise percentage of companies with a code of conduct**

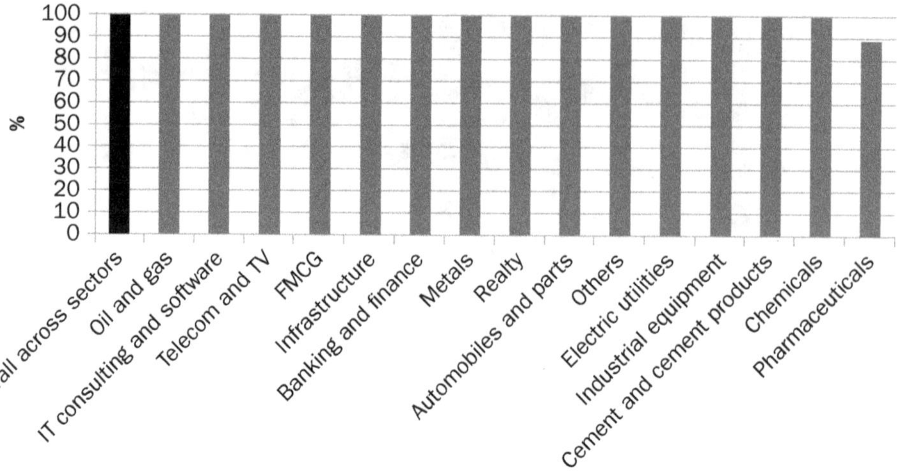

3.4.4 Voluntary sustainability principles and codes of conduct

Companies can adopt various voluntary principles and codes of conduct that are relevant to them and are designed for their specific sectors and industries. In some instances, they can join organizations as members and work together with other companies and stakeholders to enhance their sustainability practices. Over 60% of the surveyed companies had adopted voluntary codes of conduct (Figure 3.12 and Figure 3.13).

Figure 3.11 **Number of companies disclosing various elements of a code of conduct**

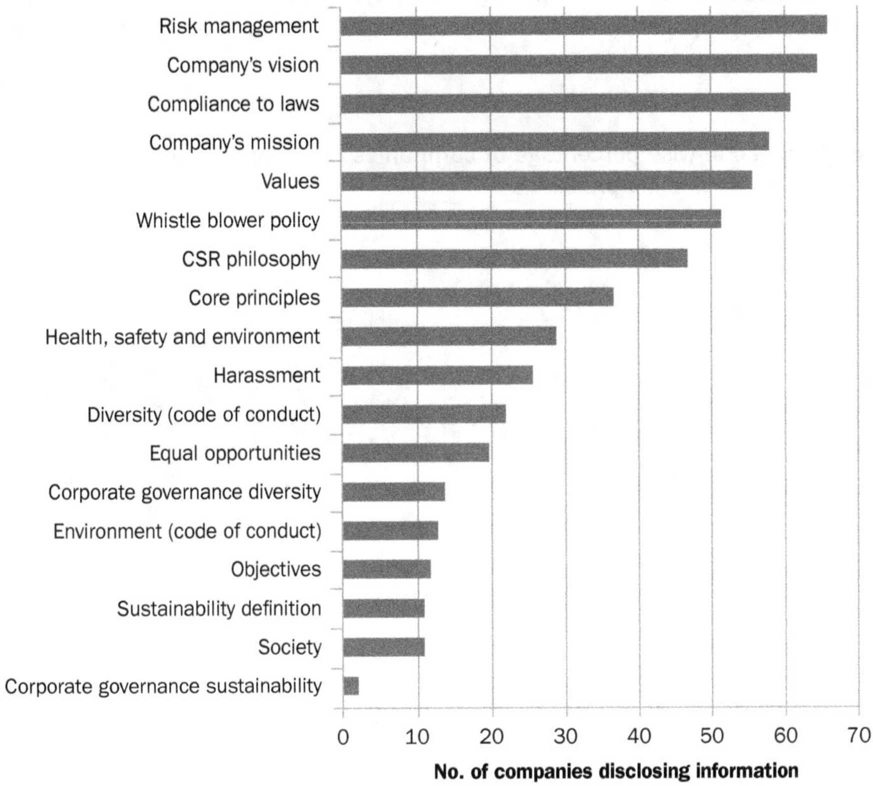

The Global Reporting Initiative (GRI) Sustainability Reporting Framework, the Carbon Disclosure project, and the United Nations Global Compact (GC) are the three most popular global sustainability initiatives that companies can become a member of; the member companies must adhere to the principles of these initiatives and use their guidelines for reporting progress on incorporating sustainable business practices. About 25% of the companies studied had published GRI-based Sustainability Reports.

Figure 3.12 **Number of companies adopting voluntary sustainability principles and codes of conduct**

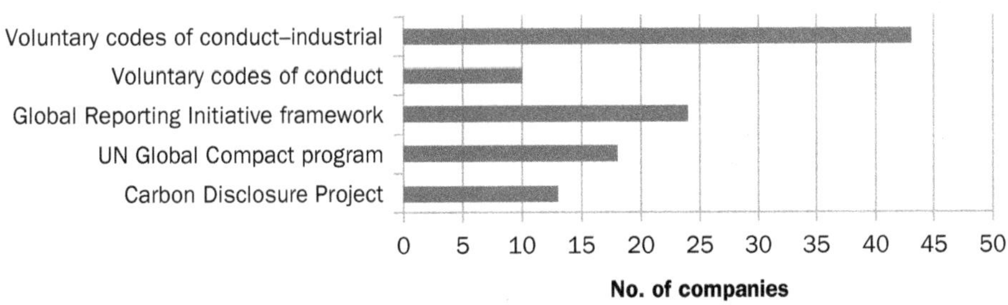

Sectors such as infrastructure, cement, electric utilities, and metals and mining were found to have the highest percentage when it came to reporting on voluntary sustainability principles. This could be linked to the requirements for a licence to operate for these sectors.

Figure 3.13 **Sector-wise percentage of companies reporting voluntary sustainability principles**

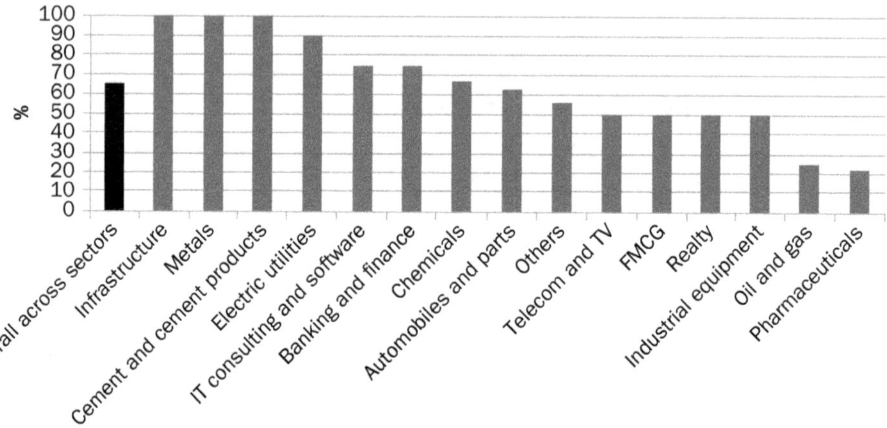

Another global initiative that can be used by companies to help them progress on their sustainability path is the Millennium Development Goals (MDGs). The MDGs include eight target goals set by the United Nations that are to be achieved by countries across the world by 2015.

Figure 3.14 **Percentage of companies reporting on Millennium Development Goals**

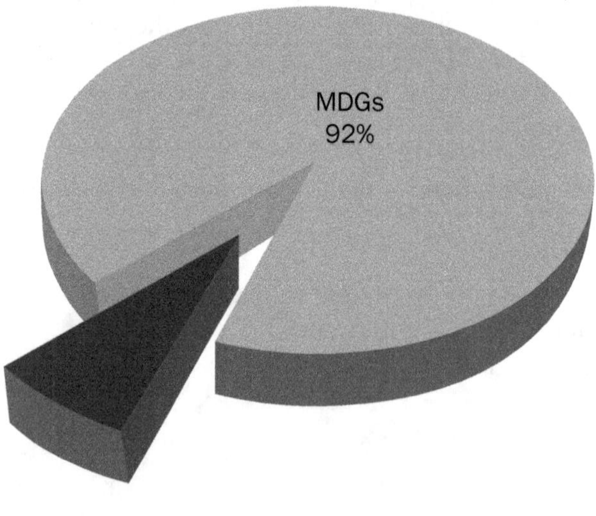

3.4.5 Certifications and audits

After implementing corporate sustainability initiatives, companies need to analyse their performance and progress towards their objectives and goals. Audits are conducted to verify and assess the implemented systems. Companies can also apply for certification for various sustainability-related initiatives such as health and safety measures, environment management, quality management, six sigma, and social accountability.

The International Organization for Standardization (ISO) has developed the ISO 14000 series and the ISO 9000 series for Environment Management System and Quality Management, respectively, which are certification schemes that can be applied by companies. The certifications are handed out by third parties after third-party audits have been conducted. Implementing ISO standards assists organizations in producing services and products through more efficient, safer and environmentally friendlier processes. Both ISO 9000 as well as ISO 14000 can be applied by service sectors, manufacturing companies, big or small organizations, private- or public-owned organizations, companies and enterprises.

A review of the certifications that the companies underwent shows that environment, health & safety, and quality are the most popular focus areas for companies (Figure 3.15). Most companies are not mature enough to undergo human and social rights certifications (SA 8000). It is also evident that audits are an emerging trend and it may take a while before more companies commit to conducting energy and safety audits. Only 17 of the 100 companies studied conducted audits. Figure 3.16 presents the percentage of companies in each sector that reported certifications and/or conducted audits.

The telecom and TV, banking and finance, and realty sectors did not seem to be as mature as the other sectors when it came to certifications and audits.

3.4.6 Communication with employees and stakeholders

Every company communicated the policies, functioning and other aspects to its employees through various mediums such as notices, emails, newsletters and so on. Almost every company provided customer services to their customers and had a customer feedback system and a complaint system. The only sector that did not seem as mature as the rest was the telecom and TV sector. Figures 3.17 and 3.18 present the data related to communication with employees and stakeholders.

Figure 3.15 **Number of companies disclosing information related to certifications and/or audits**

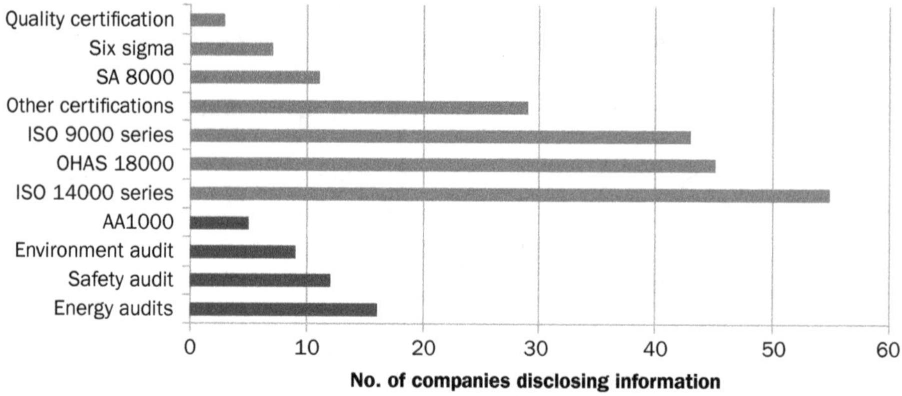

Figure 3.16 **Sector-wise percentage of companies reporting certifications and/or conducting audits**

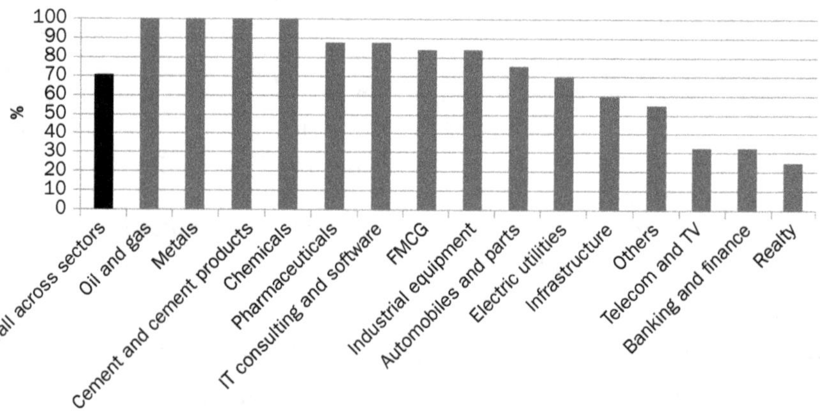

Figure 3.17 **Sector-wise percentage of companies reporting communication with employees and stakeholders**

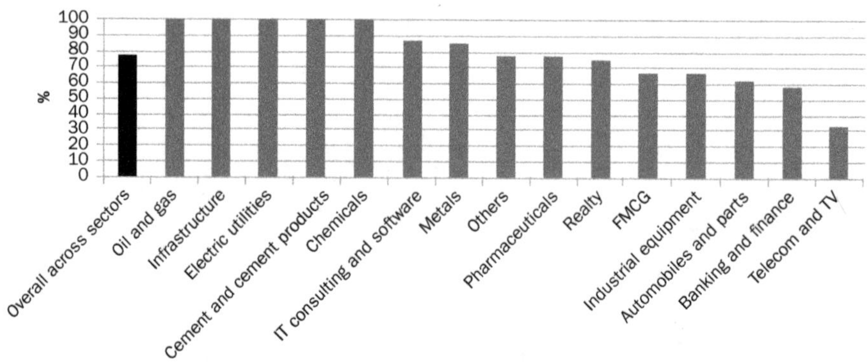

Figure 3.18 **Number of companies disclosing information related to communication with employees and stakeholders**

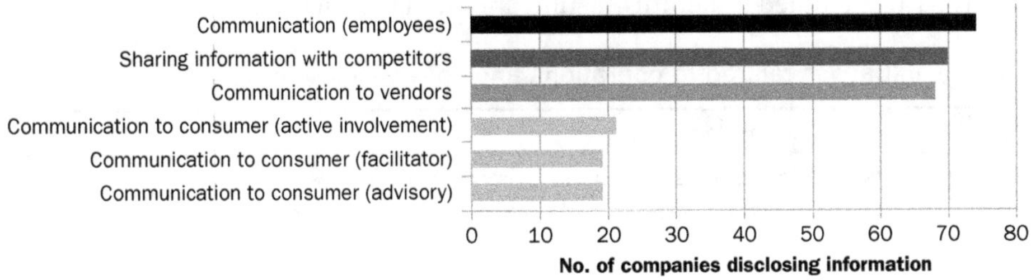

3.4.7 Awards

Most of the companies disclosed information related to the awards won for various activities. These included awards received for CSR, energy conservation, environment conservation, green building, quality, R&D, resource conservation, safety, sustainability, water conservation and so on.

Nearly 80% of the companies studied had won an award in one of these categories (Figure 3.19). This indicates that the vast majority of the top 100 companies are doing laudatory work in at least one CSR- or environment-related area. Oddly enough, there seems to be little correlation between following voluntary sustainability guidelines such as the GRI, UNGC, etc. and winning awards. For instance, the electric utilities and infrastructure sectors had the highest percentages when it came to following voluntary guidelines but seemed to lag when it came to winning awards. However, sectors like metals and cements did well in both these variables.

Figure 3.19 **Sector-wise percentage of companies that received awards**

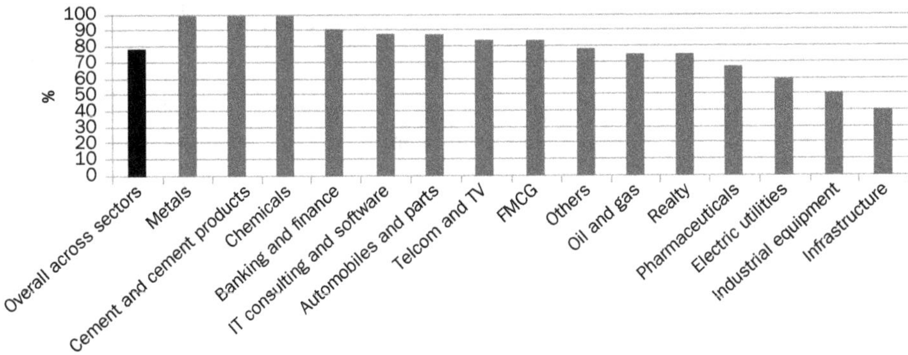

3.5 Operations and core business practices

The initiatives studied under this section are listed in Table 3.5.

Table 3.5 **Initiatives related to operations and core business practices**

CSI	Description
Green operations	Steps towards recycling and conservation of resources: · Product materials, packaging, waste materials, water, energy, offering take-back facility for recycling Controlling and prevention of air, noise, water and soil pollution Reducing emissions, eliminating toxic and hazardous elements Managing solid waste, waste-water and by-products efficiently Developing green belt
Climate change	Combating climate change through: · Carbon trading, clean development mechanisms, reduction in CO_2 emissions, reduction in other greenhouse gases (GHGs), and CO_2 sequestration
Research and development	Innovating eco-friendly processes or products as well as regularly investing in R&D for inventing them through: · Collaborating with R&D institutions, efficient finance allocation, staff allocation, and other sustainability initiatives
Greening supply chain	Initiatives carried out for greening the supply chain: · End-of-life initiatives (recycling and return facilities), efficient use of raw materials, vendor management
Renewable energy	Usage of various forms of renewable energy: · Alternate fuels, solar energy, wind energy
Health & safety	Taking care of health & safety (HS) of employees and society at large: · HS policies, HS training, and other HS initiatives
Workplace	Any procedure or practice being taken by the company: · To be non-discriminative, to be child-labour-free, to promote equality, and to provide equal opportunities for differently abled/underprivileged people

3.5.1 Green operations

In greening its business operations, a company implements measures for pollution control and environmental conservation. Manufacturing companies have their products fabricated at factories or plant units that have to adhere to particular environmental laws and regulations. For instance, in India, companies are required to maintain their emissions within the standards set under the rules and regulations as decided by the government. Service-providing companies might have less environmentally negative impacting business operations than manufacturing companies; nevertheless, the operations of service companies also have an impact on the environment.

This section focuses on the technologies and measures adopted by the companies to control emissions from their manufacturing or service units as well as the additional steps undertaken by them to protect the environment.

By far, energy seems to be the driving factor for greening operations in Indian companies. This is not surprising given that energy costs are rising and form a significant part of operating expenses. Energy efficiency initiatives are also maturing, with several companies switching to more efficient HVAC, lighting, and computing systems. The conservation of other inputs such as water and other resources (such as paper) comes next.

Managing outputs in terms of waste and emissions forms the next most important driver. These outputs can be varied and include solid waste management, recycling, waste-water treatment, and air pollution control.

About 80% of all companies that were studied reported at least one green operations initiative (Figures 3.20 and 3.21). This high percentage could be linked to the economic benefits such as lower operating costs that result from implementing such initiatives. Unsurprisingly, the sectors that had an impact on the environment such as oil and gas, mining, and other manufacturing-related companies disclosed information on their green operations. This was also true for sectors such as IT where energy and water costs make up a significant part of the operating costs. However, sectors like Telecom and TV and banking and finance do not display the same level of maturity as compared to the rest of the sectors.

Figure 3.20 **Number of companies disclosing information related to green operations initiatives**

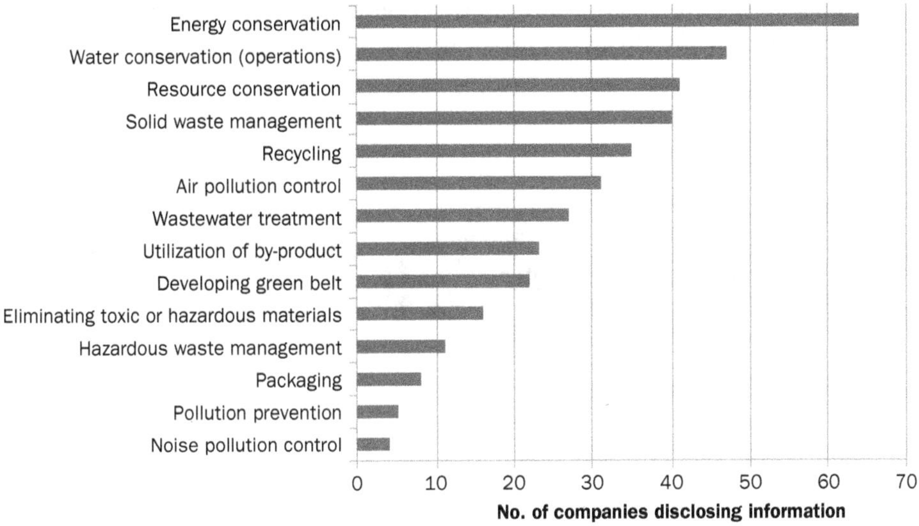

Figure 3.21 **Sector-wise percentage of companies reporting green operations initiatives**

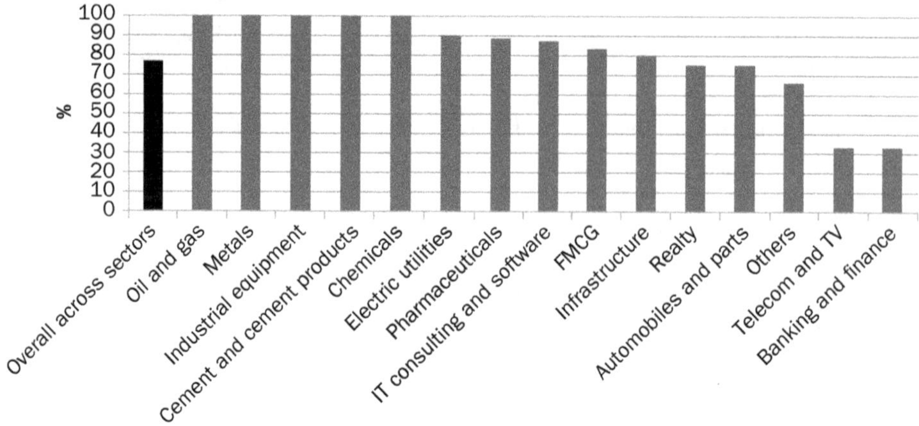

3.5.2 Climate change

Climate change initiatives can include the following:

- **Carbon trading:** Companies could be involved in trading carbon credits with other companies or any other entities. Companies could sell their credits by saving on the carbon emissions from their manufacturing units.
- **Clean Development Mechanism (CDM):** Projects are taken up by companies in adopting Clean Development Mechanism to reduce their carbon emissions
- **Reduction in CO_2 emissions:** Initiatives are taken by the companies as part of their operations to reduce carbon dioxide emissions. This includes new technologies and practices adopted by the company to curb carbon emissions from their units and other information such as emissions reduced annually by the company, new targets set by the company, etc.
- **Reduction in GHGs:** Practices are adopted by companies to reduce other greenhouse gases such as methane, water vapour, nitrous oxide, etc.
- **Sequestration:** Measures are taken by the company to sequester carbon dioxide by promoting forestry, afforestation, tree plantation, or the planting of any kind of vegetation as trees and plants help in the sequestration of carbon dioxide. Some of the other natural sequestrants include oceans and soil.

As discussed in the previous section, nearly 80% of the companies focused on greening operations. Compared to this, the focus on climate change was not as intense, with only a little over 30% of the companies disclosing information on climate change initiatives. The focus on energy conservation has the happy side effect of reducing emissions while also reducing costs, whereas solely focussing on climate change does not seem as attractive. This is evident in the distribution of the climate change initiatives undertaken by the companies—carbon and GHG reduction ruled the roost. Initiatives like sequestration and carbon trading—which may not have a direct bottom-line impact—did not seem to find favour with the companies. The data related to the number of companies reporting climate change initiatives is presented in Figure 3.22.

The cement, metals and utilities outperformed all the other sectors when it came to climate change initiatives (Figure 3.23). This may be considered part of these sectors' efforts to maintain their licence to operate.

Figure 3.22 **Number of companies disclosing information on climate change initiatives**

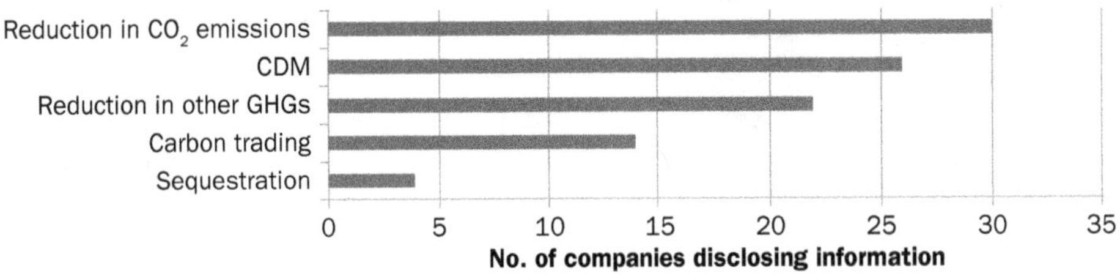

Figure 3.23 **Sector-wise percentage of companies reporting climate change initiatives**

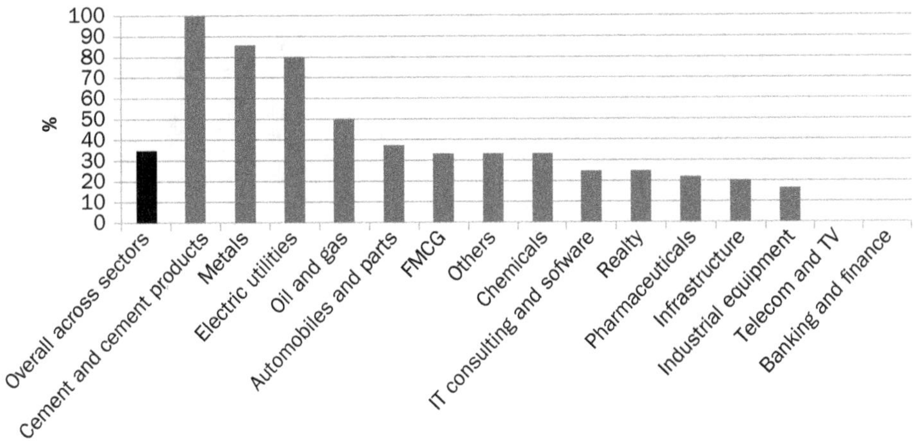

3.5.3 Research and development

Major manufacturing companies have their own research and development (R&D) centres to conduct research on improving their manufacturing processes in order to conserve energy and water, remove toxic elements, improve packaging and product development, and so on. This section looks into the R&D efforts of the companies that were studied and examines what measures they adopted to make their processes and products environment friendly. The major focus of this section is R&D from a sustainability perspective.

As shown in Figures 3.24 and 3.25, developing environment-friendly products and processes did not seem to figure high on the list of R&D priorities for these companies.

Figure 3.24 **Number of companies with R&D initiatives for sustainability**

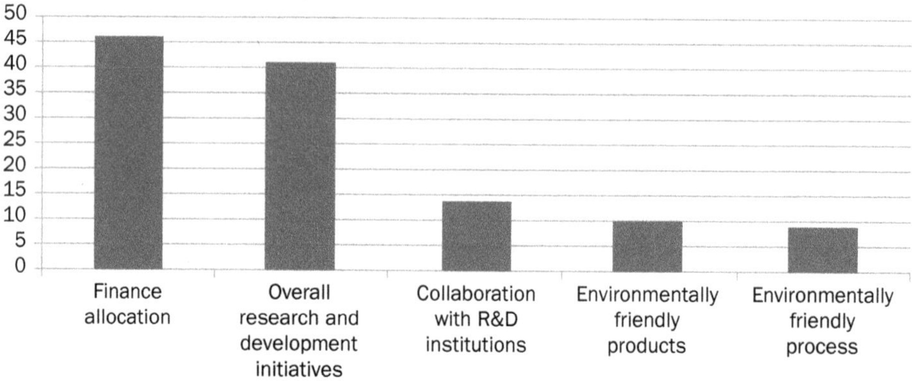

Figure 3.25 **Sector-wise percentage of companies reporting R&D initiatives**

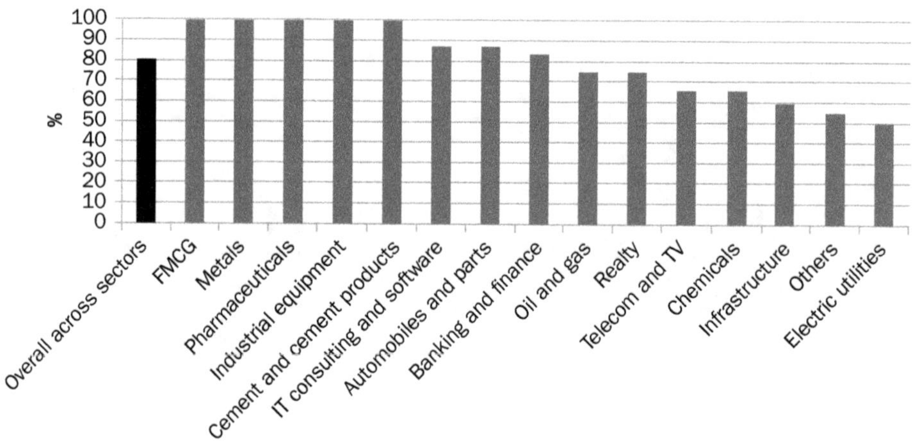

3.5.4 Greening supply chain

Greening of the supply chain refers to incorporating practices along the supply chain that cause minimum or no environmental harm. They include:

- **End-of-life:** Companies take back or recycle products at the end of their life-cycle.

- **Supply chain initiatives:** Companies could adopt green supply chain initiatives such as sourcing raw materials in a sustainable manner, emphasizing that suppliers as well as dealers should be socially and environmentally responsible, communicating supply chain policies to suppliers, and any other measures to implement greening of the supply chain.
- **Vendor management:** Initiatives could be taken by the company to manage vendors and dealers to ensure they follow green supply chain practices.

Greening the supply chain is one area where the overall maturity of the top 100 companies is very low. Barely 20% of the companies disclosed any information in this area (Figures 3.26 and 3.27). The focus here seemed to be on managing vendors and in sourcing raw materials in a sustainable manner. Very few companies focused on end-of-life supply initiatives.

The leaders in this area were the FMCG and cement sectors, with the rest of the sectors performing poorly quite uniformly. Given the relative immaturity of this area, greening the supply chain (if done right) can be a differentiating factor and a source of competitive advantage for companies.

Figure 3.26 **Sector-wise percentage of companies reporting on greening supply chain**

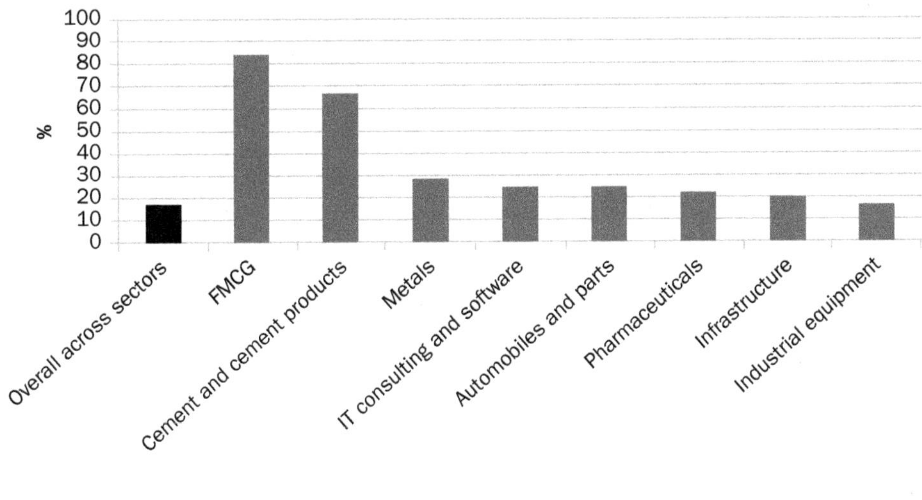

Figure 3.27 **Number of companies reporting greening supply chain initiatives**

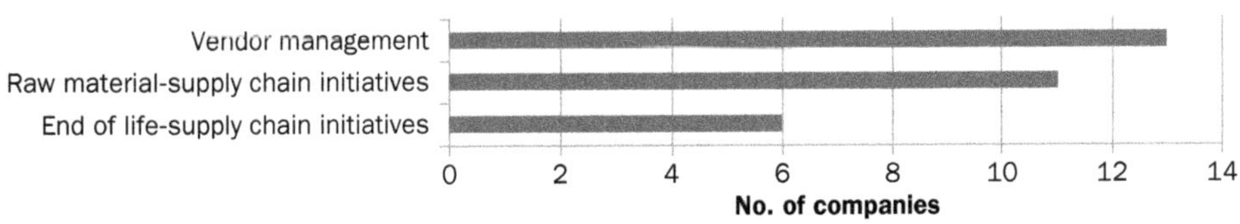

3.5.5 Renewable energy

Renewable energy in the form of solar energy, wind energy, biogas, biofuels and other alternate forms of energy are being utilized by many companies. Renewable forms of energy are cleaner and non-exhaustive. The shortage of non-renewable energy such as petrol, diesel, coal, and other fuel oils have pushed industries to look for alternatives and incorporate them into their manufacturing processes as an energy source. This study incorporated companies that promoted clean non-renewables such as LPG and CNG. In this section we considered:

- **Alternate fuels:** The use or promotion of biofuels, bagasse, biogas or other forms of cleaner fuels for production purposes that lead to energy efficiency, zero emissions and pollution control.
- **Solar energy:** The use of solar energy as a source of energy within the company for its operations.
- **Wind energy:** The use of electricity generated using wind power as a source of energy for the operations of the company.

A little over 40% of the companies studied disclosed information on using renewable fuels (Figures 3.28 and 3.29). Solar energy was by far the most popular, followed by wind energy. This focus on renewable energy is not surprising considering that 65% of the companies follow some sort of energy conservation initiative. It is heartening to see that sectors such as oil and gas, automobiles, and chemicals—which are intrinsically tied to fossil fuels—were focusing on renewable energy. It is also good that the electric utilities sector was focusing on finding cleaner sources of energy.

Figure 3.28 **Number of companies reporting use of various types of renewable energy**

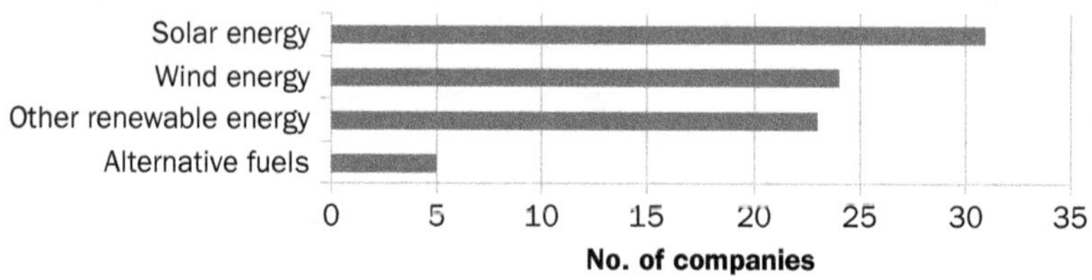

Figure 3.29 **Sector-wise percentage of companies reporting on renewable energy**

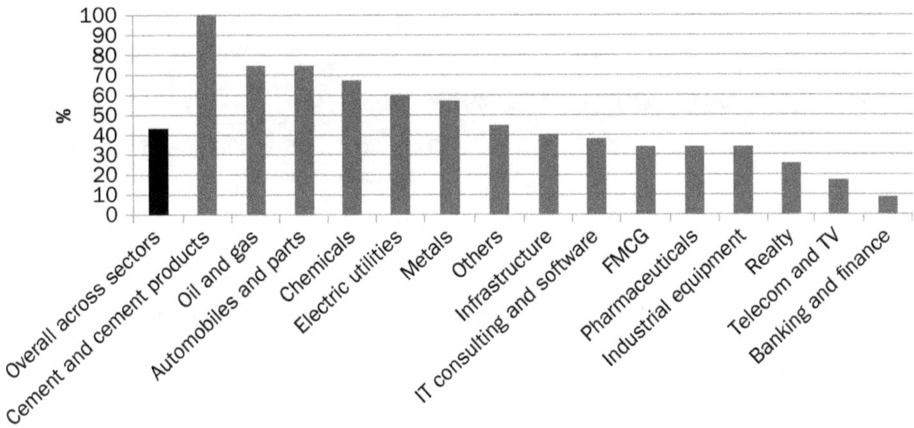

3.5.6 Health & safety

A total of 41 companies had implemented some form of HSE initiatives. The common initiatives included implementing various safety procedures, providing safety equipment, creating safety committees, setting standards, conducting meetings, reviewing procedures, and so on. The focus on safety is clearly more important for the manufacturing and the heavy industries sectors compared to the services sectors (Figures 3.30 and 3.31).

Figure 3.30 **Sector-wise percentage of companies reporting on health and safety initiatives**

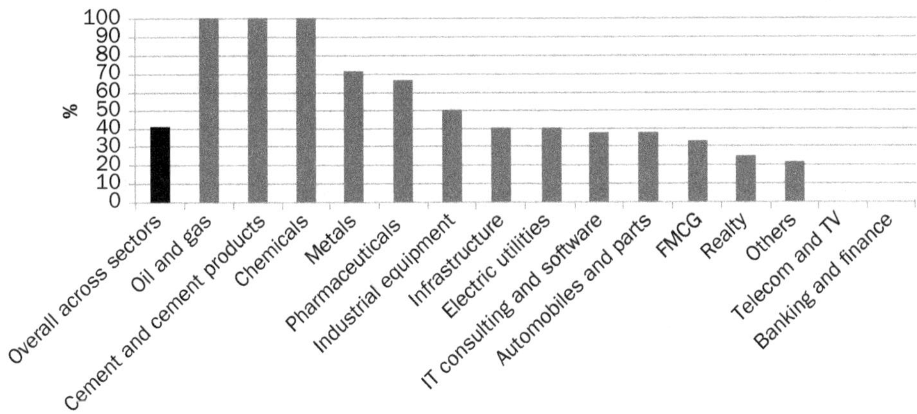

Figure 3.31 **Number of companies disclosing information on health and safety initiatives**

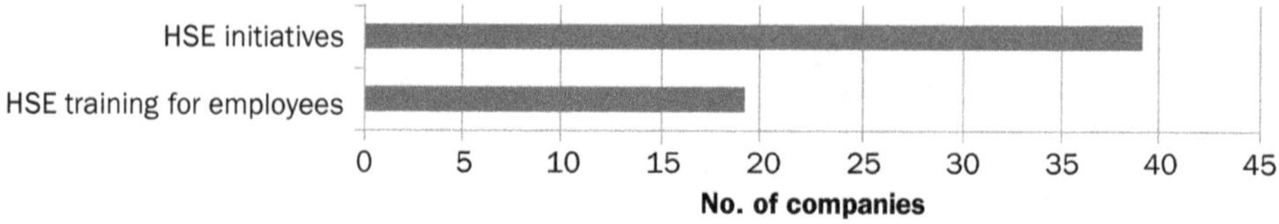

3.5.7 Workplace

Every company believes that their employees are their core strength and have various welfare programmes, incentives, rewards and other activities to improve the quality of life of their employees. Companies regularly train their employees on various operational procedures and other activities to ensure better performance. The companies that were studied gave detailed measures of their employee recognition and welfare measures. In this section, we looked at:

- **Child labour:** The HR policies of the company regarding child labour. According to the 1986 Child Labour Act, companies are required to abolish child labour practices; however, the analysis shows that very few companies clearly stated their stand.
- **Employee training:** Any training given to the employees on sustainability issues such as training on environment management, sustainable development and CSR.
- **Equal opportunities:** Does the company promote and support equal opportunities and diversity among its employees irrespective of caste, religion, creed, colour and gender?

Figure 3.32 shows that employee training was the focus area for most of the companies. While this is good, it is recommended that companies also make explicit their policies on equal opportunity and child labour.

Figure 3.32 **Number of companies disclosing information related to workplace initiatives**

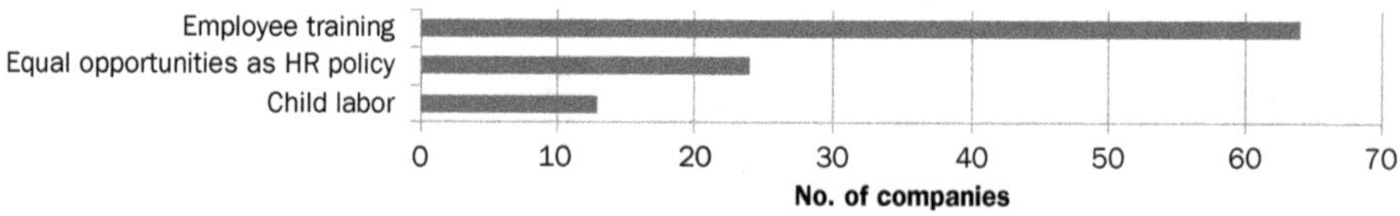

Spearheading these initiatives were the services sectors such as IT and finance for whom equal opportunities and training are a requirement for recruiting and retaining talent. Heavy industries such as oil and gas, metals, and so on also scored highly given their need for trained personnel and stringent labour policies (Figure 3.33).

Figure 3.33 **Sector-wise percentage of companies reporting workplace initiatives**

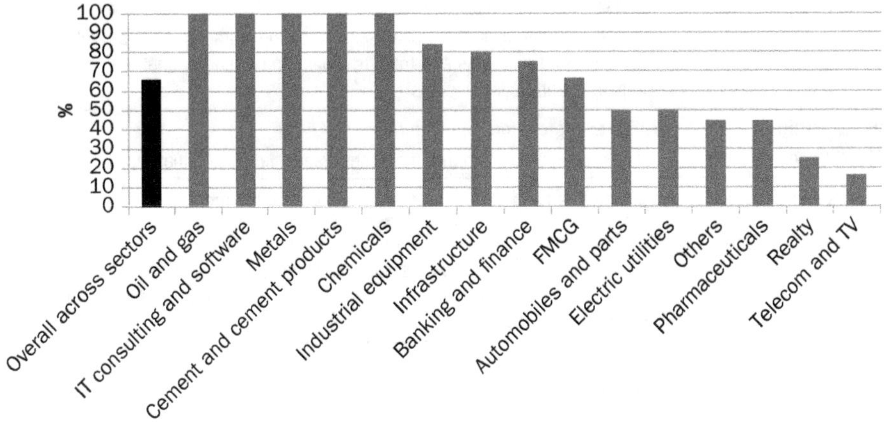

3.6 Corporate Social Responsibility

Corporate Social Responsibility (CSR) initiatives are programmes implemented by a company for the communities around its premises, for society at large, or for contributing towards environmental protection and conservation. These initiatives are philanthropic in nature—they are conducted voluntarily and free of cost for the benefit of the communities and society. These acts could include donations of money, goods, time and/or effort to support a beneficial cause, with a defined objective and with no financial or material reward to the donor. It may encompass any altruistic activity intended to promote good or to improve the quality of human life. The various CSIs that fall under this category are listed in Table 3.6.

Table 3.6 **CSIs related to Corporate Social Responsibility**

CSI	Description
CSR finances	Budget and resources allocated to operate CSIs
Donations and sponsorship	Initiatives that include charity or cash donations with a focus on the surrounding community of its operations or which address issues for public: · Offering cash or material donations, building hospitals, schools, residential homes for the elderly, and sponsoring programmes
Disaster relief	Supporting communities that are hit by disasters: · Donations to funds, infrastructure development, relief work, volunteering
Education	Steps adopted to promote education among local communities or society at large: · Building schools, scholarships, sponsoring schools, promotion of primary, secondary, and higher education

CSI	Description
Healthcare	Initiatives to offer health services: · Spreading awareness about diseases, maternal health and child mortality, setting up clinics for treatments and training programmes, blood donations, eye check-up camps and build hospitals
Infrastructure development	Activities to improve local infrastructure: · Constructing roads, sanitation and sewerage, and other initiatives
Cultural conservation	Conservation of cultural traditions and heritage and the promotion of arts
Community livelihood	Initiatives to improve quality of life in communities through: · Livelihood initiatives like professional trainings, training and activities for children, elderly and differently abled people, promoting sports, rural development, empowerment of women
Environment conservation	Contributing to environmental conservation through: · Awareness programmes, nature conservation, water conservation · Forestry, afforestation, landscaping
Other CSR initiatives	Activities part of CSR but not included in the above categories

3.6.1 CSR finances

Across all the sectors, there was little transparency when it came to disclosing the amount of money spent on CSR (Figure 3.34). Part of this may have to do with the fact that very few companies keep a detailed and auditable record of these finances, and thus these companies may be hesitant to disclose such amounts in the public domain. Apart from this, a large part of CSR has to do with non-financial support such as volunteering, which is hard to quantify.

3.6.2 Donations and sponsorship

These philanthropic initiatives taken up by companies range from offering cash or material donations (including donations for places of worship) to sponsoring programmes.

The lack of transparency was evident here, too (Figure 3.35). It is recommended that companies track their CSR spends and donations as a way of measuring the efficiency of their CSR budgets and programmes.

Figure 3.34 **Sector-wise percentage of companies reporting on CSR finances**

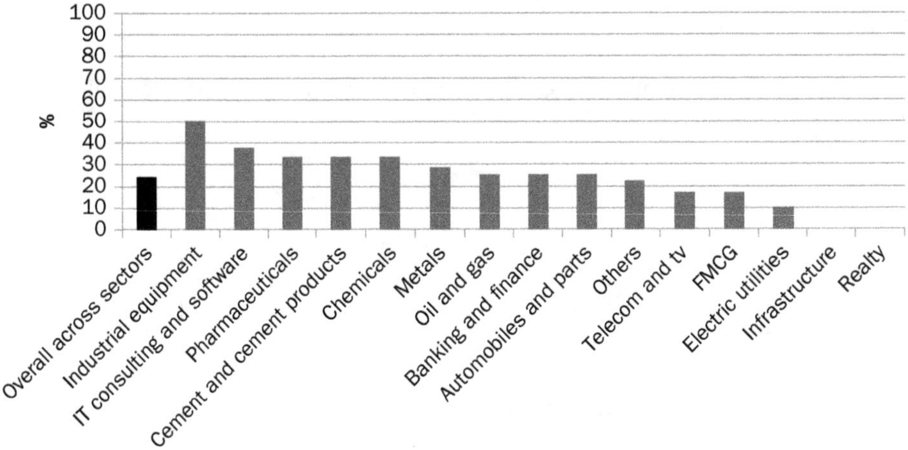

Figure 3.35 **Sector-wise percentage of companies reporting on donations and sponsorships**

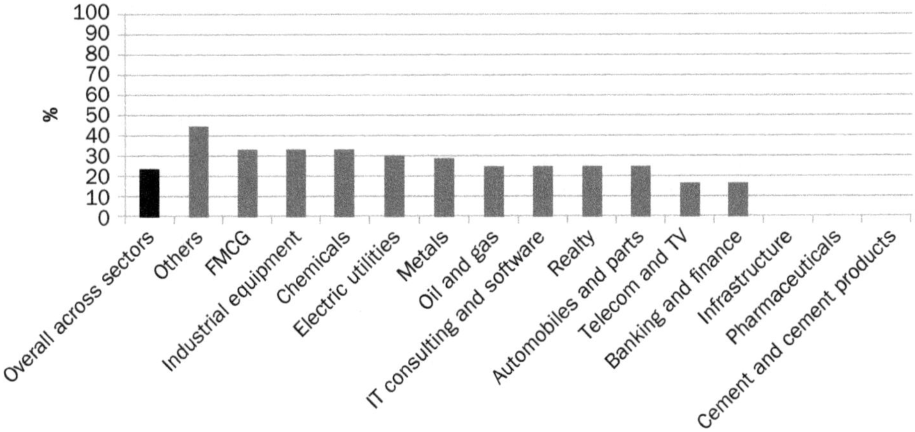

3.6.3 Disaster relief

Disaster relief includes donations to organizations helping communities that are hit by disasters. Donations could be provided in the form of food, water, medicines and clothes as well as other efforts towards providing relief to the affected public. It also includes restoring the infrastructure of places affected by disasters. This could include giving training in masonry, electrical work, agriculture, arts and crafts, and tailoring as well as running schools, clinics and hospitals, thereby bringing benefits to the community.

Overall, the extent of reporting was low for this variable (Figure 3.36), but that could be because other CSR areas such as healthcare or education were greater priorities for many of the companies.

Figure 3.36 **Sector-wise percentage of companies reporting on disaster relief**

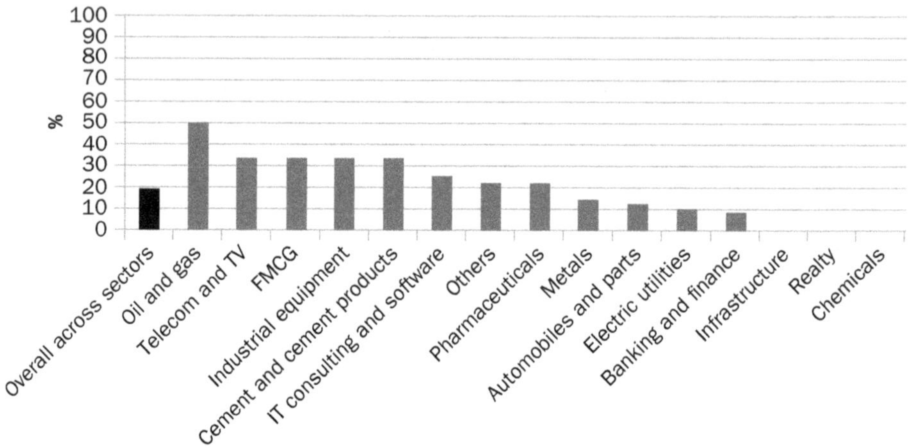

3.6.4 Education

This section includes steps adopted by the companies to promote education among the local communities or society at large. A total of 74 companies reported education initiatives in this research. These initiatives could include:

- **Building schools**: Schools built by a company free of cost or at a minimal cost to the community or the society.
- **Scholarships:** Scholarships offered by the company to underprivileged/meritorious students at various levels of education, for primary to higher studies.
- **Sponsoring or running schools**: Helping schools run efficiently by providing books, uniform, shoes and bags to children who cannot afford them or providing benches, blackboards, water coolers and other infrastructure to schools. Free education to students who cannot afford it; providing free meals also falls under this initiative.
- **Work done for secondary education:** Efforts done specifically to promote secondary education such as supporting/building secondary schools in localities that do not have one. Encouraging children to go to school by spreading awareness, helping or training teachers, providing infrastructure for the school.
- **Work done for higher/technical education**: Setting up or supporting higher or technical education institutes like vocational training centres, engineering colleges, schools offering training in other fields such as management.

Given India's large young population and weak education system, a key focus area for CSR at about 75% of the companies was education (Figures 3.37 and 3.38). The focus here is on improving access to education through scholarships as well as improving the quality of education by sponsoring or running schools.

Figure 3.37 **Sector-wise percentage of companies reporting education initiatives**

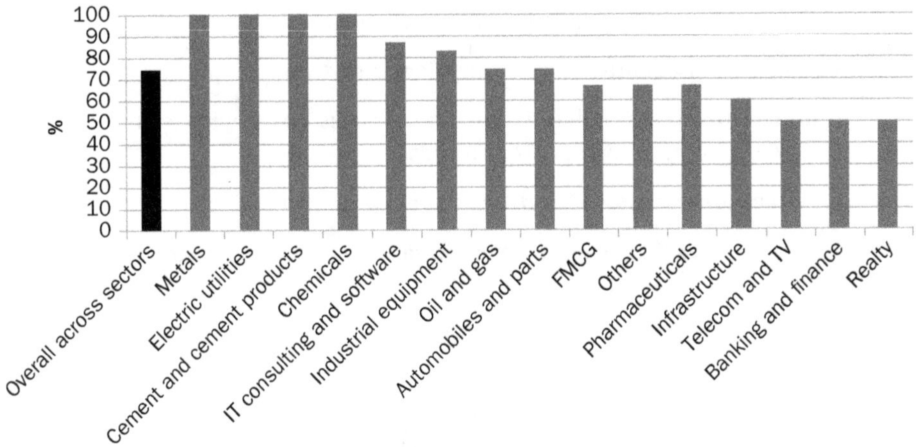

While most sectors were involved in CSR, the sectors that had an impact on the community and therefore needed a social licence to operate (such as metals and chemicals) had a very strong focus on education. While the IT sector may not have a direct impact on the community, their focus on education was driven by two things—ensuring a steady stream of talent by investing in education and providing their employees an opportunity to volunteer through CSR initiatives.

Figure 3.38 **Number of companies disclosing information related to education initiatives**

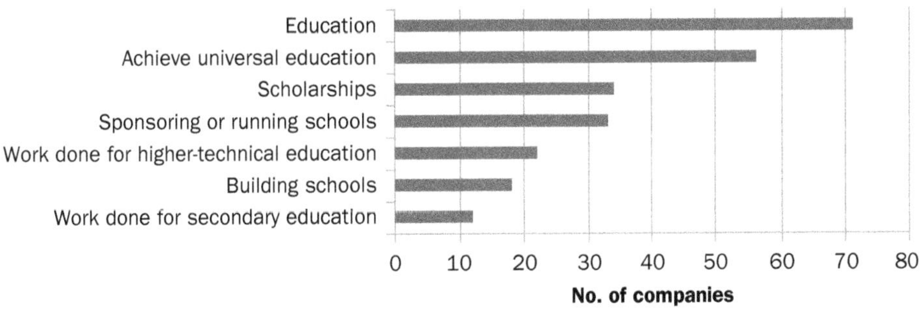

3.6.5 Healthcare

This section includes the steps initiated by the companies to offer healthcare services; to spread awareness on healthcare issues such as maternal health, childcare, HIV/AIDS, malaria, diarrhoea, cholera; to set up mobile clinics or camps for free check-ups and treatments for various diseases; and to conduct training programmes on prevention and cure. Any information that could not be stored in the sub-groups below was stored in this general section. A total of 71 companies reported healthcare initiatives. These initiatives include:

- **Blood donation camps:** Organizing blood donation camps.
- **Building hospitals:** Building hospitals/clinics to provide easy access to healthcare facilities to the communities or society.
- **Eye check-up camps:** Organizing eye check-up camps.
- **Healthcare training programmes:** Organizing training programmes for the people of the community on hygiene, childcare, nutrition, maternal care, etc.
- **Combat HIV/AIDS, malaria and other diseases (Millennium Development Goal)**

Healthcare was a focus area for almost all the sectors. More than 70% of the companies disclosed information on healthcare initiatives (Figures 3.39 and 3.40).

Figure 3.39 **Number of companies disclosing information related to healthcare initiatives**

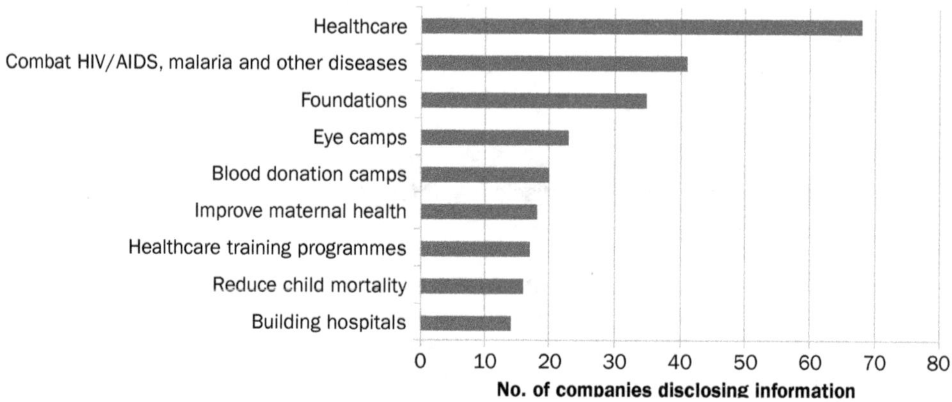

Figure 3.40 **Sector-wise percentage of companies reporting healthcare initiatives**

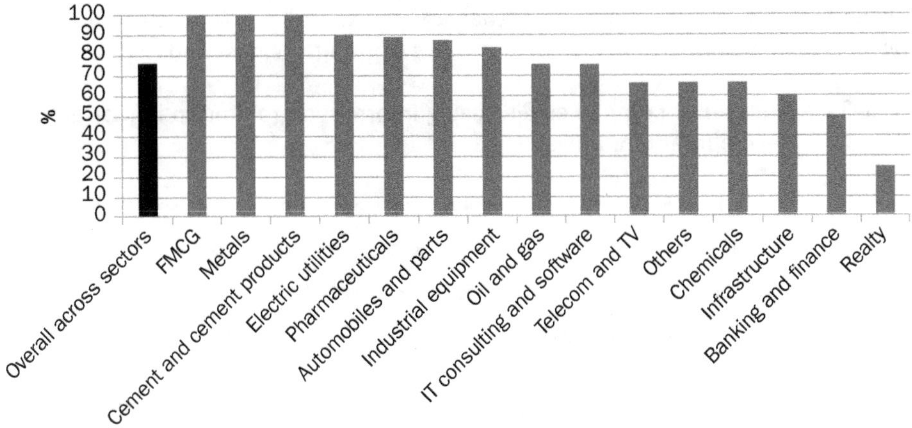

3.6.6 Infrastructure development

Infrastructure development includes the development of infrastructure, sewerage, roads and so on. Along with healthcare and education, infrastructure development formed a crucial part of the CSR strategy of many of the companies. Just under 70% of the companies included infrastructure development in their CSR initiatives (Figures 3.41 and 3.42). This is unsurprising given the pressing need to improve India's infrastructure.

Figure 3.41 **Sector-wise percentage of companies reporting infrastructure development initiatives**

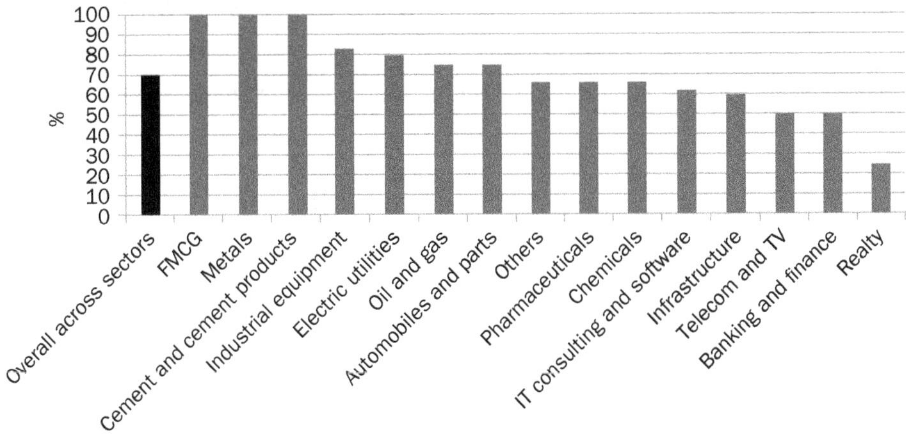

Interestingly, the FMCG sector was a leader in this area. This makes sense given that rural development and upliftment are the major focus areas of infrastructure development. For FMCG companies that seek to expand into rural markets, focusing on rural development is a great example of aligning business and CSR strategies.

Figure 3.42 **Number of companies disclosing information related to infrastructure development initiatives**

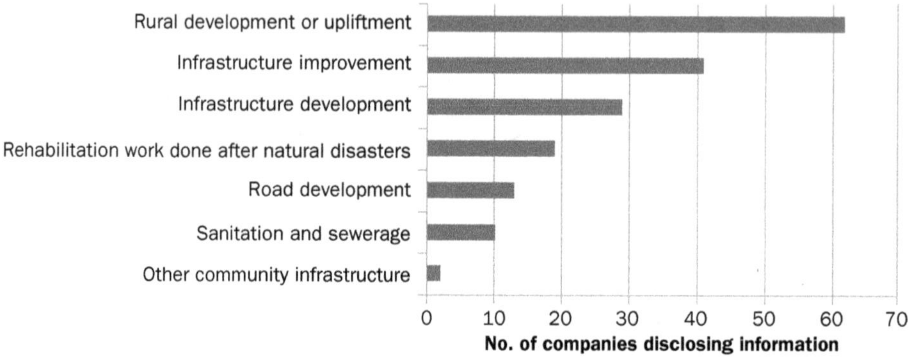

3.6.7 Cultural conservation

Companies have various means to conserve the heritage and cultural traditions of the communities in which they operate or to expose communities to various forms of arts through exhibitions and events. The measures adopted to promote local art and culture such as handicrafts, pottery, dance forms, music forms and textiles, and to support them by providing the infrastructure or helping them to sell their crafts so that they can make a living all fall under this section.

It is evident from the data in Figure 3.43 that this was not a core CSR area for most of the companies.

Figure 3.43 **Sector-wise percentage of companies reporting cultural conservation initiatives**

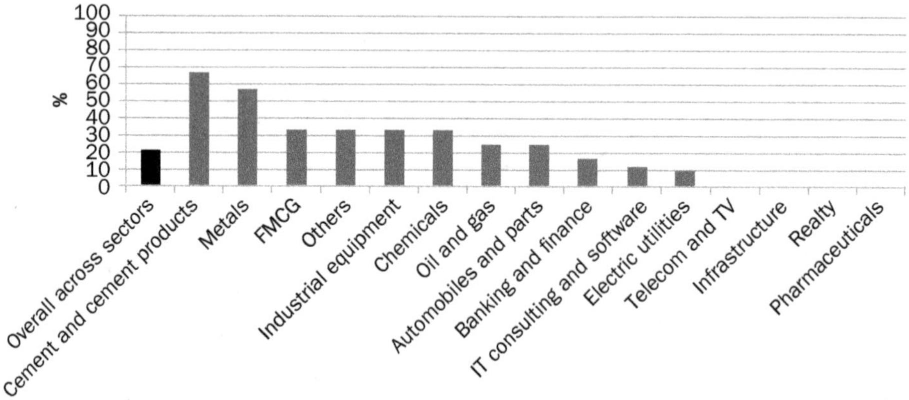

3.6.8 Community livelihood

Companies can invest in society and the neighbouring communities through the provision of training programmes to improve the livelihoods of disabled people, children and the elderly. Building skills and improving quality of life can be done through training, through the empowerment of women, disabled, children and the elderly, and by organizing relaxing and fun events and encouraging sports.

Community livelihood was found to be the most popular CSR focus area with nearly 80% of the companies disclosing some information about these initiatives. Most sectors, especially those with community impacts, focused on this area. Livelihood training is focused on imparting training. Therefore, it is not surprising that the IT sector was a leader in this area, given its focus on education as a CSR focus area (Figures 3.44 and 3.45).

Figure 3.44 **Sector-wise percentage of companies reporting community livelihood programmes**

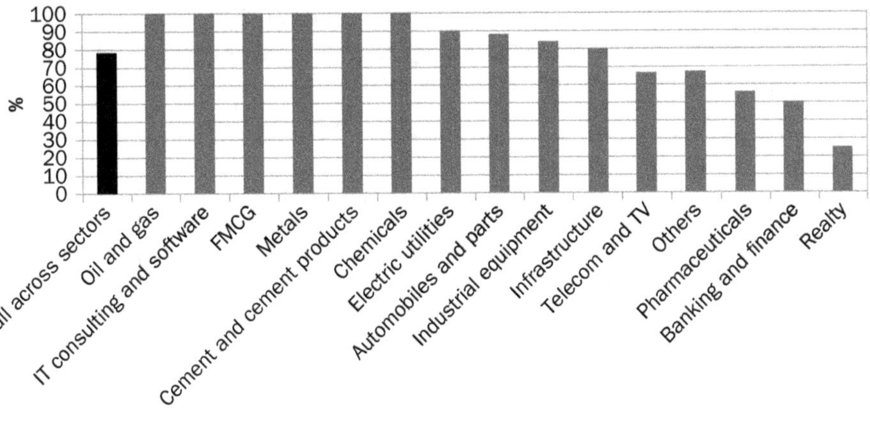

Figure 3.45 **Number of companies disclosing information related to community livelihood initiatives**

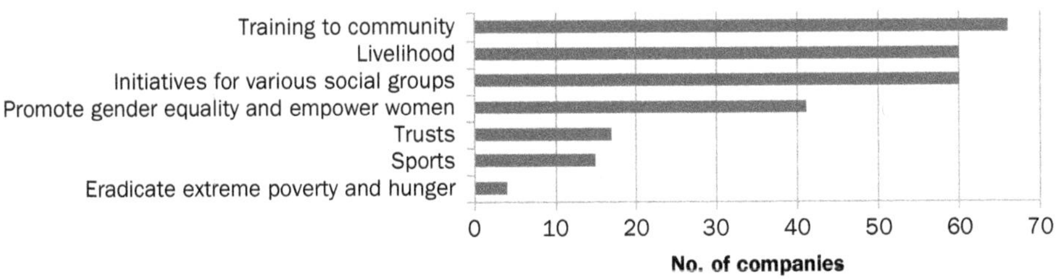

3.6.9 Environment conservation

Conserving and protecting the natural surroundings of the local community, water conservation, forestry initiatives, and spreading awareness about various environment protection initiatives were taken up by the companies as part of their CSR activities. These initiatives were not part of greening their core business operations but were of a philanthropic nature—these were deployed to create awareness among the employees and the other stakeholders, and to improve the quality of life of the neighbouring communities and society at large. To that end, companies can work with the local governments, communities and other stakeholders on initiatives such as planting trees, cleaning up the surroundings, watershed management for the villages, and organizing awareness camps in partnership with NGOs.

- **Awareness programmes:** Programmes organized or promoted by the company to spread awareness among the communities about their plants or the society at large on various issues such as environment protection, healthcare practices, conservation of water, energy, natural resources, and the importance of education and other social issues related to dowry, the girl child, etc.
- **Nature conservation**: Steps taken by the company to protect the natural biodiversity of places could include conserving natural habitats such as mangroves, forests, deserts and wildlife. The measures for implementing these could be getting involved in the conservation process or supporting/funding organizations that work towards it.
- **Water conservation**: Measures taken by the company to conserve water by promoting water harvesting practices in the community or by supporting the community to build water tanks or water harvesting units.
- **Forestry**: Planting saplings within a company's campus, external large-scale tree plantation, social forestry, and landscaping could be conducted by companies to recover natural environments and improve the quality of life in communities.

Tree plantation and nature conservation were the most popular environment-related CSR initiatives that the companies pursued. About 50% of the companies studied had such environment-related initiatives (Figure 3.46).

Figure 3.46 **Number of companies disclosing information related to environment conservation initiatives**

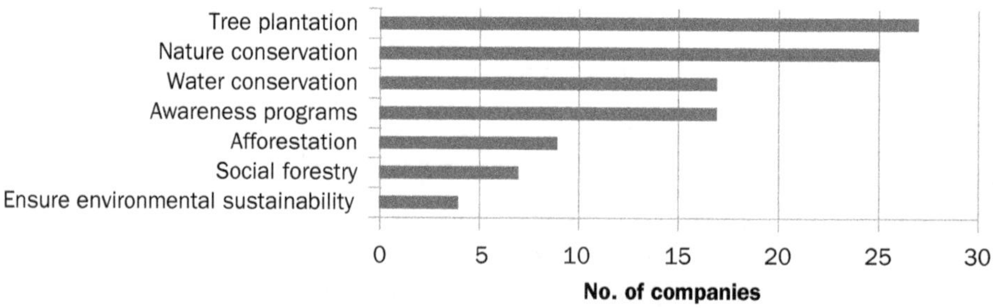

FMCG companies led the other sectors in this focus area (Figure 3.47). This could be attributed to tree plantation and similar activities being easy to implement as a customer-facing initiative that also drives brand recognition.

Figure 3.47 **Sector-wise percentage of companies reporting conservation initiatives**

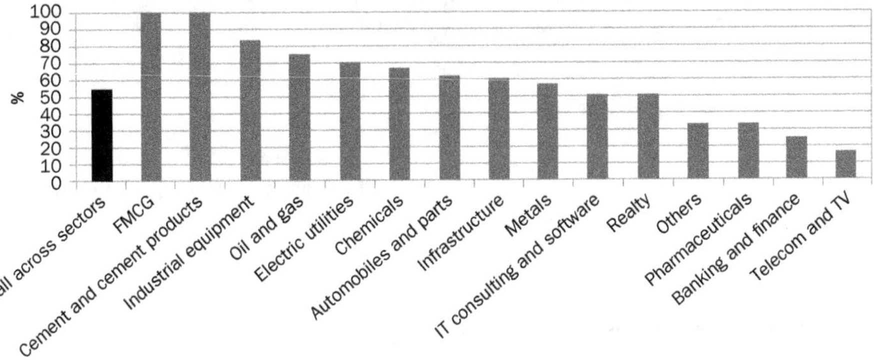

3.6.10 Other CSR initiatives

Volunteering was one of the most popular initiatives under this area. Companies encouraged volunteering because it drives greater employee engagement and satisfaction. Figures 3.48 and 3.49 present the data related to the other CSR initiatives of the companies studied.

Figure 3.48 **Sector-wise percentage of companies reporting other CSR initiatives**

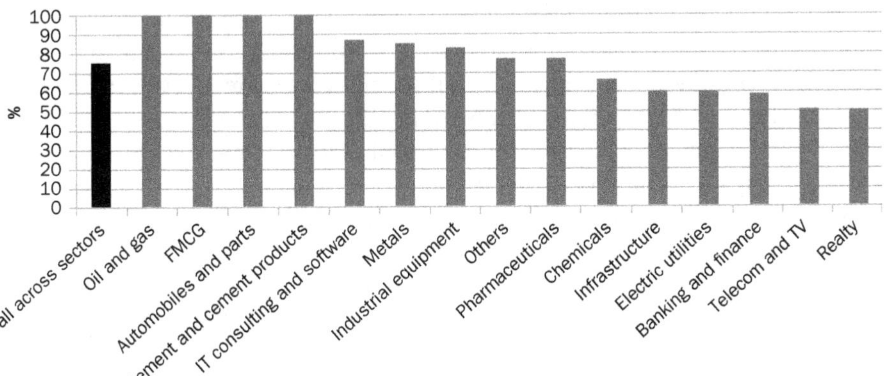

Figure 3.49 **Number of companies disclosing information related to other CSR initiatives**

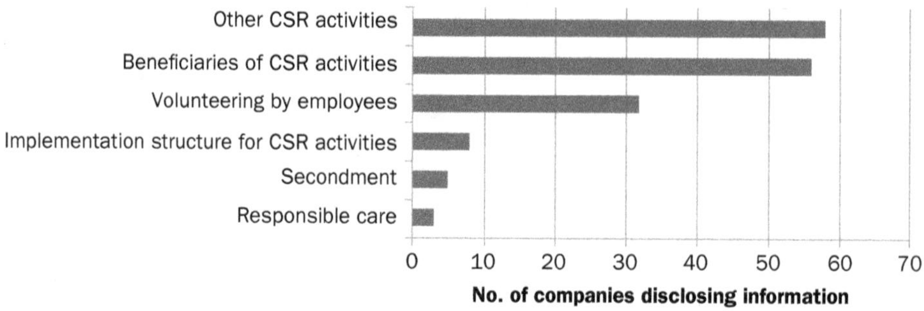

3.7 Summary and conclusions

This study analysed publicly available, sustainability-related information disclosed by India's top 100 companies in 15 industry sectors across 24 variables and 162 sub-variables. The analysis was broadly divided into three parts—organization and management; operations and core business practices; and Corporate Social Responsibility—and was also divided along industry sectors.

Overall, the study shed light on some interesting trends. There was a strong focus on corporate governance in all the companies surveyed. Nearly 90% of the companies stated that they either had developed or followed externally specified codes of conduct or internal governance policies. Interestingly, this did not translate into a corresponding focus on transparency. Only about a quarter of the companies had published reports based on widely recognized initiatives, such as the Global Reporting Initiative. Disclosures on CSR finances and donations were also low. It is in the interest of corporate India for companies to become more transparent in order to build greater stakeholder trust as well as to improve the internal processes for managing sustainability issues.

Sector-wise, heavy-industry sectors such as cement, metals and mining, and electric utilities outperformed other sectors on most indicators. This could be ascribed to their need for a social licence to operate. Some sectors such as realty, telecom and TV, pharmaceuticals, and banking and finance had not disclosed as much as the others. A notable exception was the IT and consulting sector, which performed well on several indicators and reported extensively. A generous explanation for this could be that they have a greater maturity in sustainability, driven by the need to attract and retain employees as well as global benchmarking. Alternately, one could also attribute this to the fact that with limited and less complex potential impacts compared to the other manufacturing sectors, this sector is better positioned to report on such matters.

The study highlights the following aspects related to sustainability reporting in India.

After governance, the most frequently reported initiatives were CSR-related (community livelihood, healthcare, education, etc.), operational efficiency-driven (green operations, including energy and resource conservation), or communication-centred.

More top 25 companies reported on a greater number of variables than the bottom 25 companies did, thus indicating a greater degree of reporting transparency at the top of the heap.

3.7.1 Organization and management

Nearly 85% of the companies had a published corporate governance policy. The next highest reported policy was HSE (35% of the companies). Voluntary sustainability reporting is still limited—only 25 reports based on GRI were published online at the time of data collection.

There is an increasing focus on putting systems and processes in place for managing environment, quality, safety, and so on. Nearly 55% of the companies reported having an environment management system (ISO 14000). However, very few companies currently reported on their energy audits. Given the increasing concerns about global climate change, this may be an issue that needs more transparency in reporting.

About 75% of the companies communicated regularly with the various stakeholders—employees, customers, vendors—on sustainability-related matters.

3.7.2 Operations and core business practices

About 80% of all the companies studied reported on at least one aspect related to greening of operations. Most initiatives appeared to focus on two things—resource conservation (energy, water, paper) and managing waste (emissions, solid waste, water).

The most popular initiative was energy conservation. This high percentage could be linked to the economic benefits (such as lower operating costs) that result from implementing these initiatives. Only a little above 30% of the companies highlighted their climate change initiatives. These were largely driven by emission reduction goals, which tie in to the larger energy conservation goals that the companies had.

Renewable energy adoption is also growing, with 40% companies disclosing information on the same. The leading sectors here included the oil and gas, electric utilities, chemicals, and automobile sectors.

Health and safety and providing training for employees in the workplace were the other focus areas.

The study showed two areas that companies can improve on. First, fewer than 20% of the companies disclosed information on sustainability issues related to the supply chain. This could be a great opportunity for companies to achieve operational efficiencies by working with vendors and suppliers.

Second, only 10% of the companies disclosed information on R&D in environment friendly products and processes. This could also potentially be an area of competitive advantage.

3.7.3 Corporate Social Responsibility

More than 70% of the companies studied focused on four core CSR areas—education, healthcare, community livelihood and infrastructure development.

For education, the focus was on improving access to as well as the quality of education. Companies did this by sponsoring or running schools and also by providing scholarships. Most of the healthcare CSR initiatives were driven by foundations. The initiatives themselves included blood donation drives, eye check-up camps, maternal healthcare, building hospitals, and so on.

For community livelihood, the focus was on providing training and other livelihood opportunities. Apart from heavy industries, IT companies performed very well in this area. For infrastructure development, rural infrastructure and upliftment were the main focus areas. Interestingly, FMCG companies led the way here.

Sectors with a greater impact on the community—such as metals and mining, chemicals, oil and gas, and so on—were more likely to report on their CSR initiatives. IT companies also performed very well in this section, driven by their focus on CSR as an employee engagement strategy.

Other CSR initiatives included a focus on environmental conservation (mostly through tree planting), disaster relief programmes, cultural conservation, and employee volunteering. An area for improvement for these companies is increased transparency in CSR finances and donations, which could help drive more efficient CSR programmes.

References

Bazeley, P., and Jackson, K. (Eds.) (2013). *Qualitative Data Analysis with NVIVO*. Thousand Oaks, CA: Sage Publications.

Bazeley, P., and Richards, L. (2000). *The NVIVO Qualitative Project Book*. Thousand Oaks, CA: Sage Publications.

Richards, L. (2009). *Handling Qualitative Data: A Practical Guide*. Thousand Oaks, CA: Sage Publications.

4

Voluntary green ratings in the construction industry

Exploring the underlying agendas

Ar. Shabari Shaily
Sustainability Consultant and Architect, Johannesburg, South Africa

The exceptional economic growth on the Indian sub-continent has created a demand for nearly 104 billion square feet of construction over the next few decades. This has resulted in a considerable projected carbon footprint, as well as raising alarming questions regarding the sub-continent's priorities towards environmental protection, climate change and holistic sustainability. Subsequently, the Indian construction industry has created an unanticipated demand for the development and adoption of environment assessment tools, such as the "Green Rating for Integrated Habitat Assessments" (GRIHA), alongside already established voluntary green standards such as the IGBC's LEED India. This chapter critically examines the motives that drive large and small private sector developers, along with government institutions, in fostering sustainable growth of the Indian construction industry pivoting on such voluntary standards; measured against the backdrop of sustainable development. Empirical evidence is presented regarding strategic policy formulation aimed at encouraging green building practices in India, illustrating progress, as well as magnifying the challenges that remain.

4.1 Introduction

There presently exists an overwhelming body of scientific evidence confirming that anthropogenic climate change represents one of the foremost, and potentially devastating, global environmental concerns facing the world in the 21st century. This is further confirmed with the emission of greenhouse gasses (GHGs) having firmly been established as the main contributor to global warming (IPCC, 2007). Concurrently, the marked increase in the environmental footprint of the built environment industry in recent years has endorsed the view that buildings and their integrated systems represent a significant contributor to CO_2 and other GHG emissions.

On a global scale, buildings in an urban environment have similarly demonstrated a significant impact on land, water, energy and material resources. Buildings, with their heavy dependence on heating and cooling systems, place a heavy burden on Earth's depleting resources; this subsequently leads to sustainability being included in the criteria against which a building's value is judged (Reed *et al.*, 2009).

As an ever-increasing population demands an exponential growth in construction, especially given the rising number of developing countries and emerging economies, it is imperative to identify means to mitigate the resultant environmental degradation. However, in order to develop effective mitigation strategies, it is necessary to first identify the quantity and quality of the *full* life-cycle impact of building projects on the environment. In response to this need, several countries developed sustainability assessment tools that are capable of efficiently quantifying the impact of projects, and rank the sustainability of future and existing building stock. Regardless of the geographical factor, however, the ultimate objective remains the same, i.e. to provide a judicious appraisal of projects to all relevant stakeholders in the industry.[1] Some authors, however, maintain that environmental assessment of buildings has a greater contribution to make, and thus, instead of merely providing a means to determine cost effective measures to mitigate adverse effects of individual projects, it underlies a broader agenda in that it provides a means to advance the industry towards increased responsible environmental behaviour (Gibson *et al.*, 2005).

This chapter accordingly considers these divergent viewpoints, particularly within the context of the Indian built environment industry. The development of various policy frameworks implemented in India is discussed, followed by an examination of the economic, environmental and social factors underlying these developments, and which manifest as different drivers behind the support for green ratings by government and industry.

1 Given the multifaceted nature of the built environment industry, stakeholders represent a plethora of parties and interests, including builders, developers, property evaluators, owners, architects, and governmental and industry regulatory bodies.

4.2 Development of green building practices in India

The vernacular architecture in various regions of India demonstrates key climate-responsive strategies that indirectly minimize their adverse impact on soil, efficiently utilize water and energy, and reduce pressure on material resources. These strategies are collectively referred to as "green building practices" in the traditional layperson nomenclature. However, due to changes in Indian urban climate over the preceding decades, coupled with an increased building footprint, the challenge arising is to maintain that same quality of space with these green strategies.[2] Reed makes this point by stating:

> [A]rchitects and engineers address the efficiency of buildings while failing to understand the earth systems, the very systems we are trying to sustain. It is time to change our mental model to one that better reflects the new understanding of how the universe actually works, and also enables us to design, build and heal with the whole system in mind—a deeply integrated worldview (Reed, 2007, pp. 674-680).

The concept referred to above is "whole systems approach", and represents a novel development in terms of which each component of a building (from cradle to grave) is accounted for during the conceptual design of the internal spaces.[3] As will be seen later on in this chapter, the incorporation and acceptance of such an approach into the attitude of the built environment stakeholders is vital to ensure sustainable growth of the Indian construction industry. However, green building practices globally have come about to rely heavily on a regulatory body that is capable of facilitating such a holistic sustainability framework that integrates necessary key systems.

In order to provide for such a framework, and following on from the successful practices in other developed and developing nations, green building rating tools were introduced to India in early 2001 through Indian Green Building Council's LEED–India (IGBC), a bespoke version of USGBC's LEED. This in turn was followed in 2007 by the introduction of Green Rating for Integrated Habitat Assessments (GRIHA)—an indigenous and domestic building rating system, which was endorsed in a collaborative effort by The Energy and Resources Institute (TERI), and the Ministry of New and Renewable Energy, India. According to the official statements by IGBC and GRIHA, although these rating bodies function independently, they have nonetheless jointly achieved a 145 million m^2 green building footprint in India since their respective inceptions (as of 2014). This figure illustrates

2 For the purpose of this chapter, quality of space is represented in terms of daylight quantum, ventilation rate, and thermal comfort achieved through a balance between temperature, humidity and airflow.

3 For example, in terms of this approach an architect in the conceptual stages of design would take into account factors such as building envelope, space functionality, and equipment.

a positive step towards achieving a reduced carbon footprint in the coming decades, and at first glance provides a fair indication of the significant growth in acceptance of rating tools by stakeholders within the Indian building industry. However, this view can be misleading when regarded within the context of the drivers that influence this apparent acceptance. Generally, "green buildings" can be expected to be only 9–12% higher in initial cost than conventional buildings (*The Hindu*, 2014). With project costs potentially running into the billions, this represents a significant financial burden to developers. From an economic perspective, such a ready acceptance is therefore somewhat suspicious, and requires examination of the different factors that may contribute to this shift towards environmental sustainability.

As per the latest report by McGraw Hill Construction Analytics on world green building trends (McGraw Hill Construction, 2013), during 2012, client and market demand (35% and 33% respectively) were identified as the most influential factors for the growth of green buildings. This was closely followed at 30% by branding benefits and lower operating cost over the long term (See Figure 4.1). These figures clearly indicate that green building has undertaken a paradigm shift from being a specialized field, to a potential business opportunity created by the market despite the increase in initial costs.

Figure 4.1 **Global responses on drivers of green building activities in 2012**

Source: data adapted from McGraw Hill Construction, 2013

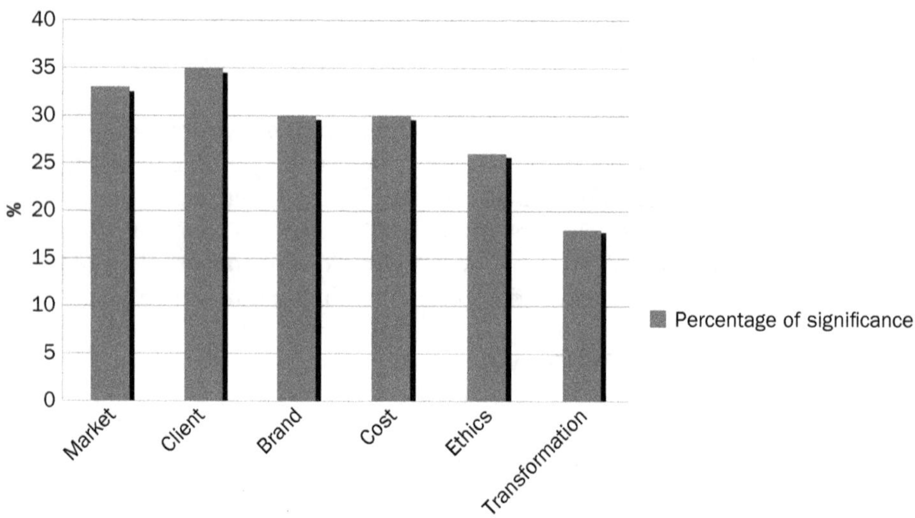

This market-driven increase in the incorporation of green building standards is, however, not only limited to the independent non-profit organizations working in the built environment industry. The incorporation of green ratings by the government has also shown a noticeable increase in both encouragement, and enforcement, over the last decade. The question then arises as to whether the underlying factors influencing government assimilation of green standards relate to those of the industry and, if so, what the common denominator might be. This question is examined in the following section.

4.3 Government integration in the assessment process

In their early days, green building ratings had a conservative approach to entering the mainstream industry. The system was marketed as a business model for large sector developers to achieve sustainability via a defined standard and get it recognized. Gradually, in order to reach small-scale developers from Tier II cities, the rating bodies were required to collaborate with national government and local municipal bodies.[4]

This approach adopted by rating bodies had resulted in the promotion of the concept of "green building" in the public domain, while simultaneously allowing for a degree of regulatory supervision, despite the fact that the adoption of green building ratings by projects remained voluntary. A recent example of such collaboration on a national level includes the issuance of a memorandum by the Ministry of Environment and Forests (MoEF), India that ensures the expediting of clearances for "green building" certified projects. Various public councils across the country have likewise introduced fiscal incentives for the adoption of green ratings. For example, the Pimpri Chinchwad Municipal Corporation in Maharashtra state has introduced property tax rebates for GRIHA-certified buildings; and in Northern India, Noida Development Authority is awarding 5% additional "Floor Area Ratio" (FAR) to "green building" certified projects (GRIHA, 2013a).

Existing regulatory frameworks have also been seen to evolve, albeit slowly, in order to incorporate the concept of green ratings. Historically, the Town and Country Planning Organization enforced a series of "Model Building Bye Laws" as per the 74th Constitutional Amendment Act, 1992, with the aim of guiding local bodies, urban development authorities and state governments towards orderly construction of urban areas (MoUD, 2011). Despite being over two decades old, these bylaws still govern contemporary building massing, architectural and construction techniques, building footprint and height. Given the growing awareness regarding the viability of sustainable construction among both the industry and government, however, new developments regarding sustainable building have been incorporated into the National Building Code–2005. In addition, the MoEF initiated an Environmental Clearance Process for projects with a built-up area greater than 20,000 m^2 (MoEF, 2010), in terms of which the committee scrutinizing the proposals are able to challenge the project proponents to provide for basic environmental

4 Tier II cities in this instance refer to those with nearly 1 million population. These are mostly state capitals or highly industrialized or commercialized cities.

management infrastructure, such as water recycling plants, rainwater harvesting systems, and organic waste management. These provisions have therefore become an indirect, yet integral, part of most building rating tools, including GRIHA and the IGBC LEED–India, and illustrates that development policy framework in India has progressed to a considerable overlap between government-regulated mechanisms, and the independent building assessment methods.

The scope for this joint enforcement of regulatory practices seemingly does provide for a mutually beneficial relationship, with good returns over the long term to both parties. Since the rating tools remain voluntary in nature, subsidies and incentives floated by the government provide an encouraging, and potentially lucrative, offer to building industry stakeholders to get involved with green building practices.[5] Conversely, concerning government assets, buildings falling under the auspices of the Central Public Works Department (CPWD) are required to achieve minimum three-star rating in terms of GRIHA. Such interplay encourages sustainable construction by means of established and detailed assessment tools, without having to revert to subsidiary regulation governing the state assets.

In order to accommodate the above government incentives, and to ensure a more efficient collaboration, the Indian rating tools further evolved into a two-stage process. The first stage allows projects to achieve so-called "pre-certification" by documenting future green commitments towards sustainable site management, water efficiency, energy efficiency, material resources conservation, and indoor environmental quality. Once a project is awarded pre-certification at the design stage, the onus transfers to the MoEF to consider the application and process the same within *six* to *seven* months. If a project is able to demonstrate its ability to meet the prescribed set of environmental norms, this represents a considerable potential incentive to project developers, as it considerably minimizes the regular processing time of at least 15 months for a non-rated project. Although this approach is commendable with regard to fostering commitment towards green building, the critical aspect, however, lies with the probability of these projects being able to proceed to final certification. As a project requires the submission of extensive documentary evidence regarding environmental compliance in order to proceed to final certification, the real test to ascertain environmental commitments only becomes possible at this later stage of groundwork. The various processes and mechanisms to conduct assessment in terms of green building standards are well documented and

5 Such interplay between government and rating systems are not unique to India though, with such governmental strategies thriving in global markets. See, for example, the case of Canada, which is currently proceeding through a sustainability transformation phase. Apart from federal government subsidies, a cap and trade system has also been introduced in the country that exerts pressure on business with larger carbon footprints to purchase tradable permits. In addition, all buildings of federal stock—owned and leased—are required to comply with green building standards (Tripathi, 2011).

therefore fall outside the scope of this chapter. Nonetheless, a pressing question that arises is that of the appraisal of direct and indirect effects where the success of the appraisal depends upon the implementation quality, and concurrently, the level of authority divested to the governing body responsible for appraisal within the construction industry.

These "incorporations" of green ratings into government policies relating to the construction sector convey a weighty responsibility on the rating systems, as they effectively become the image of government policy regarding green commitments. This further suggests a level of accountability on the part of the rating systems, and necessitates continuous verification to ensure that commitments are not eschewed in order to accommodate a political agenda. It should be noted, though, that this does not suggest critique of the ratings, but rather highlights the need to cautiously analyse the underlying agenda for such policy strategies, and to determine the potential of these strategies to successfully deliver on sustainability goals.

4.4 Sustainable development agenda and the Indian construction industry

To this day, the Indian approach to government subsidization discussed in the previous section has been well received by the industry in terms of the number of projects registered for pre-certification. The overlapping of government regulations and green building rating frameworks further allows for the scenario where a project that meets the prerequisites as per the local regulations (such as water efficiency and site management), can effortlessly accomplish the rating criteria as well.[6] Although there is no data available on the exact figure, approximately 2,200 projects are registered under various rating systems and currently going through evaluation process (as of 2014). Out of this figure, nearly 80% of projects are pre-certified, a figure predominantly owing to the MoEF memorandum of fast-track environmental certification (GRIHA, 2013b).

These figures are quite commendable when considered in terms of a mere decade of operation, and, as such, have been used to indicate positive progress towards sustainable construction. However, these figures must be cautiously interpreted as they merely represent commitment, and not *actual* implementation of green standards. In comparison to the number of projects registered for pre-certification,

6 More stringent, though, is energy efficiency and building physics, which are more critically examined under the rating systems. For example, in terms of GRIHA, more than a third of allotted points (34 out of 100 points) pertain to energy optimisation through efficient mechanical and electrical systems and building design. Water, site, material and indoor air quality share the remaining two-thirds (66 out of 100 points) (GRIHA, 2013b).

only 350 projects are at present fully certified and at operation stage. This may indicate a motivation by developers that appears to be more inclined towards marketability and branding, i.e. corporate reputation, rather than an agenda towards the progression of sustainable construction.

4.4.1 Marketability: role of quality and quantity

The urbanization of Indian cities has led to a significant growth in the construction industry, and has led to a spate of corporate firms acquiring interests in the sector. As was discussed previously, the prospect of profitable branding and a good return on the property are market driven factors that have an undeniable influence on decisions to adopt green building.

Some authors have emphasized this "marketability mentality" towards building tools by built environment stakeholders (Alwaer *et al.*, 2007). Sustainability assessment methods in general consist of two quite distinct aspects—quantitative and qualitative—that are often in contradiction with each other. Whereas quantitative aspects account for energy, water, waste and other such measurable parameters, quality aspects explore the social-psychological impact of green buildings. Quantitative aspects being measurable against established benchmarks, there are no definitive standards defining qualitative value of green buildings, which further complicate this distinction. This presents a challenge when a performance comparison has to be drawn between green certified, and non-green certified buildings, particularly when considered in terms of profitability.

However, this assumption regarding an industry bias towards non-certified projects because of the lack of qualitative information is challengeable in terms of the Indian building industry. Qualitative values such as daylight, ventilation and thermal comfort are expressly defined by set parameters in the National Building Code–2005, as well as in the Energy Conservation Building Code–2007, by the Bureau of Energy Efficiency, India. The availability of these standards enables architects, engineers and contractors to make an informed decision prior to drafting of the design specifications. Additionally, building rating tools prescribe the benchmarks that are over and above the government set codes, thus ensuring that green building projects represent an advance on conventional designs, and enhancing the overall quality of green rating certified buildings. However, in terms of this context, two concerns become apparent. Firstly, the standards are voluntary, and thus only affect projects that register in terms of the ratings. Secondly, a lack of capacity regarding assigned auditing agents results in compliance verification becoming unfeasible for every new project in urban and rural areas. Although, local development authorities may issue demolition orders for projects, which are in breach of the building by-laws, this does not include environmental and social aspects.

This complexity in maintaining a well-balanced approach towards quality and quantity of sustainable buildings, at various instances, fails to drive the greener marketability and thus extensively influences the decision-making towards adoption of voluntary standards.

4.4.2 Social factors

Similar to the concept of Corporate Social Responsibility (in terms of which the socially conscious activities by corporate entities are publicized), green ratings systems have also adopted a focus on visibility, and subsequently, the promotion of a "green agenda" within popular society. The resultant impact of such a growing awareness is easily illustrated by the construction industry in the Indian state of Maharashtra. The region, which is endowed with vast natural resources, has encountered substantial environmental challenges on various instances. These challenges have consequently driven awareness campaigns within the local population, thus creating a demand for environmentally conscious infrastructure. For example, the *Gadgil Panel Report*, which incorporates guidelines for a controlled development in the Western Ghats belt, highlights the need for the involvement of locals in decision-making prior to any proposal approvals by the ministry (*The Hindu*, 2013). Similar instances have arisen in southern India, where mining operations were suspended after determined protests by environmental protagonists (*The Hindu*, 2004). These events illustrate the influence that popular society, and often those at the bottom of democratic structure, can make a significant impact to help achieve sustainable living.

Social awareness is therefore quite capable of moulding the market to generate a demand for green practices for building infrastructure, as much as the market-driven incentives. Greater calls for transparency and accountability in terms of sustainable development by society, is further driving developers towards the adoption of systems that are able to provide a breakdown of broader subjects, such as sustainable development and environmental awareness, into smaller components, including energy and water security, resource depletion, land degradation and occupant health and well-being. These rating systems additionally ensure an auditing process at the *operational* stage to verify the sustainability claims. It is therefore evident that projects must attempt a balance by considering the economic benefits in green building against the consequential environmental and social benefits.

This "triple bottom line approach", the attempt at balancing such seemingly dissimilar interests, is reflected on a micro, or individual project, basis as well. Any construction project represents the culmination of collaborative work by the developer, architect, engineer and project manager. This suggests that green building practices can likewise only be effectively accomplished once these four stakeholders unequivocally share the ideas that form the basis of sustainable design. This view is clearly demonstrated by the McGraw Hill study, in which responses from these four key stakeholders are recorded regarding multiple factors that are assumed to trigger the green building growth globally (McGraw Hill Construction, 2013). According to the study, engineers, developers and project managers form a consensus on the market demand and low operating costs, while most architects adopt sustainability purely because of *design* ethics.

It is important to take note to these differences, as they relate to the broader drivers that lead building developers towards rating tools. For example, it would be unfair to criticize industry's project leaders for their profit-driven approach since it is after all the foundation of a mixed-economy market. Engineers' duties generally revolve around ensuring efficiency and low operating costs, and therefore cannot be unduly criticized for this focus. However, given the growing awareness of environmental issues within popular society,[7] it has become necessary for these stakeholders to adapt their mind-set towards building energy-efficient infrastructure with minimum GHG emissions and long-term sustainable benefits.

Given the above, green building rating tools are undoubtedly an effective means to promote sustainable improvements in the built environment. Ratings assist in the increased awareness among stakeholders regarding broader, theoretical concepts, such as sustainable development, environmental protection and energy efficiency. They further provide an effective practical illustration as to potential benefits of "going green", as ratings can be incorporated into projects over a relatively short span, with immediate paybacks if applied correctly. Roychowdhary conceptualizes this view when he states that "[T]he advantage of the rating system is that it helps to disseminate green building practices outside the realm of regulations that are often impeded by structural and institutional barriers. This is a quicker way of increasing market outreach and build consumer support and awareness at the societal level" (Roychowdhary *et al.*, 2012).

However, though such incentives both encourage and mandate developers to adopt the rating tools, even if merely to expedite a lengthy bureaucratic process, it is essential to recognize that statistics indicating an increase in pre-certified green buildings may be painting a rather vague picture of the conscience of built environment industry stakeholders.

Thus far, this chapter has illustrated that various underlying factors have influenced the trend towards green building ratings. Both industry and government are influenced by economic and social factors, as well as environmental factors in the form of low-carbon construction. The question that remains though, is how these underlying factors work in practice, and is further discussed in the following section.

4.5 Green rating tools in practice

The minimum prerequisites for an assessment tool have been well established, and can by summarized as "a method that shall identify, describe and assess, in an appropriate manner, the direct and indirect effect of a project on: human beings,

7 The growth of sustainable development is an expansive topic that is well documented within academic literature. Though it falls outside the scope of this chapter, readers are encouraged to see: *Silent Spring* by Rachel Carson (1962), IPCC Reports and *Sustainable Design: Ecology, Architecture, and Planning* by Daniel Williams (Wiley, 2007).

flora and fauna, ecology, the interaction between the[se] factors and the material assets" (Roaf, 2004).

The objective of *green* building assessment methods is to create a built environment that is climate-responsive, conserves material and water resources, reduces energy consumption, and provides a healthy indoor environment for the users. Though these characteristics can be achieved in non-certified projects as well, the critical aspect relates to reliability of life-cycle performance. Non-certified projects may not be monitored for necessary environmental standards at the post-occupancy stage. Conversely, certified or rated buildings are expected to perform to the committed standards throughout the life-cycle of the building, and in case of any deviation from the standards, a commissioning body is tasked to resolve the issues identified through auditing processes. Thus, rating tools can, through a systematic implementation process, pave the way for a verified sustainability, and are able to address, indirectly, any gaps in existing policy frameworks.

The key to this argument lies in user satisfaction, which is assessable only after a certain period of occupancy. In case of residential projects, the buildings remain occupied for comparatively longer periods than commercial buildings.[8] During hours of occupation, a user experiences multiple elements that define his/her comfort, indirectly or directly. For example, in a naturally ventilated residential or commercial space located in a warm and humid climate, temperature, air velocity and relative humidity will collectively play a significant role in achieving comfort for the occupant during daytime in summer months. An architect would deal with these parameters through designing window opening percentage against the floor area to balance daylight and ventilation and optimum orientation to control solar heat gains from critical facades and through efficient material selection. An engineer would analyse and verify the structural implications of the architectural design, while the contractor would execute the project. These stakeholders, however, contribute primarily in a supporting capacity, and are typically not responsible for long-term functioning of the project. Throughout a project, the client (or project owner) would typically assume the top level of the project hierarchy, and would ultimately be responsible for the decisions that will affect the life-cycle of the project. Well-marketed "green" projects attract a premium, and as user satisfaction drives the profitability of *a single project*, it is in the best interest of the client or project owner to ensure continued compliance with permitting commitments. Conversely, a well-marketed project, but with a low user satisfaction will not merely hamper the profitability of a single project, but may influence the profitability of *all* future projects.

Another challenge that surfaces is with respect to the initial cost. As has previously been stated in the chapter, green design modifications to a conventional proposal require 8–10% higher initial costs to be borne by the owner. At this initial design stage, while architects and engineers are more ready to come to a consensus

8 This refers specifically to commercial and residential projects, as the two building types share a significant percentage of green certified or registered buildings in India.

regarding the green building concept, most project owners prioritize simpler and cost-effective strategies under the rating system. Even though certain strategies show rewarding long-term paybacks,[9] in order to represent a project's sustainability, owners choose to incorporate only those measures from the rating system's requirements that are already mandated by the regulatory bodies such as MoEF to obtain environmental clearance. To avoid such dubious practices by private sector developers, Indian building rating tools are structured to require the design to comply with energy performance requirements, failing which the project can be denied the rating.[10] Therefore, the owner is the key decision-maker in the hierarchy of a construction team's structure, where the design briefs are streamlined according to the owner's project requirement.

This vertical structure of a project team influences the working principle of any green certified building, from its design stage to execution and to operation and maintenance. As a process, one can divide the certification into multiple stages. It commences with a self-evaluation tool. This matrix enlists criteria under various issue categories, and allots a series of points based on their impact scale on the overall sustainability of the project. It highlights mandatory and optional criteria and a basic rating is awarded only upon compliance with certain criteria, entailing the project achieving minimum points required. This mechanism ensures an open-ended and flexible system for the stakeholders, i.e. the project owner, engineer, architect and contractor must be selective in their project specifications so that the rating's constraints do not compromise the client or project owner's requirements, whilst reflecting commitments that are achievable. However, due to the divergence in prioritization of green building issues and strategies among the client and the remaining stakeholders, green buildings are undergoing a non-uniform growth in principle, which is posing significant challenges to research institutions tasked with developing the assessment methods, and governmental bodies striving to enforce the sustainable development agenda.

Final mention should be made regarding the challenge of "Westernization" by the Indian construction market. This refers to the regrettable practice by building professionals of capriciously adopting Western standards and *not* adapting architectural details from Western culture for Indian urban areas. For instance, architects encounter fierce opposition by the uninformed audience while prioritizing relationship of building design to occupant comfort as against the conventional yet marketable approach of the client. The unapprised demands resultantly create a pseudo-market that struggles to survive with the accompanying innovative ideas addressing sustainability. The adoption of rating systems, therefore, endeavour to

9 For example, water recycling and installation of energy-efficient systems conserved resources for the long run with low energy and water bills.

10 Under the GRIHA rating system, project design is required to show compliance with Energy Conservation Building Codes and demonstrate a minimum 10% reduction in the building's annual energy consumption per square metre.

align the market expectations with sustainable development goals by introducing simpler strategies that can lead to economic, environmental and social sustainability. Under such a mechanism, with apt functioning, the future demand of nearly 104 billion square feet of construction in India by 2030 can sit smoothly under the green building guidelines (CSE, 2012).

4.6 Conclusions

The arguments, theories and practical realities presented in the above sections clearly highlight the gravity of the challenges currently faced by the regulatory bodies and research organizations to arrive at a common consensus with private sector developers and other building professionals. In order to maintain greater credibility in sustainability assessment methods, Indian rating bodies have opted for a longer-term "cradle-to-grave" approach, and while technical expertise is abundant with the design logics that drive sustainability, the business aspect contradicts with the underlying objectives of the green movement propagated by the building assessment methods. This rating tool template is unquestionable; however, the implementation methodology requires more scrutinizing. The involvement of government should serve as a boon to these voluntary mechanisms, which exist to streamline the private sector towards meeting national goals. Incentives call for close monitoring for their ultimate outcomes on the ground level. The glitches in the system must be resolved proactively and pragmatically through constant revision to the regulations responding to the immediate transformations in the development sector.

The conservative belief by stakeholders in the built environment that sustainable building is a *profit-oriented* business strategy (i.e. through positive branding) has been shown to be a rather narrow interpretation. As green assessment tools provide for a systematic mechanism to identify buildings as "green" based on their attributes and life-cycle performance against an established set of benchmarks, it suggests that the popularity of these standards are influenced as much by economic factors, as concerns for a lower carbon footprint.

However, additional factors in the form of social awareness have been shown to be a major driver. In fact, the popular understanding of sustainable development by society has been highlighted as an influential contributing factor to both government policy and rating systems. It is therefore imperative that the built environment industry take cognizance of the broader agenda for environmental protection and resource conservation, as increased efforts to incorporate sustainable development into mainstream policy frameworks, and subsequently into green building systems, will undoubtedly increase.

Moreover, it has been shown that successful incorporation of the "green mentality" can only be accomplished when the four primary key stakeholders—project owner, architect, engineer and contractor—address the sustainability of a project with sheer commitment and prioritize each section pertaining to economic, social and environmental challenges on an equal scale. However, projects must utilize rating tools as a guideline to attain holistic building efficiency, and not merely as a bypass towards rapid sanctioning and clearance. The pre-certification stage is intended to create awareness among a larger audience, and in particular the small-scale developers that generally shy away from the concept of green buildings as a costlier affair.

In conclusion, the statement by Leaman and Bordass, that "...green buildings are often more 'fragile' in their performance, so it is more important that everything works well together" (Leaman and Bordass, 2007) indirectly communicates the fact that diverging motivations for incorporating green building processes, merely frustrates the very aims of a more efficient and greener construction industry. It is therefore imperative that projects not only align with the broader interests of society, but manage to find an internal common goal among each other.

References

Alwaer, H., Sibley, M., and Lewis, J. (2008). Different stakeholder perspectives of sustainability assessment. *Architectural Science Review,* 51(1), 47-58.

Centre for Science and Environment (2012). Why "green" buildings? Retrieved from www.cseindia.org/userfiles/01%20WHY%20GREEN.pdf.

Gibson, R.B., *et al.* (2005). *Sustainability Assessment.* London: Earthscan.

GRIHA (Green Rating for Integrated Habitat Assessment) (2013a). Compendium: GRIHA Incentives. Retrieved from www.grihaindia.org/index.php?option=com_content&view=article&id=109.

GRIHA (Green Rating for Integrated Habitat Assessment) (2013b). No title. www.griha.org.

IGBC (Indian Green Building Council) (2013b). No title. Retrieved from www.igbc.in.

IPCC (Intergovernmental Panel on Climate Change) (2007). *Climate Change 2007: The Physical Science Basis. Contribution of Working Group I to the Fourth Assessment Report of the Intergovernmental Panel on Climate Change.* Cambridge, UK: Cambridge University Press.

Leaman, A., and Bordass, B. (2007). Are users more tolerant of "green" buildings? *Building Research and Information,* 35(6), 662-73.

McGraw Hill Construction (2013). *World Green Building Trends.* Bedford: McGraw Hill Construction. Retrieved from www.worldgbc.org/files/8613/6295/6420/World_Green_Building_Trends_SmartMarket_Report_2013.pdf.

Ministry of Environment and Forests (2010). Environmental Protection Act: Notification. *New Delhi: Gazette of India.* Retrieved from envfor.nic.in/legis/eia/so1533.pdf.

Ministry of Urban Development (2011). Model building bye laws. *New Delhi: Town and Country Planning Organisation.* Retrieved from moud.gov.in/legislation/model.

Reed, B. (2007). Shifting from "sustainability" to regeneration. *Building Research and Information,* 35(6), 674-680.

Reed, R., Bilos, A., Wilkinson, S., and Schulte, K. (2009). International comparison of sustainable rating tools. *Journal of Sustainable Real Estate,* 1(1). Retrieved from www.deakin.academia.edu/RichardReed/Papers/151515/International_Comparison_of_Sustainable_Rating_Tools.

Roaf, S. (2004). *Closing the Loop.* London: RIBA Enterprise.

Roychowdhary, A., Kishan, S., and Dasgupta, S.C. (2012). Green building-rating: Overrated. *Centre for Science and Environment.* Retrieved from www.cseindia.org/content/green-building-rating-overrated.

The Hindu (2004). Locals mining in Western Ghats suspended following protests: Andolana. Retrieved from www.hindu.com/2004/06/22/stories/2004062202330300.htm.

The Hindu (2013). Locals need final say on development of Western Ghats. Retrieved from www.thehindu.com/todays-paper/tp-national/tp-kerala/locals-need-final-say-on-development-in-western-ghats/article4790420.ece.

The Hindu (2014). Green homes are not "costly". Retrieved from www.thehindu.com/features/homes-and-gardens/green-living/green-homes-are-not-costly/article5900985.ece

Tripathi, A.K. (2011). Building a momentum: Green buildings. *Akshay Urja*, 4(5), 11-17.

5

Coping with globalization and climate change

Lessons learned from pro-poor business in South Asia

Venkatachalam Anbumozhi
Economic Research Institute for ASEAN and East Asia, Jakarta, Indonesia

Over the last few years, inspiring strategies and fruitful policies have evolved in the developing countries of Asia to integrate their economic activities, tackle climate change and accelerate green growth. Domestic stakeholders initiate and support these actions, not only because of perceived climate impacts, but also due to non-climate benefits such as energy security, reduced local pollution levels and inclusive growth. This chapter examines the impacts of globalization and climate change in a South Asian context, paying attention to how they present opportunities and risks for doing pro-poor business under integrated economic scenario. Analysing selected examples, it explores the factors that drove corporate to do pro-poor business and adopt green corporate practices. It concludes that an affirmative public–private partnership agenda is needed to transform value chain activities for the benefits of the society while reinforcing corporate strategies.

5.1 Introduction

National policy-makers and development practitioners alike increasingly recognize the potential role of the private sector in tackling poverty and global environmental problems like climate change. As early as 1992, the Rio Conference on Environment and Development created Agenda 12 to promote partnerships involving business; more recently, there has been the Business Call to Action (2008). Many firms in South Asia address poverty and environmental sustainability in their "core" businesses. This is a marked shift away from "philanthropy" (charitable gifts to worthy causes) and "corporate social responsibility" (essentially, doing no harm). The premise is that business can be carried out on a commercial basis but also be sustainable and benefit the poor, particularly in developing countries of South Asia. At the World Economic Forum Annual meeting 2013 in Davos-Klosters, three leading economic voices—the presidents of the International Monetary Fund (IMF) and the World Bank (WB), and the Secretary-General of the Organisation for Economic Co-operation and Development (OECD)—delivered the troubling message that it will not be possible to emerge from the current global economic crisis without addressing resource scarcity and climate change. Countries in the South Asia region, business actors within the national economy, eco-systems and communities are confronted by both the impacts of climate change and consequences of globalization. Globalization and its outcome trade liberalization also impact the energy industry and natural resources, creating new patterns of winners and losers within the corporate sector. This chapter examines the impacts of both elements and the causal relationship between them. Later it pays attention to how responding to globalization and climate change presents both opportunities and risks. The general argument of the chapter is that the private sector is the engine of economic integration and growth and the provider of solutions to global environmental issues like climate change. Pro-poor green growth goals will not be achieved by commercial activities alone. In many cases, governments must offer incentives for private companies to trade with the poor and adopt green corporate practices, and public–private partnerships can close the gap between the outcomes of private commercial activity and development goals.

5.2 Globalization, climate change and economic integration in South Asia

5.2.1 Trade integration and environmental risks

Globalization—a growing degree of interdependence among economies, businesses and societies through cross-country flows of information, ideas, technologies, goods and services, capital, finance and people—has ushered in a new era of contrasts: of fast-paced change and persistent sustainability problems. Expanding and maintaining this impressive growth rate, however, requires trade integration to ensure the free flow of goods, services and capital across borders (ADBI, 2013). Indeed, interplay of market forces and increased participation in trade have been decisive in the growth of emerging Asian economies. In East Asia's export-oriented industries, market-led de facto regionalization preceded formal *de jure* integration. Since the early 1990s, several attempts have been initiated to boost South Asian economic integration through a number of trade pacts at the bilateral, sub-regional and plurilateral levels. The South Asian Preferential Trading Arrangement (SAPTA), the South Asian Free Trade Area (SAFTA), and more recently the SAARC Agreement on Trade in Services (SATIS), which was signed in 2010, accelerated investments across the borders. As indicated in Table 5.1, South Asia's intra-sub-regional trade share increased from 2.7% in 1990 to 4.3% in 2011. Also, Figure 5.1 provides a comparative picture of intra-sub-regional trade shares for the member states of SAARC, the Association of Southeast Asian Nations (ASEAN), and ASEAN+3. It clearly shows that South Asia is progressing in terms of sub-regional integration, but lagging behind other regions. For example, in 2011, SAARC's intra-sub-regional trade was only 4.3%, whereas the corresponding figures for ASEAN and ASEAN+3 were 26% and 39%, respectively. But the positive trend is clear; as such, policy-makers and business communities in South Asia have become increasingly interested in economic integration in South Asia and the potential benefits that may come along with it.

Table 5.1 **South Asia's total trade within the sub-region and with the world**

Source: Asia Regional Integration Centre (ARIC) Integration Indicators Database

Reporter	**South Asia**				
Partner	**South Asia**			**World**	
Indicator	**Total trade, in billion US$**	**As percentage of South Asia's total trade with the world**	**Total trade growth (%)**	**Total trade, in billion US$**	**Total trade growth (%)**
1990	1.8	2.7	N/A	66.2	N/A
1995	4.4	4.2	43.3	104.4	26.9
2000	6.2	4.3	21.7	142.8	10.6
2005	17.3	5.3	30.6	324.1	32.5
2010	33.2	4.6	45.9	719.9	33.8
2011	40.5	4.3	22.1	951.1	32.1

Figure 5.1 **Intra-regional trade within South Asia and other regions**

Source: Asia Regional Integration Centre (ARIC) Integration Indicators Database

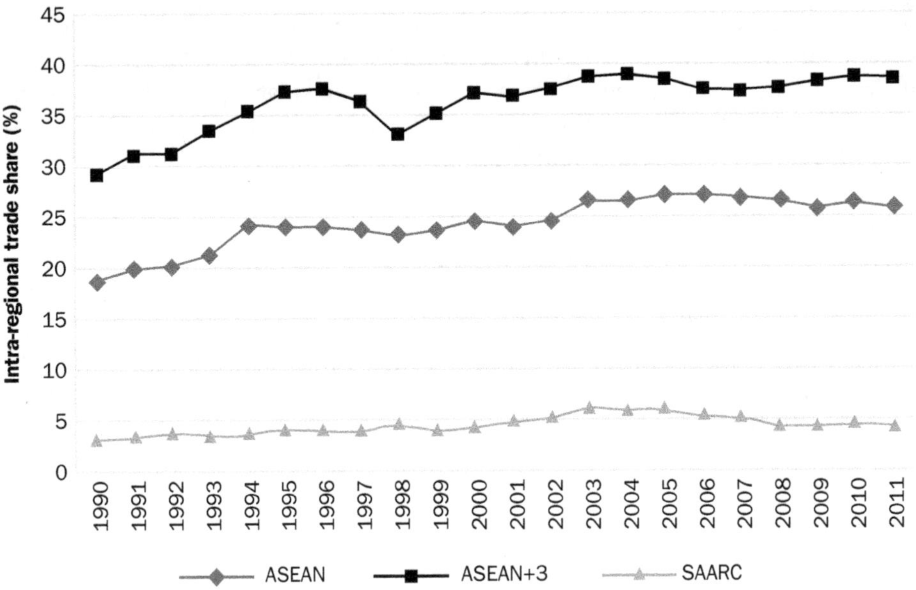

ASEAN: Association of Southeast Asian Nations;
SAARC: South Asian Association for Regional Cooperation

This globalization and economic integration can have both positive and negative effects on the environment and hence the necessity for corporate responses. It exacerbates environmental problems as well as providing new means of addressing them (Anderson *et al.*, 1999; Jobes, 2003; Speth, 2003). Corporate strategies and choices can also shape the path of globalization as national regulatory choices may act as barriers to liberalized trade or trigger a convergence towards higher international standards agreed by corporate houses. The challenge is that to establish an approximate mix of competition and cooperation, market forces and collective action must be planned for the protection of the poor and the environment.

5.2.2 Effects of climate change on corporate business strategies

Corporate executives typically manage environmental risks as threefold problems of regulatory compliance, potential liability from industrial accidents, and pollutant release mitigation. But climate change presents business risks that are different in kind because the impact is global, the problems is long-term, and the harm is essentially irreversible. Though the South Asia region is estimated to be the hardest hit by climate change effects (ADB, 2013), government policies have not offered companies both international and national guidance as to how climate policy may change in the future. Ignoring the financial (e.g. weather-related damages) and competitive consequences (e.g. emission reduction efficiency measures) of climate change could lead a company to formulate an inaccurate risk profile. While this obviously has been the case for utilities and energy-intensive industries like chemical and manufacturing, it now holds true for most industries in South Asia. In fact, the most important distinctions to be made when considering environmental risk assessment are not between sectors but within sectors, where a company's climate-risk-related mitigation and product strategies can create competitive advantage.

Government regulators are not the only ones monitoring individual companies for adequate climate-related practices. Big investors are beginning to demand more disclosure from companies. For example, the Carbon Disclosure Project, a coalition of institutional investors representing more than $31 trillion assets, annually request information from large companies about their climate positioning. Its most recent report, released in 2013, showed a marked increase of 170 companies in Asia—which includes 23 from India—indicating the awareness of climate change on the part of respondents in the best practices being developed to manage exposure to climate risk.

5.3 Competitive advantage of doing pro-poor green business in globally integrated economies

5.3.1 Key drivers of corporate climate strategy

The far-reaching effects of globalization and climate change become clear when the corporate think about different kinds of risk—most of which can be transformed into opportunities—and how they could affect the value of the company. The corporate risks associated with climate change can be grouped into: regulatory risks, supply chain risks, product and technology risk, litigation risk, reputational risk and physical risk (Lash and Wellington, 2010).

Companies operating in South Asia, such as Anglo American, BP, GE, Toyota, Unilever and Vodafone, belong to the World Business Council for Sustainable Development (WBCSD). The above-mentioned Business Call to Action was supported by 80 of the world's leading CEOs. Its purpose is to enhance inclusive growth and help achieve the Millennium Development Goals. Smaller companies are developing strategies with similar objectives. Halgolle Estate of Kelani Valley Plantations, Sri Lanka, is promoting smallholder cultivation of forest plantations. In Pakistan, Five Rivers Corporation is purchasing smallholders' production of Jatropha and promoting the use of sustainable agricultural methods. Gramin Sakthi in Bangladesh is selling environmentally friendly solar-powered lanterns to rural people

The experiences of the above companies indicate that there are four key drivers to consider in establishing balanced responses to globalization and climate change risks. They are summarized in Table 5.2.

Table 5.2 **Firm-level business drivers, opportunities and risks associated with new climate strategies**

Driver	Opportunity	Risks
Revenue generation	Design, manufacture and marketing of climate-friendly products and services	Loss of market share from changes in customer perceptions, as well as competitive and substitute changes
Regulation	Tax incentives, stimulus funding and subsidies at global, regional, local and sectoral levels	Extra investments and possible additional financial penalties for companies that are reactive rather than proactive in responding to climate change
Cost reduction	Integrating clean technology into the business and greening the supply chain to achieve greater energy efficiencies in operation	Possible increase in prices of raw materials, energy and water as suppliers respond to change in the regulatory environment
Stakeholder expectation	Meeting stakeholders, employees, customer and media demands for higher levels of commitments to climate change; being aware of the actions of competitors and staying ahead of industry's response	Being seen as laggard for not having climate change strategy—stakeholders can influence the bottom line by choosing to support or abandon organizations based on their core corporate or Corporate Social Responsibility (CSR) strategies.

5.3.2 The business case of reaping the rewards of a climate change strategy

The Tata Group is one of the largest and most respected business conglomerates in India. Established 140 years ago by Jamsetji Tata, the group's businesses encompass power, software, automobiles, steel, hotels and chemicals among other interests. The Group employs more than 350,000 people worldwide, and 27 Tata Group companies are publicly listed. In addition to its strong business model, the Tata Group is also acknowledged as a socially conscious pro-poor business organization and is well known for its philanthropy.

Tata Group leadership recognized early the need to address the risks associated with climate change and the need to formulate a long-term mitigation strategy for the Group. Mr Ratan N. Tata, Chairman, Tata Sons, stated, "We should sensitize ourselves to what our processes are doing and how we can reduce the pollutants and the emissions in our processes today."

The Tata Group, through Tata Quality Management Services (TQMS), measured its carbon footprint and attempted to identify abatement levers for the largest companies in the group. This included its automobile, chemical, power and steel businesses. The plan was to address at least 80% of the total emissions of the Group. The Tata Group had trade links and operations in India, Singapore, Indonesia, Thailand, Europe and the United States. As a part of coping with globalization and climate change, and identifying the opportunities, the Tata Group undertook the following steps

- **Estimate the carbon emissions of its major facilities.** The goals were to understand each unit's operations, identify the major sources of emissions and accurately estimate the emissions. Tata followed the WBCSD guidelines as well as relevant International Organization for Standardization (ISO) standards.
- **Identify potential mitigation opportunities within the organization.** Once the carbon blueprint was complete, the individual companies are advised on how to improve their operations and develop an approach with respect to carbon reduction.
- **Formulate a clear, detailed climate change strategy.** Having assessed the ways in which climate change could affect the organization, the individual companies are prepared to develop strategies and make moves to mitigate the risks and enhance the opportunities available to make more informed decisions regarding their future growth in light of carbon constraints.
- **Sensitize its employees to the effects of global warming.** Individual companies of Tata Group conducted several training sessions with participating senior-level functionaries. Through these sessions, Tata identified champions to drive the processes within their respective companies.

Figure 5.2 **Direct carbon emissions relative to market capitalization**

Source: Goldman Sachs, 2010, p. 128

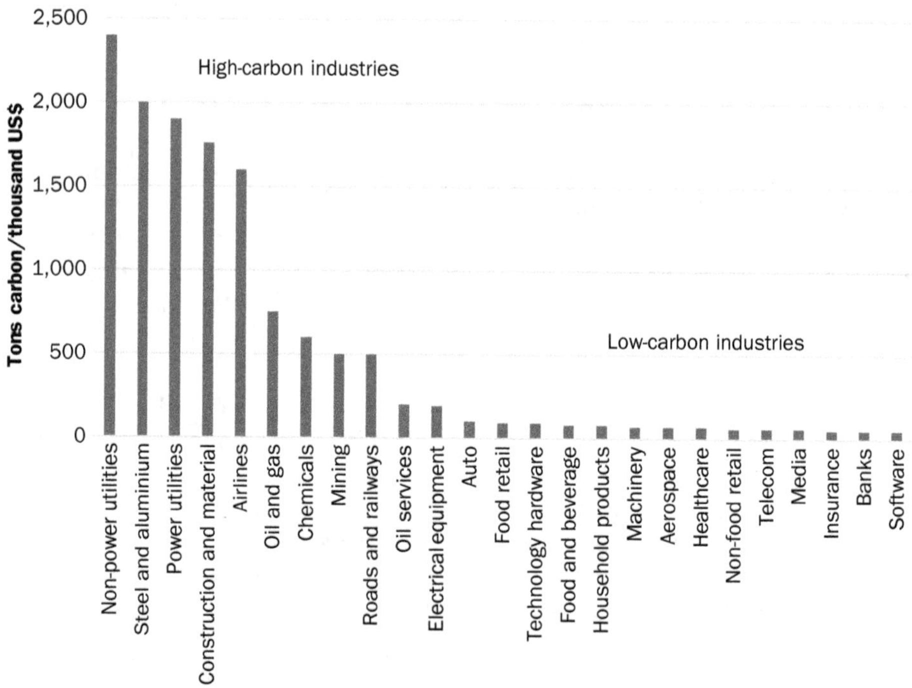

Carbon-intensive industries such as utilities, steel and aluminium, oil and gas, and mining have huge opportunities to reduce carbon emissions (Fig. 2). In other low-carbon sectors, Tata is looking more broadly at ways to reduce their environmental impact. Measuring the emission footprint is only part of the story. After determining the direct and indirect impacts of climate change, Tata broadened its analysis and thought strategically about how climate risks could hurt—or offer opportunities that better position its business. Its automobile unit is investing in making its already relatively low-emission diesel engines more efficient. It has also found opportunity in the risk of greater regulation by building a new business that makes particulate filter systems to be retrofitted on its own and other's engines. Its steel unit is studying turbines that run on alternative fuels, as well as combined heat and power generation turbines that recover waste heat. It is poised to commit significant R&D funds to these projects. Creative moves are not restricted to heavy manufacturing and other industries traditionally unfriendly to environment. Tata Telkom is in the middle of three plans to improve energy efficiency up to 30%. This initiative was launched not only to support the government's Nationally Appropriate Mitigation Action Plans but also improve the bottom line of profits. In a lower-emission sector, IT services, Tata has implemented a coordinated environmental policy framework that, among other things, requires the measurement and reporting of resources (energy, water, material, waste) attributable to its internal operations. Tata is already well on its way to reaching perhaps the most critical element of climate strategy: increasing profits. Its R&D programmes and energy efficiency programmes are already paying off, with a reported 49% increase in earnings.

The aggressive moves by Tata and other forward-looking South Asian companies show that tackling globalization-related risks and climate change is not a strategy issue to be considered for future action. It is already influencing the competitive dynamics in the market in South Asia. Companies with the vision to provide technology, products and services that address climate risks or other pressing globalization issues will enjoy a competitive advantage.

5.4 Why are climate strategies and inclusive business not mainstreamed by all?

Two forces are driving commercial relations between business and the poor. The first is the rising spending power of people in emerging economies. The second is innovation on the supply side. The high rates of growth that have been attained in recent years in South Asia have led to a general increase in spending power and the lifting of millions out of poverty. India, Maldives, Pakistan and Sri Lanka have led the way, with Bangladesh, Nepal and Bhutan all enjoying growth rates well in excess of those achieved by the their counterparts in South East Asia. This has created new market opportunities for local and international businesses. At the same time, there has been a burst of innovation by the private sector in its effort to take advantage of these new opportunities.

Indian Oil and Reliance Ltd have started selling renewable energy products and services to rural households with limited budgets. In this context, the idea of innovation must be reconsidered. This may involve: technology breakthroughs, incremental improvements to products and processes, or stripping products down to their bare essentials. Firms are complementing technical innovation with a new understanding of poor people. This is leading them to open new markets, squeeze costs, narrow their margins, and go to scale (increase the scale of production in order to spread overheads and support the narrower margins they are accepting).

Beyond philanthropy and corporate social responsibility, the goal of a private business is to make a profit. This normally involves seeking out the cheapest source of inputs and the markets best able to bear a viable price. Incorporating measures into the production and supply process that protect the environment and reduce climate change usually involve additional costs, which reduce profit margins. Moreover, there are difficulties doing business with the poor.

Anbumozhi and Bauer (2013) noted that there are five main constraints on businesses seeking to be more inclusive and low-carbon:

- Information: Poor consumers are often unaware of new products; firms often do not understand the needs and desires of the poor.
- Institutions: Markets in which the poor trade often lack regulation; it is difficult to enforce rules and contracts.
- Infrastructure: In poor countries, public infrastructure is often inadequate for the needs of a growing economy, and it is usually the worst in the poorest areas.
- Spending power: People subsisting on a couple of dollars a day do not make much of a ripple in the markets.
- Finance: The ability to save and to borrow can create spending power where it otherwise might not exist. Yet small and medium enterprises are poorly served by banks and other financial institutions.

5.5 Role of public–private partnerships in enhancing the corporate climate strategies

Private firms produce low-carbon goods and services, provide employment and income, buy farmers' crops, and pay taxes. In this way, the private sector acts as an engine of economic growth and delivers a range of socially useful services. The "externalities" of this growth, however, may not always be to the benefit of society, or to the liking of government. Accelerated Foreign Direct Investment (FDI) in mining, logging and heavy industry can damage the environment. As economies grow, the rising consumption of fossil fuels and the destruction of forests lead to a build-up of carbon that contributes to global warming and climate change. The poor are often the last to benefit from new consumer opportunities and the first to suffer from a degraded environment. "Private sector as an engine of growth" is therefore not necessarily synonymous with "private sector as a means of low-carbon green growth".

There is a huge need for complementary government spending on health and education and special programmes that target the poor (Karnani, 2009). There are many firms that pay little regard to poverty and environmental problems. It is here that governments, international development agencies and social entrepreneurs see a role for themselves. The private sector may be encouraged to move closer to producing the desired outcomes of poverty alleviation and low-carbon growth through advocacy and incentives. The questions then are: "How should it be done?" and "How far should we go?", i.e. to what extent should governments intervene? There is a broad range of public–private partnership choices.

A public–private partnership (PPP) is a government service or private business venture that is funded and operated through a partnership of government and one or more private sector companies. In some types of PPP, the cost of using the service is borne exclusively by the users of the service (e.g. by means tariff for clean energy use). Alternatively, a company will invest capital for the purposes of providing agreed services, with the cost borne mostly or wholly by the government. The government then makes payments to the company over a period of years to cover running costs and give the company a return on its investment. A notable example of this is Pakistan's private finance initiative. Infrastructure projects that have successfully involved PPPs include power generation and distribution, water and sanitation, refuse disposal, pipelines, hospitals, school buildings and teaching facilities, stadiums, air traffic control, prisons, railways, roads, and housing.

Early attempts at introducing PPPs in India were largely motivated by a desire to reduce the level of public debt. Private investment in infrastructure was appealing because public accounts did not distinguish between recurrent and capital expenditures. By privatizing investment, governments could create the illusion of reducing debt by taking investment out of the budget.

Now, increasingly, governments (and international development agencies) are using PPPs for the purpose of providing incentives for private sector investment to support a wide range of sustainable development activities. For example, "product development partnerships" focus on energy efficiency product development in response to global warming. PPPs have also been recognized for their potential for promoting food security: "Protection of intellectual property rights encourages private sector investment in agrobiotechnology, but in developing countries the needs of smallholder farmers and environmental conservation are unlikely to attract private funds and new and imaginative public–private collaboration can make the gene revolution beneficial to developing countries" (Serageldin, 1999).

Therefore talk about PPPs should be in the sense of a broader partnership that might also include international development agencies and social enterprises. They may also be focused on a wide range of activities, not just on the provision of infrastructure. Approaches begin with co-sponsorship of specific projects, continue through sector-wide cooperation, and go on to the establishment of supportive national legislation and regulatory regimes.

In South Asia, various mixes of these PPP initiatives measures were observed:

- In Gujarat, the Agricultural Research and Development Institute cooperated with Amul to develop disease-resistant, high-yield fodder crops. This reduced the risk to Amul of the long gestation period of the research and development effort, which took ten years. Now over 500 indigenous farmers are using advanced cultivation techniques to earn income from a high-value fodder crop.
- In Bangladesh, Grameen Bank partnered with the Department of Energy (which provided a subsidy), local government units, NGOs and microfinance institutions to deliver affordable solar power to rural communities that were beyond the reach of the electricity grid.
- In Pakistan, Five River Corporation is working with the government's Centre for Bio-technology in Forestry to produce improved jatropha phenotypes. The government is reclassifying marginal and unproductive land for jatropha cultivation and has mandated that petro-diesel include a 5% blend of bio-diesel by 2015. All of this makes it possible for Green Energy Biogas to work with poor smallholders who can in turn increase their incomes by cultivating land previously considered unproductive.
- Tokyo Marine Insurance, is piloting insurance against extreme weather for rice farmers in Maharashtra State. The government-owned Agricultural Cooperatives acts as distributor and prime promoter of the insurance with farmers. The State Meteorological Department is investing in new weather stations that provide the insurance company with more comprehensive rainfall data. The Japan Bank for International Cooperation initiated and coordinated the pilot project.

Leaderships and supportive public policies are critical for upscaling these models economy wide. The current economic systems combined with climate change has placed enormous pressure on both the public and private sector actors to act quickly. Traditional approaches to business and policy-making need reorientation and they have to develop innovative solutions. That will happen only when executives and policy-makers recognize a simple truth: tackling globalization and climate change need innovation and new corporate strategies.

5.6 Conclusion

Both globalization and climate change are affecting businesses in South Asia, no matter what industry the business is in. This demands coordinated and collective action by both the corporate sector and governments. Emerging experiences from South Asia indicate that an extraordinary mix of idealism and pragmatism are needed to tackle the challenges. But the risks also offer new sources of competitive advantage to the multinational companies and small-scale domestic economic operators. How to seize the opportunities? Early experiences from India, Pakistan and Sri Lanka indicate that innovative firms first estimate their contributions to global warming, before assessing the climate-related risks and seize opportunities. Then they reinvent business strategies—to mitigate those risks and seize the opportunities. South Asia houses more poor than the rest of the world. Making profit, while preserving the environment and serving the poor need innovations at firm and policy level. Leading organizations in South Asia know the benefits of acting early and some of them have seized the opportunities, taken the risks, and are now reaping the rewards. That example also emphasizes that an affirmative public–private partnership agenda is needed to transform value chain activities for the benefit of society while reinforcing corporate strategies. It is time for the governments to aim for new, forward-looking and more efficient public policies that will better serve environmental and business needs. Success in tackling climate change very much depends on the public sector developing a multi-tier governance structure supporting vibrant efforts made by the corporate sector.

References

Anbumozhi, V., and Bauer, A. (2013). How low-carbon green growth can reduce inequalities. ADBI Working Paper, #420. Tokyo: Asian Development Bank Institute.

Anderson, K. (1992). Agricultural trade liberalization and the environment: A global perspective. *World Economy*, 15(1), 153-71.

Anderson, S., Cavanagh, J., and Lee, T. (1999). Ten myths about globalization. *The Nation*, 6 December 1999.

Ashley, C. (2009). *Harnessing Core Business for Development Impact: Evolving Ideas and Issues for Action*. London: Overseas Development Institute.

Asian Development Bank (ADB) (2012). *Economics of Reducing Greenhouse Gas Emissions in South Asia, Options and Costs*. Manila: ADB.

Asian Development Bank Institute (ADBI) (2013) *Low-Carbon Green Growth in Asia: Policies and Practices*. Tokyo: Asian Development Bank Institute.

Business Call to Action (2008). About BCtA. Retrieved from www.businesscalltoaction.org/about.

Goldman Sachs (2010). *Global Outlook: New Energy Perspectives*. Boston.

Jobes, P.C. (2003). Globalization and regional renewal revisited. *Australian Journal of Social Issues* 38(1).

Karnani, A. (2009). The bottom of the pyramid strategy for reducing poverty: A failed promise. Retrieved from www.un.org/esa/desa/papers/2009/wp80_2009.pdf.

Lash, J., and Wellington, F. (2010). Competitive advantage on a warming planet. *Harvard Business Review*, Spring, 69-77.

Serageldin, I. (1999, July 16). Biotechnology and food security in the 21st century. *Science* 387.

Speth, J.G. (Ed.) (2003). *Worlds Apart: Globalization and the Environment*. Washington, DC: Island Press.

United Nations Development Programme (UNDP). 2008. *Creating Value for All: Strategies for Doing Business with the Poor*. New York: UNDP.

6

The dyestuff industry in Gujarat

Environmental issues

Prem Pangotra and P.R. Shukla
Indian Institute of Management, Ahmedabad

India's dyestuff industry is concentrated in the state of Gujarat along the Golden Corridor which runs from north to south of the state. The dyestuff industry is one of the major causes of river pollution in the region. In 1997, the Gujarat High Court ordered a shutdown of all polluting industries in the three industrial estates of Ahmedabad city, many of those being dyestuff manufacturers. Eventually these industrial units were allowed to restart operations after Common Effluent Treatment Plants (CETPs) were set up and the polluting firms joined as members. The problem of pollution in industrial estates has not been mitigated and the performance of CETPs has been less than satisfactory. This chapter discusses the problems of managing environmental impacts of the dyestuff industry in India. The focus is on issues related to the presence of large number of small-scale firms, the problems of managing CETPs, and the role that industry and government could play to achieve environmental objectives.

6.1 The context

The Indian dyestuff industry has registered an impressive growth (both domestic sales as well as exports) during the financial year 2007–08." The industry recorded better-than-expected growth for three years in a row and finally emerged from a phase of near stagnation. It was expected that, in the coming years, supportive government policies and restructuring within the industry would improve long-term growth prospects. Rising incomes and increased levels of consumption in developing countries would have positive impacts on the growth of domestic market for dyestuffs while the demand for specialty dyes from developed countries would help in the growth of exports.

Along with the emerging opportunities for growth, the industry faced the challenges of providing better products while not harming the environment. It had learnt its lesson from the crisis in the mid-1990s. There was no room for complacency in complying with environmental norms. It needed to push towards raising product quality and striving to achieve the highest environmental standards. Both small-scale and large-scale industries were equally responsible for reducing the burden on the environment.

In 2008, the industry faced another formidable challenge. Increased environmental concerns in developed countries, and the European Union's decision to implement REACH regulations, were exerting enormous pressure on the dyestuff industry to adopt greener measures.[1] The leading companies were shifting their focus from traditional end-of-pipe treatment to cleaner technologies and greener products. In India, the government announced its intention to establish a strong environmental protection agency modelled after the USEPA (United States Environmental Protection Agency). There was also a trend towards greater media scrutiny and public pressure for greater transparency on the environmental impacts of industrial activity. The Indian dyestuff industry faced stiff competition from China and neighbouring South East Asian countries. The industry felt the need to innovate in order to respond effectively to the emerging trends in demand for better and safer products.

6.2 The dyestuff industry in India

After the introduction of the first commercial synthetic dye in Europe in the middle of the 19th century,[2] the international dyestuff market expanded rapidly, leading to the discovery of an array of dyes, pigments and dye intermediates, commonly

1 REACH is a new European Community Regulation on chemicals and their safe use. It deals with the Registration, Evaluation, Authorization and Restriction of Chemical substances. The new law that came into force on 1 June 2007 requires manufacturers and importers of substances in the EU to obtain information on the substances they manufacture or import and assess the risks arising from the uses and to ensure that the risks, which the substances may present, are managed properly. The chemical could be restricted from use in cases, where there is an unacceptable risk to health or the environment or the prohibition of any of these activities, if necessary (EU, 2007).

2 The first synthetic dye was produced in 1856 by William Henry Perkin of the Royal College of Chemistry in London when he accidentally discovered the colour purple during one of his experiments. He had filed for a patent in August 1856 and the first batch of commercial dye was ready in the following year.

referred to as "dyestuff".[3] Subsequently, American and Japanese companies also entered the market, which was until then dominated by the Europeans. The dyestuff products were widely used in a variety of industries such as textile processing, leather tanning, paints, paper, printing inks and cosmetics (Table 6.1).

Table 6.1 **Types of dyes* and their applications**

Group	Application
Acid	Wool, silk, paper, synthetic fibres, leather, cosmetics, jute, straw, etc.
Azoic	Printing inks and pigments
Basic	Dyeing of real silk, cotton, photographic and medical purposes
Direct	Cotton, cellulosic and blended fibres
Disperse dyes	Synthetic fibres
Reactive	Cellulosic fibre and fabric
Organic pigments	Cotton, cellulosic, blended fabric, paper
Sulphur	Cotton, cellulosic fibre
Vat dyes	Cotton, cellulosic and blended fibre

* As per the US International Trade Commission

The Indian dyestuff industry was established in the 1960s, although a few companies were set up earlier. In the initial years, most of the manufacturing was in the unorganized sector. Sensing the rising demand for chemical dyes, and rapid growth of the industry, major players from the organized sector stepped in. These included companies like Amar Dyechem, Indian Dyestuff Industries (IDI) and Atul Limited in the 1950s and 1960s. Later, several multinationals like ICI, Hoechst, Geigy and Sandoz entered the Indian market.

India became a major exporter of dyestuff within two decades, exporting nearly 50% of the total domestic production (Table 6.2). From 1985 onwards, India's exports of dyestuff and dye intermediates grew at a remarkable rate, as high as 40% in some years (Figure 6.1). During this period the share of Europe, USA and Japan in global dyestuff production went down significantly as they closed some of their production facilities and started sourcing their requirements from Asia, mainly China, India, Taiwan, Korea, Thailand and Indonesia.

3 The term "dyestuff" encompasses three product segments: dyes, pigments and dye intermediates. Dyes and pigments are both colouring agents, the main difference being that dyes are water soluble whereas pigments do not dissolve in the medium of application. Dyes are primarily used in the textile industry whereas pigments are used as printing inks, wall papers, rubber and PVC products, cosmetics, coloured pencils, etc. Dye intermediates are petroleum downstream products which are further processed into finished dyes and pigments. These have important applications in major industries like textiles, plastics, paints, paper and printing inks, leather and packaging.

Table 6.2 **Export of dyes and dye intermediates (Rs. million)**

Source: Annual Reports of Basic Chemicals, Cosmetics & Dyes Export Promotion Council, CHEMEXCIL (various years) (https://chemexcil.in)

Year	Dyestuff	% growth over previous year	Dye intermediates	% growth over previous year	Total	% growth over previous year
1995-96	10,326	-6	5,132	27	15,458	3
1996-97	14,146	37	5,304	3	19,450	26
1997-98	16,722	18	5,668	7	22,390	15
1998-99	15,563	-7	4,387	-23	19,950	-11
1999-00	17,829	15	4,655	6	22,484	13
2000-01	21,280	19	4,890	5	26,170	16
2001-02	20,440	-4	5,130	5	25,570	-2
2002-03	24,240	19	8,840	72	33,080	29
2003-04	39,594	63	7,506	-15	47,100	42
2004-05	47,936	21	5,524	-26	53,460	14
2005-06	64,046	34	8,956	62	73,020	37
2006-07	89,210	39	15,480	73	104,690	43
2007-08	102,320	26	12,250	-21	114,570	-9
2008-09	98,290	-4	12,140	-1	110,430	-4
2009-10	98,700	0.4	12,200	0.5	110,900	0.4

* 2003–04 and 2004–05 breakdown is not available

Figure 6.1 **Growth of dyestuff exports from India**

Source: Based on Annual Reports of Basic Chemicals, Cosmetics & Dyes Export Promotion Council, CHEMEXCIL (various years) (https://chemexcil.in)

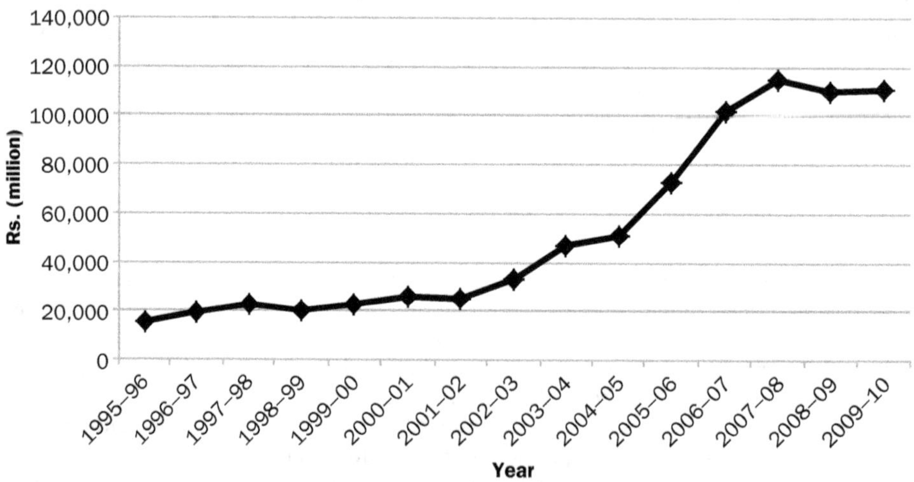

In India, a regime of favourable tax policies during the 1980s and lax environmental regulations led to rapid growth of small-scale units, especially in the western states of Gujarat and Maharashtra. However, the 1990s saw a slowdown and major restructuring within the industry. The government reduced the rates of excise duty levied on manufacturers in the organized sector.[4] This decreased the relative cost advantage of the unorganized sector, which was previously fully exempt from these duties. The larger firms in the organized sector, being more technologically sound and having better market reach, began to gain competitive advantage over small manufacturers.

Around 1993–94, global markets were undergoing a major upheaval. Environment awareness in developed countries was on the rise as many research studies started documenting the hazardous effects of dyestuff manufacture on the environment and on human health. Following public health concerns over the use of certain classes of azo dyes, the German chemical industry association decided to ban the import of amine-based azo dyes and their use in any application—including clothing, leather goods and buttons—that could come direct in contact with human skin. The ban came into effect in 1996 and, subsequently, many other countries imposed stricter environmental regulations. In India, while the larger companies were able to phase out the banned azo dyes, some of the smaller producers had to exit the industry.

During the 1990s, the production of dyestuff in the USA, which was previously around one-quarter of total world production, declined considerably with the closing-down of manufacturing operations in giant companies of DuPont and American Cyanamid. Manufacturers in Western Europe, Japan and Russia also scaled down their operations, as companies started relocating their production facilities to Asian countries. The lower costs of setting up manufacturing plants, as well as cheap labour and easy availability of raw material in many Asian countries including India, were the other driving factors that facilitated this shift. Apart from exports to developed countries like Germany, the UK and the USA, the Indian dyestuff exports to Singapore, Malaysia, Indonesia and Pakistan have grown substantially since 2002–03 (Table 6.3).

4 From 2% in 1993–94, the government reduced the excise duty rates to 20% in 1994–95 and further to 18% in 1997–98 (IRIS, 2009).

Table 6.3 **Top 15 countries of exports of dyes and dye intermediates from India during 2009–2010 with comparative figures for previous years (Rs. million)**

Source: Annual Reports of Basic Chemicals, Cosmetics & Dyes Export Promotion Council, CHEMEXCIL (various years) (https://chemexcil.in)

Countries	2009–10	2008–09	2007–08	2006–07	2005–06
Pakistan Ir	12,404	13,009	16,888	11,087	7,764
Indonesia	10,439	14,366	1,668	14,711	12,843
China P. Rep.	10,286	6,566	10,079	10,079	3,762
Saudi Arab	10,104	6,234	2,282	4,341	1,596
USA	8,334	9,120	8,906	7,909	4,329
Malaysia	7,170	2,789	2,973	3,596	4,060
Korea Rep.	3,789	6,101	8,639	4,505	2,886
Singapore	3,571	3,356	3,924	5,272	5,386
Turkey	3,498	2,769	2,835	2,275	1,565
Brazil	3,406	2,210	1,932	1,430	1,049
Belgium	3,389	4,002	3,378	2,916	1,383
Germany	3,288	5,717	5,673	4,665	3,551
Italy	3,152	2,806	3,131	2,857	2,116
Netherlands	3,026	2,717	2,660	1,990	1,768
Thailand	2,325	2,039	1,329	1,329	1,282
Total exports to top 15 countries	**88,181**	**83,801**	**76,297**	**78,962**	**55,340**

In 2006, the Indian dyestuffs industry's share in global dyestuff production was around 6.8% with total output of about 100,000 tons of intermediates and 28,700 MT of dyes and pigments, making it the second largest producer of dyes and intermediates in Asia. The industry was an important segment of the large chemical industry in India and a major foreign exchange earner for the country. The Indian dyestuffs industry produced 700 varieties of dyes and dye intermediates, chief categories being direct dyes, acid dyes, reactive dyes and pigments (United Colours of Industry, 2005). The textile industry was the largest consumer of dyestuff produced in India, accounting for nearly 80% of the total domestic consumption of dyestuff.

Figure 6.2 **Share of regions/countries in the global dyestuff market (2006)**

Source: Based on Cygnus Business Consulting and Research (2006)

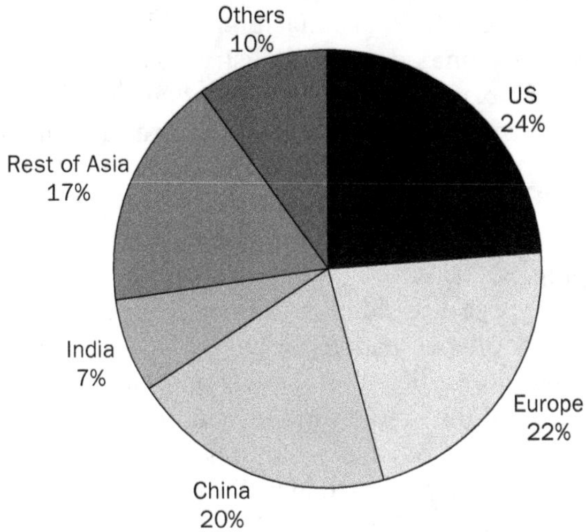

There were around 50 units in the organized sector (large and medium) mainly producing specialty dyes, pigments and intermediates and about 1000 units in the small-scale sector that manufacture a variety of dyes. The large and medium-sized companies, including multinationals, accounted for about 65% of the production in 2006, whereas the small-scale units made up the remaining 35%.

6.3 Emerging trends in global markets

At the turn of the century, the overall trends in production as well as consumption of dyestuffs began to change. The production of dyes in Western Europe, USA and Japan, which had dominated until the 1990s, decreased while production in Asian countries, mainly in China, India, Taiwan and South Korea, began to increase. In 2004–05, the share of Asian countries exceeded 50% of global dyestuffs production (*Chemical Business*, 2005). Similar trends were observed in the consumption patterns. While the consumption of dyes had decreased in developed countries like US, some European countries and Japan, it was increasing in Asian countries. Major reasons for this growth were increase in population, consumer spending levels, demand for textiles, leather and other coloured products (Ishikawa, Y., *et al.*, 2008).

Among the Asian countries, China had the highest market share in both production and exports. Although it had been a late entrant into the dyestuff market, the Chinese dyestuff industry had managed to gain a strong foothold in the global dyestuffs export market capturing more than 25% of the total market share. By 2006, China had a total installed capacity of 800,000 tons and about 500 units engaged in the manufacture of dyes and dye intermediates compared to about 65,000 tons capacity in India with about 1,200 manufacturers (Planning Commission, 2006).

The rapid growth of China's dyestuff industry was a result of supportive government policies, low tax rates and availability of cheap labour. In addition, the Chinese industry had several other advantages such as availability of basic infrastructure, free land and cheap electricity. However, many of their dyestuff products were in the medium- and low-grade category, with little emphasis on specialty products of greater sophistication that represented the emerging preferences of consumers (Xianping, S., 2004).

The Indian industry was also suffering from falling margins and over-capacity as the demand from developed nations varied considerably and caused volatility in the markets. In 2005, immediately after the removal of the textiles quota system, Chinese industry flooded the markets in the USA and Europe with cheap goods. This reduced orders for dyes from these countries. In addition, due to smaller profit margins, Indian players hardly invested in R&D for inventing new dyes or for modern applications such as specialty products. Compared to 5% of total sales revenue spent by developed countries for R&D, Indian manufacturers hardly spent 1–2%. Although the demand for natural dyes was increasing, the Indian industry failed to capitalize on this trend and occupied only a marginal presence in the natural dyes market.

6.4 The crisis in Gujarat

6.4.1 The golden corridor

The state of Gujarat accounted for nearly 80% of total dyestuff production in India in 2006. Most of the dyestuff producers were located in the 11 industrial estates set up by the Gujarat Industrial Development Corporation (GIDC) at various locations in the corridor extending from Ahmedabad to Vapi. The 450 km long and 40 km wide stretch was called the "Golden Corridor" because of the large-scale investment it had been able to attract during the 1980s and 1990s. Positive industrial climate, strategic location and high market potential for products were some of the factors that attracted investment in the area. The Golden Corridor hosted more than 60% of the total small-scale industries in Gujarat. These industries, which mainly comprised of organic chemicals, dyestuffs, textiles and pulp and paper industries, generated as many as 50,000 direct jobs and many more indirect jobs (DMAI, 2007).

However, this development came at a huge cost in terms of environmental degradation. The dyestuff manufacturing industries, being highly water-intensive and chemical-intensive, generated large quantities of highly polluting effluent. This effluent had very high levels of COD, BOD, acidity, chlorides, sulphates, oil and grease, phenolic compounds and various heavy metals (Box 6.1). Some of these pollutants were non-biodegradable and inflicted severe irreversible damage to the environment. In the absence of proper treatment facilities, many of these industries routinely dumped toxic effluents on nearby land or in open surface water channels.

Box 6.1 **Waste-water generation from the dyestuff industry**

- Typical effluent generated from this industry is dark in colour with very high levels of COD, BOD, acidity, chlorides, sulphates, oil and grease, phenolic compounds and various heavy metals.
- When large amounts of these wastes are dumped untreated, they exceed the carrying capacity of these rivers and render them unfit for human use. Effluents containing very high amounts of salts threaten the groundwater sources and ecology of the area.
- Some of these dyes are non-biodegradable and are not easily removable by conventional processes. When this coloured effluent is released into the receiving water bodies, it interferes with the transmission of light, as a result of which photosynthetic activity is inhibited. This leads to deficiency of oxygen in the water body, sometimes converting a clean water body to a stinking drain.
- Some dyes contain heavy metals such as chromium mercury, copper, nickel and cobalt. In addition to toxicity to the human body and ecosystem, metals are non biodegradable and may persist in the environment for many years.
- Raw materials used in the process can cause allergic reactions to the respiratory systems and in some cases extreme skin irritation. Some dyes and dye intermediaries are potent carcinogens.
- Waste-water treatment from these industries is basically a three-step process:
  - Primary treatment is a physico-chemical process that generally employs equalization, pH adjustments, solids removal, and oil and grease removal. This is mainly done by industries themselves in their own premises.
  - Secondary treatment mainly includes biophysical and chemical treatments which can be carried out by CETP or industries themselves. Secondary treatment achieves very high reduction of BOD. The treated effluent is disposed of to a nearby water source or to the sea.
  - Some other pollutants such as heavy metals and organic contaminants cannot be removed by standard primary and secondary waste-water treatment processes and require sophisticated technical treatment processes such as reverse osmosis, electrolytic treatment or ozonization. These processes, also referred to as advanced or tertiary treatments, require significant investment as well as recruitment of trained personnel and therefore are not willingly adopted by industries.

For many years, the industries and the government ignored this continual abuse of the environment. In the 1980s, factories in the three industrial estates in the city of Ahmedabad were discharging high volumes of effluents into the nearby Kharicut canal,[5] which flowed into the river Khari. Large-scale emissions of poisonous gases, release of toxic chemicals and hazardous solid waste had led to severe contamination of air, water and land. In the early 1990s, there were reports of loss of fertility of agricultural lands and a decline in agricultural yield. In downstream villages, water was reported to have reddish colour even at a depth of 300 feet. The borewells in the area were heavily contaminated and villagers were forced to consume this water. Environmental activists organized public protests against the industry claiming that industrial effluents were causing irreversible damage to the environment. At one point, public outcry had reached a climax and anti-industry campaigns gained momentum.

6.4.2 Clean up or shut down

Irked by the indifference of industries and the state government towards their plight, the farmers of one of the affected villages filed a Public Interest Litigation (PIL) in the Gujarat High Court in 1995. The PIL alleged that industrial effluents from the three industrial estates—Naroda, Odhav and Vatva—in Ahmedabad city were polluting the Khari river. The writ petition sought action against the State of Gujarat, the Gujarat Pollution Control Board (GPCB), the Gujarat Industrial Development Corporation (GIDC) and the Ahmedabad Municipal Corporation (AMC) for failing to control pollution in the Khari river. The petitioners also sought compensation for the losses they had suffered.

During the court proceedings, three expert committees were appointed to assess the extent of pollution and make recommendations to address the problem. All of them came to the conclusion that most of the industrial units in the GIDC estates were in violation of pollution control norms and there was urgent need to establish an effective system for handling the effluents. Following the recommendations of these committees, the Gujarat High court ordered the State of Gujarat to direct the closure of the 756 chemical units in and around Ahmedabad for non-compliance with environmental regulations and causing large-scale air, water and land contamination. The affected units were mostly involved in the manufacturing of dyes, chemicals, textile processing and rolling, and stainless steel mills.

The High Court also ordered that the closure of these industries should not be treated as closure under the Industrial Dispute Act and consequently the workers would continue to receive wages. The industries were asked to contribute 1%

5 The canal was originally constructed to supply irrigation water, but had practically become a channel for carrying the waste-water of the Naroda, Odhav and Vatva industrial estates which then flow into the Khari river and finally into the Sabarmati river downstream of Ahmedabad city. On its way to Sabarmati, the Khari passes several villages which were severely affected by the toxic effluent discharge into the river.

of the gross turnover for the year 1993–94 or 1994–95, whichever was greater, into a special fund. This fund was to be utilized for socio-economic development in the affected villages and for the betterment of educational, medical and veterinary facilities, and agriculture.

Following the court order, the state government made it mandatory for industrial units to set up their own effluent treatment plants or become members of the Common Effluent Treatment Plants (CETPs). Some industries decided to set up individual primary treatment plants and gave written assurance to the court that they would take responsibility for secondary treatment either on their own or through the CETPs. In 1998, most of the closed factories were allowed to reopen and, by the end of 1999, all three industrial estates in Ahmedabad had installed Common Effluent Treatment Plants to treat the effluent generated by the industries. CETPs were to act as buffers between industry and the environment, a solution then perceived to be an ideal one. By 1999, 11 CETPs were functioning in Gujarat with one each in the three industrial estates of Ahmedabad: Vatva, Odhav and Naroda.

6.5 Common Effluent Treatment Plants: a solution or a problem?

Common Effluent Treatment Plants (CETPs) had advantages of scale economies. Even by conservative estimates, the cost to an industry of treating waste at its own facility could cost five times more as compared to sending it for treatment at a common effluent treatment facility. For small-scale industries, setting up treatment facilities on their own would have been too heavy a burden to shoulder. CETPs minimized the problems of availability of land, professional and trained staff, and financial constraints. For these reasons, the CETPs were readily accepted by the industries. The regulatory agencies also favoured CETPs, as monitoring a single treatment facility was easier than monitoring a large number of individual plants.

The newly established CETPs in the industrial estates of Gujarat collected the waste-water from individual industries and charged these industries for treatment. Members had to pay operational costs usually based on the pollution load. Typically, the financing pattern for CETPs consisted of 25% of the project cost as a grant from the central government, a matching contribution from the state government, a 30% contribution from the promoter, and 20% to be borne by the units. There were three popular arrangements for managing the CETPs:

1. A cooperative or registered association of industries in the estate
2. A private or public limited company
3. A public sector enterprise operates the plants

The Ankleshwar CETP formed by the association of industries had introduced effective mechanisms to control pollution such as separation of ownership from membership, incentives for pre-treatment, and inducement for early payment of user charges (Kathuria, 2004). The cost-sharing method adopted here was proportional to the toxicity of influent. External consultants conducted monthly audits and submitted reports to GPCB on a regular basis. This was also the first CETP in India to receive the Environmental Management System standards ISO 14000 certification. The Vapi CETP, which was managed by the Vapi industrial Trust, had evolved efficient management system which included rigorous penalties for defaulters. Repeated defaulters were fined heavily and, in extreme cases, industries had been forced to shut down.

A survey of 160 dyestuffs manufacturing units in six industrial estates of Gujarat carried out in 1999 by the Indian Institute of Management Ahmedabad found that a majority of industries (98%) surveyed were members of CETPs. The Gujarat High Court's closure order in 1995–96 had affected about two-thirds of those units. All six estates had made impressive progress in setting up CETPs and developing landfill sites for disposal of hazardous solid wastes. The respondents blamed GIDC and municipal authorities for not providing adequate infrastructure. Most of the respondents felt that setting up CETPs, mixing treated effluents with municipal sewage and final disposal in the sea through pipelines, were the best solutions for controlling pollution.[6]

However, the overall experience of CETPs in Gujarat, as well as in rest of India, was quite disappointing. Systems for operating and maintaining the CETPs were not very effective. Most of the CETPs did not have a strong management structure—for enforcing inlet norms, collecting user charges and laying down penalties. For instance, where there were no underground pipelines and effluent had to be delivered via tankers, some units would simply dump them in nearby areas in order to avoid the expense of paying treatment costs to the CETPs. In some cases, some non-complying units did not pay the charges, as a result of which those who paid shouldered the burden of the free riders. CETPs directly managed by industry associations faced problems related to the absence of separation between ownership and membership. In these cases, the defaulters were themselves the regulators of the system leading to malpractices in the regulation of CETPs. The absence of an autonomous body to take action against defaulters was one of the major causes for the inefficiency of the CETPs in meeting objectives. Many of the CETPs could not even recover the cost of operation and were making huge losses (Box 6.2).

6 The survey was carried out by students of the Indian Institute of Management, Ahmedabad (IIMA).

Box 6.2 **Why CETPs fail**

Source: Summary based on *Down to Earth*, 15 January 2003

Although Common Effluent Treatment Plants (CETPs) were seen as the most effective solution for the problem of pollution in industrial estates, the actual experience has been quite disappointing. A study by the Centre for Science and Environment (CSE) explained why most CETPs in India have been a dismal failure.

- ***Weak institutions.*** Neither the State Pollution Control Boards nor the industry associations that managed the CETPs had the capabilities needed to ensure smooth functioning of CETPs. In Delhi, for example, the CETP users' society, which was responsible for setting up and operating the CETP, did not have the powers to set the dues or to recover unpaid dues from users.
- ***Monitoring and enforcement issues.*** The Pollution Control Boards lacked the capacities for monitoring and enforcement, although they had been given powers to shut down polluting units. In Maharashtra, some unit owners managed to bribe MPCB officials to obtain zero discharge certificates and thus evaded paying user charges.
- ***Non-cooperation from industry.*** In a number of instances, members of CETPs continued unregulated dumping of effluents showing complete disregard for the environment and the pollution control laws. Non-payment of dues made the operations of CETPs financially unviable.
- ***Cost sharing.*** Ineffective cost sharing led to malfunctioning of the system in many cases. Often charges were not related to quantity and quality of effluent. In a number of cases user charges were not updated and firms continued to pay a pre-designated amount even after the quality of effluent had changed.
- ***Technical flaws.*** Some CETPs failed because of design flaws and non-adherence to contracted quantity and quality of effluents. In Delhi, many industries misreported the actual quantity of effluent in a survey prior to designing the CETPs. The CETPs failed due to the mismatch between design specifications and actual effluent loads.

The concept of CETP, which was hyped as a solution to manage water pollution, had failed. It had only compounded the issue, producing larger volumes of toxic content. In addition, these CETPs were conventionally designed to handle large fluctuations in influent volume; this under-capacity was a problem for plant operation and functioning. Reverse osmosis, Granulated Activated Carbon, ultra-filtration ion exchange and other tertiary treatment methods, which could be effective, in this case were not used by CETPs mainly for economic reasons. With the growing pace of industrialization, CETPs were unable to cater to the need of industrial clusters, which resulted in industries bypassing the treatment and directly discharging untreated effluents in water bodies.

One of the many problems with the existing regulations was that they operated on a "one size fits all" basis. There was no flexible approach that differentiated between the size and capacity of industries. End-of-pipe technologies such as on-site pre-treatment facilities required high capital investment, financial costs and specialized technical skills. Lack of access to these inputs created a disincentive framework for many small and medium enterprises (SMEs).

Many industries diluted their high concentration residues to make them acceptable to common facilities. This increased hydraulic loads and waste volumes. In any case, by sending their wastes to CETPs, the industries washed their hands of the problem. There was no incentive for them to invest in cleaner production. Internationally, several countries had resorted to economic instruments such as water charges, pollution taxes, non-compliance penalties and environmental performance-based ratings to encourage environmental friendly processes in potentially polluting industries (Table 6.4). The government of Gujarat still relied on the traditional "command and control" approach of formulating environmental policy.

Table 6.4 **Common effluent treatment plants in five industrial estates of Gujarat**

Sources: Status of CETPs in Gujarat, GPCB, March 2010; Viability of Common Effluent Treatment Plants, CPCB, 2002

	Naroda	**Odhav**	**Vatva**	**Ankleshwar**	**Vapi**
Name of the Implementing agency	Naroda Enviro-Project Ltd	Odhav Enviro-Project Ltd	Green Environment Co-op Society Ltd	Enviro Tech. Ltd	Vapi Waste Effluent Management Company
Type	Limited company	Limited company	Co-operative Society	Limited company	Limited company
Promoters	Industries of Naroda GIDC	Industries of Odhav GIDC	Industries of Vatva GIDC	United Phosphorous Ltd	Vapi industrial association
CETP members	180	54	671	268	786
Design capacity	3 mld	1.2 mld	16 mld	10 mld.	6.6 mld
Capacity utilization	60%	58%	63%	75%	65%
Internal collection system	Sump and underground pipes	Sump and underground pipes	Sump and underground pipes	By tankers	Pipeline of 73 km
Cost of the project	Rs. 79.5 million	Rs. 41.5 million	Rs. 300 million	Rs. 59.90 million	Rs. 204 million*
System of user Charges	Based on COD in the effluent	N.A.	Based on the total organic carbon in the effluent	Based on effluent characteristics viz: acidity and COD	Based on water consumption by the individual unit

* Cost of conveyance and disposal not included

Some reports indicated that pollution in industrial areas of Gujarat had receded to some extent. This was partly attributed to the closure of a large number of industries and partly due to the operation of CETPs. In 2000, the government laid down a pipeline with the help of contributions from industries to carry waste from these industrial estates into Sabarmati at Pirana. Here, industrial effluents mixed with treated domestic sewage also discharged by AMC and thus diluted the toxicity of metals and other pollutants in the effluent to a permissible level. In 2002, the government widened the Kharicut canal and converted it into a live canal by diverting the Narmada water into it.

From 2006, the GPCB became more vigilant and took a tougher stand against industrial units found discharging waste-water into the Kharicut canal or Khari river. Top GPCB officials maintained that pollution of the Kharicut canal was completely under control and they monitored industries in Ahmedabad regularly to ensure that they complied with environmental norms.

However, some newspaper reports stated that many of the earlier environmental problems persisted. According to some villagers residing around these industrial estates, pollution was still rampant. There were instances of frequent leakages from the manholes connected to the mega-pipeline. Some factories continued to discharge effluents underground through tubewells, a phenomenon known as "reverse bore pumping" to save treatment charges of the CETP.

Similar problems existed in CETPs outside Ahmedabad. In 2007, GPCB issued notices to 124 units in Ankleshwar for failing to pay CETP charges. Fifteen of those industrial units that failed to achieve environmental norms were forced to shut down (Ahmedabad Mirror, 2008). Amid reports of severe pollution in Vapi and Ankleshwar industrial estates, the central government delivered another major blow to the industries. In July 2009, the Ministry of Environment and Forests directed the GPCB to refrain from giving environmental clearance to all new units in these estates as well as further expansion projects until the CETPs complied with the prescribed norms. The state government also decided to take over the operations of CETPs, which were originally set up for respective industrial associations.

6.6 Problems of small-scale units

Small-scale industries held a significant presence in the dyestuffs industry mainly due to the incentives provided by the Indian government in the form of excise duty exemptions and tax concessions. An indirect tax exemption on pollution control equipment, imports and goods made from industrial waste was provided.[7] This

7 Until 1991, the 900 small-scale units with total turnover of Rs. 30 million were exempted from excise duty, while the 48 large and medium units had to pay 31.5% excise duty. After 1991, the tax structure was changed and small-scale units had to pay excise if the turnover exceeded Rs. 7.5 million. Zero excise duty was allowed for units with turnover below Rs. 3 million and 15% duty for units with turnover up to Rs. 7.5 million. In addition, these units were given a depreciation allowance of 100% since 1991–92 and an investment allowance of 35% since 1983. Also dyestuff industries with a capital investment of less than Rs. 10 million were not required to obtain environmental clearance.

incentive structure boosted the small-scale segment and exports from the small-scale segment shot up considerably in the 1980s and 1990s. A large number of these industries were involved in the manufacture of dyestuffs.

It was widely believed that the small-scale sector did not invest in pollution control measures. As a result, they produced dyes at lower costs while compromising on environment responsibility. However, there were problems inherent in the small-scale industries. Technological constraints compelled many of these enterprises to make do with inefficient processes thereby generating high pollution loads. In addition, a number of them were operating with obsolete technology and outdated equipment. Shortage of land, unavailability of trained technical personnel and financial constraints stalled modernization of production as well as installation of infrastructure for effluent treatment.

Ineffective utilization of raw materials and use of large volumes of water in manufacturing scaled up the volume of effluent. According to regulations, even small-scale operators had to either set up their own effluent treatment plants or become members of CETPs. Effluent treatment in the dyestuff industry was an expensive proposition and, according to industry estimates, could account for as much as 10% of the price of the product. SSIs felt that the additional investment required for pollution control would threaten their financial viability or render them uncompetitive in the global market.

Box 6.3 **Indian dyestuff industry at a glance (2004–06)**

• **Output**	
– Total production	29,500 tons (FY 2005–06)
– Share in world production	6%
– Growth rate	(CAGR)
– 2001–2005:	0.1%
– 2006–2007:	3.5%
– Projections for 2010:	2.5%
• **Capacity utilization**	
– Installed capacity	55,000 MT/yr (FY 2004–05)
– Production	28,700 MT/yr (FY 2004–05)
• **Exports**	
– Value of exports	Rs. 51 billion (FY 2004–05)
– Growth rate	8% (FY 2004–05)
• **Imports**	
– Value of imports	Rs. 16 billion (FY 2003–04)
– Growth rate	20% (FY 2003–04)

- **Structure**
  - Organized sector (large and medium)—about 50 units
  - Unorganized sector (small)—about 1,200 units

Earlier, the Ministry of Environment and Forests (MoEF), Government of India under its Environmental Impact Assessment Notification, 1994 had suggested that the presence of SSIs be restricted in these sectors. The EIA report also suggested that the government of Gujarat should come up with a policy by which no unit be allowed to be set up in identified polluting sectors below a certain minimum economic size after internalizing full cost of compliance with environmental standards. However, closure of SSIs could mean huge economic losses for the state.

Industry operators stood united in their opinion that, if the government wanted a clean environment, it should share the cost of infrastructure. The GPCB, the agency responsible for curtailing pollution in Gujarat, had been ineffective in enforcing pollution control norms. Though environmental standards were in place, GPCB had failed to provide technical guidance to achieve those standards. In addition, it did not have the internal capacities to keep up with the task of monitoring such a large and heterogeneous mix of industries that had come about as a by-product of accelerated industrialization in Gujarat. Insufficient workforce, lack of expertise and inadequate infrastructure were some constraints faced by GPCB.

6.7 Quest for sustainable growth

At the end of 2008, environmental consciousness was rising and some dye manufacturers had begun to switch over to more environment-friendly processes. The industry was at a threshold of momentous change. Individual companies could either grow and become stronger, or could flounder in the changing environment.

It had become clear that all stakeholders wanted to improve the environment—the industries, GIDC, government of Gujarat, and citizens. The message that rang loud and clear was that the future of the industry depended on the course it would take as far as environmental issues were concerned. The government had realized the importance of preserving the environment and the GPCB had become more vigilant in enforcing norms.

Table 6.5 **Effluent charge system in various countries**

Sources: * "Selected Experiences with the use of Economic Instruments for Pollution Control in non-OECD countries", Joachim von Amsberg, 1995; ** *Greening Industry: New Roles for Communities, Markets, and Governments*, The World Bank, 2000; *** *Economic Instruments for Pollution Control*, OECD, 1999

Country	Charge basis	Effectiveness
Brazil*	· Volume and concentration of effluent (price per pollution unit) including BOD, TSS, heavy metals	30–57% reduction in industrial BOD emissions over a two-year period in São Paulo state
Columbia**	· Charge per ton of BOD and TSS	Reduction in BOD charges to targeted river by 52% and TSS by 16% in the first six months of implementation
Malaysia**	· Charge per ton of BOD · High charges for levels exceeding the discharge standards · Waivers for research in BOD reduction technologies	40% reduction in BOD in the fist year of implementation
Philippines**	· Charge per unit BOD discharge below standards and additional charge for discharges beyond standards	88% reduction in BOD discharges into Laguna Lake within two years of implementation
Russia***	· A combination of non-compliance penalties and emission charges · Rapid increase in charges above ambient standards	Not successful in inducing optimal pollution levels. But created revenues for mitigating damages

However, these initiatives did not address the problem in totality. Over the long run, an integrated long-term plan was needed. While industries did recognize the importance of "going green", only a handful of industries voluntarily adopted environment-friendly business practices. For a larger part of the industries, sending waste to CETPs meant washing their hands of the problem. In the case of effluent treatment through CETPs, what started as a relatively simple solution had now become an extremely complex management issue.

The government needs to encourage industries to find mechanisms to self-regulate and develop new products and treatment technologies that do not harm the environment. The Pollution Control Board must ensure a fair process of enforcement of norms, and CETPs should develop a sound management structure, comply with regulations—inlet and outlet standards—and invest in upgrading to manage the plants more efficiently. The Government needs to encourage the CETP associations to explore options with the ownership structure to eliminate conflict of interest and devise uniform charging systems to achieve better compliance from industries.

The government must recognize the value of the industry and the growth opportunities that exist in the future. Until now, the industries and the government have always been at loggerheads over the issue of pollution. However, environmental issues cannot be neglected any longer. For a sustainable growth of the dyestuff industry, all stakeholders—firms, industrial estates, CETPs, Pollution Control Board and citizens—must cooperate with the government. Manufacturers should no longer stop at treating wastes but also try to incorporate environmental concerns into their production processes. All manufacturing units must safeguard the long-term interests of the community at large. Industrial estates must provide good infrastructure facilities for pollution treatment and ensure that member industries comply with environmental standards.

For the Indian dyestuffs industry, many issues need to be resolved. Its importance to the country's economy is paramount. At the same time, if the industry continues to function in absence of proper regulatory enforcements, the consequences of long-term environmental damages are grave.

References

Ahmedabad Mirror (2008, February 12). No title. *Times of India. Chemical Business* (2005, February). The dyestuff industry in India. *Chemical Business.*

CHEMEXCIL, Basic Chemicals, Cosmetics & Dyes Export Promotion Council, Ministry of Commerce and Industry, Government of India. Retrieved from: https://chemexcil.in

Cygnus Business Consulting and Research (2006). *Indian Dyestuff Industry and Global Opportunities: White Paper.* FICCI, New Delhi, 2006. Retrieved from: documents.mx/documents/indian-dyestuff-industry-ficci-whitepaper-180906.html

DMAI (Dye Manufacturers Association of India) (2007). *Budget 2008–09.* New Delhi: DMAI.

Down to Earth (2003, 15 January). For a good churn. *Down to Earth*

EU (European Union) (2007). REACH. Retrieved from ec.europa.eu/environment/chemicals/reach/reach_en.htm.

IRIS (2009). My IRIS. Retrieved from www.myiris.com.

Ishikawa, Y., Glauser, J., and Janshekar, H. (2008). CEH marketing report research abstract: Dyes. Retrieved from chemical.ihs.com/nl/Public/2008Mar.pdf.

Kathuria, V. (2004, June). Controlling pollution in small industry. *Economic and Political Weekly.*

OECD (1999). *Economic Instruments for Pollution Control and Natural Resources Management in OECD Countries.* Working Party on Economic and Environmental Policy Integration.

Planning Commission (2006). Chapter 3.2: Dyestuff sector. Working Group on Indian Chemical Industry. Retrieved from planningcommission.gov.in/aboutus/committee/index.php?about=11strindx.htm.

Status of CETPs in Gujarat, GPCB, March 2010. Retrieved from: gpcb.gov.in/status-of-cepts-in-gujarat.htm

United Colours of Industry (2005). Down to earth. Retrieved from www.downtoearth.org.in/coverage/united--colours-of--industry-9113.

Viability of Common Effluent Treatment Plants, Parivesh: A Newsletter from ENVIS Centre—Central Pollution Control Board (CPCB), 2002. Retrieved from: cpcbenvis.nic.in/cpcb_newsletter/Common%20Effulent%20Treatment%20Plants.pdf

Von Amsberg, J. (1995). Selected experiences with the use of economic instruments for pollution control in non-OECD countries. Draft. Washington, DC: World Bank.

World Bank (2000). *Greening Industry: New Roles for Communities, Markets, and Governments. A World Bank Policy Research Report.* Oxford, UK: Oxford University Press.

Xianping, S. (2004, November). Problems in the development of the dyestuff industry. *China Chemical Reporter.*

7

An approach for assessing the multi-stakeholder perspective

A case study of an integrated steel plant

Rajesh Kumar Singh
Thinkstep, India

A.K. Dikshit
Centre for Environmental Science and Engineering, IIT Bombay, India
School of Energy, Society and Environment, Malardalen University, Sweden

The importance of organizational–stakeholder relationships has and continues to be of interest in the organizational studies literature. However, there is lack of clarity on the linkage between proactive sustainability management practices by the firms and their understanding of the needs and expectations of stakeholders. It is still not clear that firms initiating proactive sustainability management practices have better insight of stakeholder pressure. This study investigates the various aspects of the importance of stakeholder relationships and of stakeholder views on the sustainability performance of the organization. Results are presented from an empirical study conducted at a typical integrated steel plant located in a central-eastern part of India, determining the key stakeholders, assessing their expectations, examining the interaction of stakeholders with the organization, and the views and perceptions of managers and stakeholders. Stakeholder typologies were studied and appropriate strategies were suggested. The outcome of the research is that stakeholder relationships can be improved by categorizing the stakeholders, developing

stakeholder-specific strategies, and strengthening communication. Instruments like Importance–Performance Analysis (IPA) were used to assess the Stakeholder Satisfaction Level (SSL).

7.1 Introduction

The importance of organizational–stakeholder relationships has been given key consideration in the deployment of sustainability management within the organization. Stakeholder dialogue aims to fulfil the needs and expectations of both partners: the stakeholder and the company. Stakeholder theory has been specifically applied in the areas of sustainability and Corporate Social Responsibility (Ullmann, 1985; Roberts, 1992; Clarkson, 1995; Davenport, 2000). Stakeholder theory has also been used quite extensively in the management literature since Freeman's landmark book *Strategic Management: A Stakeholder Approach* was published in 1984.

According to Freeman (1984), "current approaches to understanding the business environment fail to take account of a wide range of groups who can affect or are affected by the corporation, its stakeholders". There is significant risk of an organization losing legitimacy when it does not respond to stakeholder pressures and social expectations (DiMaggio and Powell, 1983). Stakeholder influences need to be evaluated and, accordingly, organizations' responsibilities allocated to address their concerns (Rowley, 1997; Wood, 1994).

Stakeholders are persons or groups who are directly or indirectly affected by an organization, as well as those who may have interests in the company and/or the ability to influence its operations, either positively or negatively. Stakeholder engagement can be described as an organization's efforts to understand and involve stakeholders and their concerns in its activities and decision-making processes. The overall purpose of stakeholder engagement is to drive strategic direction and operational excellence for an organization. It can result in learning, innovation and enhanced performance that will not only benefit the organization, but also its stakeholders and society as a whole. In addition to serving as a key tool to support a facility's sustainability reporting efforts, stakeholder engagement can be seen as a foundation that supports a facility's broader sustainability efforts to set strategic goals, implement action plans, and assess its performance over time.

Donaldson and Preston (1995) discussed three different aspects—namely, descriptive/empirical aspects, instrumental aspects and normative aspects—in their stakeholder theory of corporation. Mitchell *et al.* (1997) proposed that classes of stakeholders can be identified by the possession or attributed possession of one or more of three relationship attributes: power, legitimacy and urgency (Figure 7.1).

Figure 7.1 **Stakeholder typology**

Source: Mitchell *et al.*, 1997

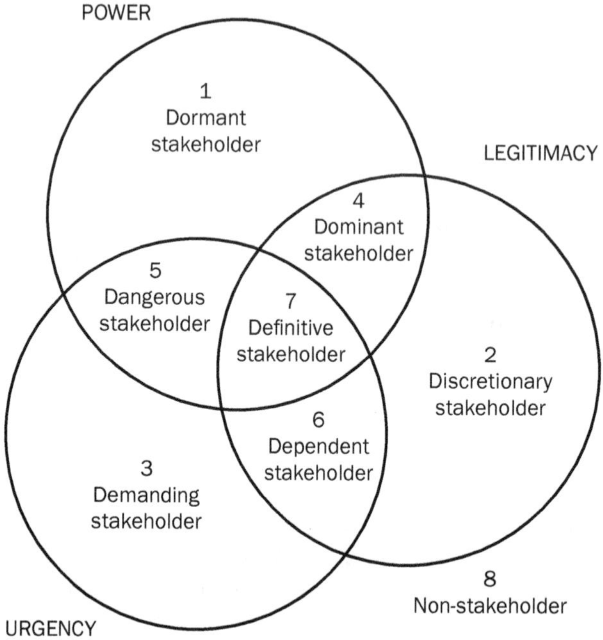

Frederick (1992) classified stakeholders into internal, external, key and secondary stakeholders, each carrying a different level of influence over the enterprise. The relationships between firms and their stakeholders are as complex as the ways to manage them.

Wheeler and Sillanapää (1998) have described two basic principles of stakeholder inclusion. The first principle stresses importance of dialogue and effective communication to share values, perspectives and beliefs in order to understand expectations. The second principle focuses on enhanced dialogue resulting from empowered relationships.

Savage *et al.* (1991) suggested four steps for a stakeholder strategy process which includes identification of stakeholders, creation of stakeholder maps, classification of stakeholder relationships and assessment of likely outcomes in different scenarios. The types of stakeholders and strategies are divided into four categories according to the potential for threat or cooperation, categorized as per a two-by-two matrix.

Taking all the above into account, this chapter investigates the determinants of both stakeholder relationships and of their views, particularly in the context of the sustainability performance of an organization. In order to illustrate the same, a case study has been conducted at a typical integrated steel plant located in a central-eastern part of India in order to determine the key stakeholders, assess their expectations, their interactions, and their views and perceptions within the organization. Stakeholder typologies were studied and appropriate strategies were suggested.

The outcome of the research is expected to improve the stakeholder relationships by categorizing the stakeholders and to help develop stakeholder-specific strategies and strengthening the communication.

7.2 Research methodology

The research work outlined in this chapter aims to bring out the potential of stakeholder interaction and to find methods to help assess the expectations of stakeholders. This study investigates the determinants of stakeholder relationship importance and their views on the sustainability performance of the organization. The key research topics are:

- The internal and external stakeholders involved and the key stakeholders in the steel company
- The key sustainability issues for each stakeholder and their most important expectations of the company
- The significance of stakeholders' powers to influence the steel company's sustainability issues and company's influence on stakeholders
- The significance of stakeholders' legitimacy and urgency in influencing the steel company's sustainability issues
- The threat and potential for cooperation posed by the stakeholders to the steel companies on sustainability issues
- The level of engagement with the stakeholders
- Dependence Influence Matrix
- Stakeholders' perceptions on key sustainability issues viz. importance, expectations and performance

The goal of this work is to systemize stakeholder interaction as part of promoting sustainability management in the organization. The typologies of Mitchell and Savage (1991) were selected as the best approaches which are further used to categorize stakeholders and provide suggestions for strategies specific to stakeholder types. The method employed was a case study of a typical integrated steel plant located in a central-eastern part of India which covers analysis of sustainability issues of the organization and relationships with stakeholders.

7.2.1 Survey process

This study was conducted in the above-mentioned integrated steel plant located in a central-eastern part of India. From over 3,000 managers and workers, 300 managers and workers were identified who are directly or indirectly contributing to addressing the sustainability issues of the organization. The respondents are classified into four categories: viz. top management (TM), middle management (MM), front-line executive (FM) and workers (W). The sample has been selected from three levels of executives and one level of non-executive, i.e. worker category. Seventy-five per cent of the employees work as shop-floor personnel irrespective of executive or non-executive, which includes coke ovens, blast furnaces, sinter plants, BOF, mills, utilities, energy, water supply, environment, maintenance, waste management, etc. The remaining 25% were drawn from different disciplines such as R&D, marketing, materials management, HRD, administration, personnel, quality, project, design, etc. Bearing in mind educational levels and general understanding about sustainability, only senior-level workers were chosen for the study. A structured questionnaire was formulated to capture their views on various issues. To ensure that the questionnaire was clearly understood and easily answerable by respondents, it was pre-tested twice during the developing period. The pre-test included two experts on sustainability and CSR issues from the steel companies. Furthermore, these individuals were interviewed to probe their interpretation of each question and to solicit suggestions for clarifying them. All 300 respondents were requested to answer part A.

Part B of the survey aimed to capture views of stakeholders and managers about the importance of, expectations of and performance on the various sustainability issues of the steel plant. Eleven stakeholder groups along with one group of managers from the steel plant were identified who were directly or indirectly affected by the sustainability issues of the organization. The questionnaire was sent to 25 participants in each group. The objective was to receive responses from at least 10 participants from each group. The two parts of the questionnaire are discussed in next two subsections.

7.2.1.1 Managers' perspective about stakeholders

The first part of the questionnaire was constructed from the insights gained from the literature on strategic management, Corporate Social Responsibility and stakeholder engagement. The questions were framed as per Likert scale points: 1—least important, 2—minimally important, 3—moderately important, 4—considerably important, and 5—very important. Results were obtained from a written questionnaire and face-to-face interviews with the managers. On some occasions, group interviews were also conducted. The questionnaire and interviews were conducted on the basis that the individual results would be non-attributable and that all information provided directly to the author would remain strictly confidential. Of these, 112 persons responded representing a 44.8% response rate. According to Hart (1997), response rates in industrial or business surveys vary from 17% to 60%, with an average of 36%. Therefore, the response rate of 44.8% was found to be within an acceptable range for business surveys. The breakdown of responses received from various categories are as follows:

- Top management. Questionnaires circulated: 50; responses received: 28
- Middle management. Questionnaires circulated: 75; responses received: 31
- Frontline executives. Questionnaires circulated: 75; responses received: 29
- Workers. Questionnaires circulated: 100; responses received: 24

The Cronbach alpha for reliability measurement (Tabachnick and Fidell, 2001) for the scale used in the survey was found to be 0.734–0.823. This exceeds Nunnally's (1978) suggested reliability range of 0.50–0.60, which is considered sufficient for this type of research.

7.2.1.2 Stakeholder perspective

The second part of the survey aimed to capture views of stakeholders and managers about importance, expectations and performance on the various sustainability issues of the steel plant. As mentioned already, 11 stakeholder groups along with one group of managers from the steel plant were identified who are directly or indirectly affected by the sustainability issues of the organization. The questionnaire was sent to 25 participants in each group. The objective was to receive the responses of at least 10 participants from each group. A structured questionnaire was formulated to capture their views on sustainability issues. To ensure that the questionnaire was clearly understood and easily answerable by respondents, telephone discussions with the stakeholders were conducted at regular intervals. Furthermore, these individuals were interviewed (face to face/over the telephone) to probe their interpretation of questions and to solicit suggestions for clarifying them. Conditioning of stakeholders was done over the telephone for ensuring clarity about sustainability issues.

Stakeholders were asked to identify the most important sustainability concerns. Accordingly, the four most important stakeholder concerns for each category were identified. Questionnaires were sent to identified stakeholders and the following information was sought:

- *What is important to you?* Stakeholders were asked to rate on a 5-point Likert scale (ranging from extremely important to not at all important) the four key stakeholder concerns.
- *What are your expectations?* Respondents were then asked to rate on a 5-point Likert scale (ranging from very high expectations to no expectations) the same four stakeholder concerns. Subsequently, respondents were asked the following:
- *How was the performance of the organization?* This questionnaire asked respondents to rate on a 5-point Likert scale (ranging from very high to low) the same stakeholder concerns under each stakeholder category.

The response rate varied from 40% to 72% for each stakeholder groups. The Cronbach alpha for reliability of measurement for the survey was found to be 0.711–0.768, which is acceptable being higher than 0.5.

7.3 Results and discussion of the study

The results of the questionnaire concerning managers' perceptions towards stakeholders and views of various stakeholders towards sustainability issues in the steel industry are presented in the following sections. Though the analysis has been carried out function wise, the figures discussed in the results are based on average values.

Managers were asked to identify the company's stakeholders. Since the organization is a public sector unit, 97% of employees identified the government as a stakeholder. The results also indicate that customers and shareholders were identified by 92% and 88% of respondents. Figure 7.2 represents the percentage of respondents identified by the various stakeholders.

Figure 7.2 **Percentage of respondents identified by the stakeholders**

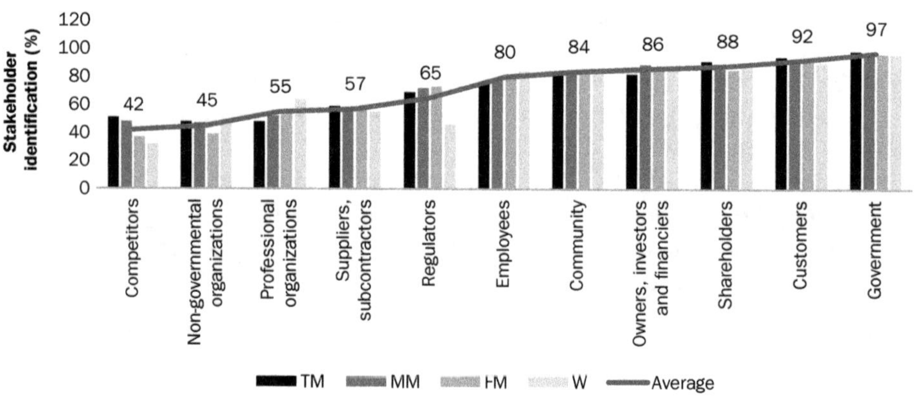

Respondents were asked to give their perception on the importance of stakeholders with respect to the organization on a scale from 1 (for least important) to 5 (most important). The respondents' ratings were evaluated and a mean score for each stakeholder was calculated. The survey result as shown in Figure 7.3 indicates that customer (4.74) is the most important stakeholder. The second and third most important stakeholders are the government (4.66) and shareholders (4.22) respectively.

Figure 7.3 **Importance of stakeholders**

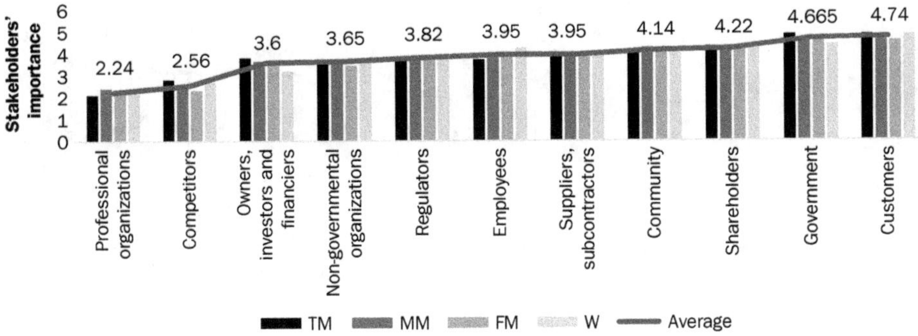

It is essential to ascertain the stakeholder's power to influence the company's sustainability issues. Respondents were asked their views about the stakeholder's power to influence, based on a scale going from 1 (negligible) to 5 (very high). The four significant stakeholders with power to exert influence are customers (4.47), the government (4.45), regulators (4.21) and financial companies (3.63). The extent of influence over the company's decisions is depicted in Figure 7.4. In the fourth question, respondents were asked how significant the company's influence was on the stakeholders on the scale 1 (not at all) to 5 (very high). It is interesting to note that a company can significantly influence employees with mean score of 4.64. The other stakeholders who can be influenced by a company are shareholders (4.23), the community (4.10) and suppliers/subcontractors (3.98). Figure 7.5 represents the mean score of the significance of company's influence over various stakeholders.

Figure 7.4 **Stakeholders' power to influence a company's sustainability issues**

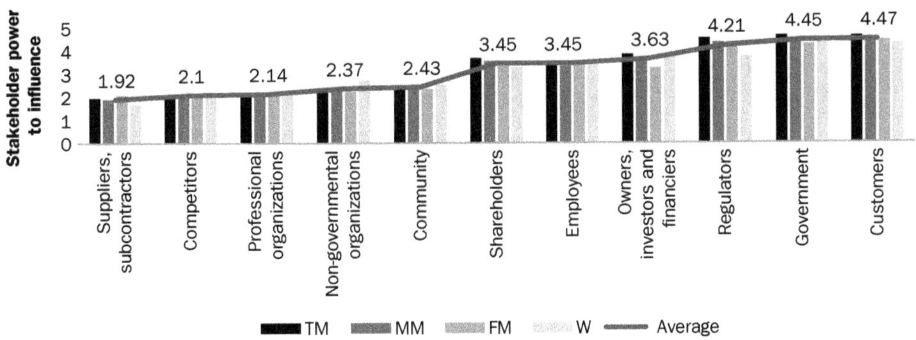

Figure 7.5 **Company's influence on stakeholders**

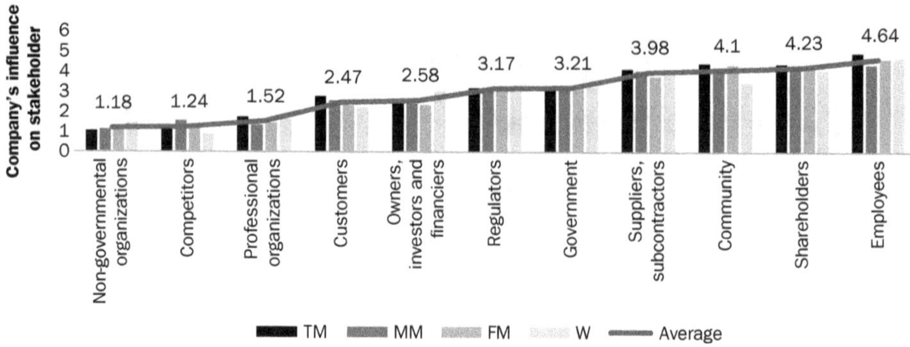

The intention of the fifth question was to evaluate the stakeholder's legitimacy to influence the company's sustainability issues. The level of a stakeholder's legitimacy to influence was evaluated on the scale of 1 (not at all) to 5 (very high). It is perceived through the survey results that the customers (4.48) followed by the government (4.27), employees (4.22) and regulators (4.11) can have significant levels of legitimacy in influencing the company. The overall picture is shown in Figure 7.6.

The objective of the sixth question was to evaluate the stakeholder's urgency to influence the company's sustainability issues. The level of stakeholder's urgency to influence was evaluated on the scale of 1 (not at all) to 5 (very high). According to respondents, the stakeholders, viz. the community (4.17), employees (4.12), NGOs (3.98) and regulators (3.92), have a significant level of urgency in influencing the company's sustainability issues.

Figure 7.6 **Stakeholder legitimacy to influence**

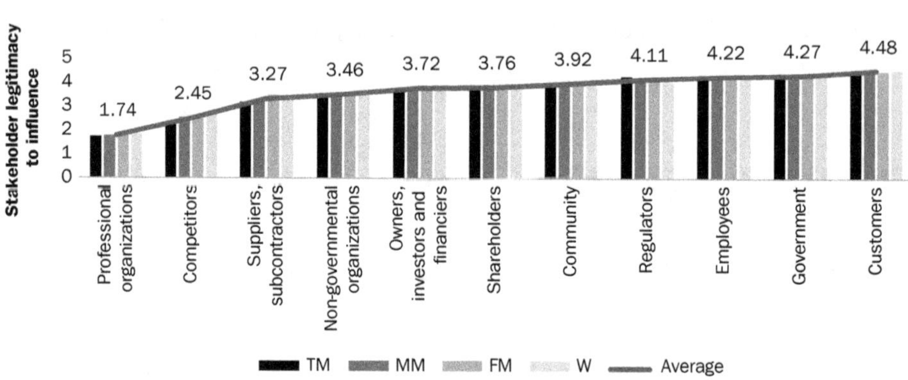

Figure 7.7 represents the mean score of various stakeholders for the significance of urgency in influencing the company's sustainability issues. The comparison of various stakeholders with respect to their power, legitimacy and their urgency in influencing a company is jointly depicted below.

Figure 7.7 **Stakeholder urgency to influence**

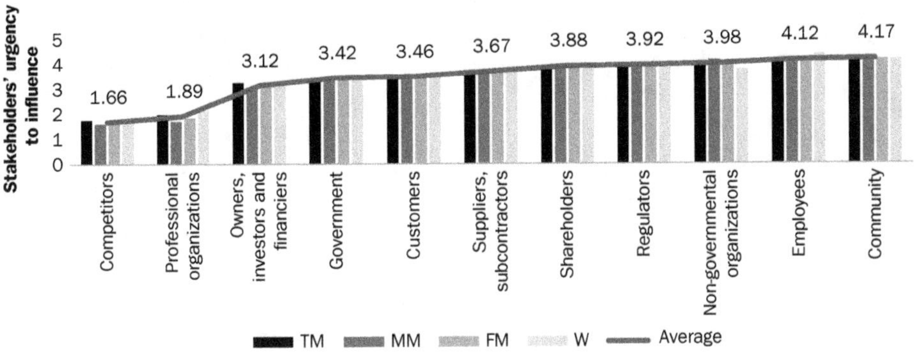

Based on the respondents' views, the mean score of stakeholders' influence and their dependency have been displayed in a diagram to depict the level of influence and dependence. Figure 7.8 shows that professional organizations, competitors and NGOs fall into the low influence and low dependence zone. However, the government, customers and regulators are categorized in the high influence and low dependence area. Employees and shareholders occupy the high influence and high dependence zone. The suppliers and community fall into the low influence and high dependence area.

Figure 7.8 **Influence–dependence matrix**

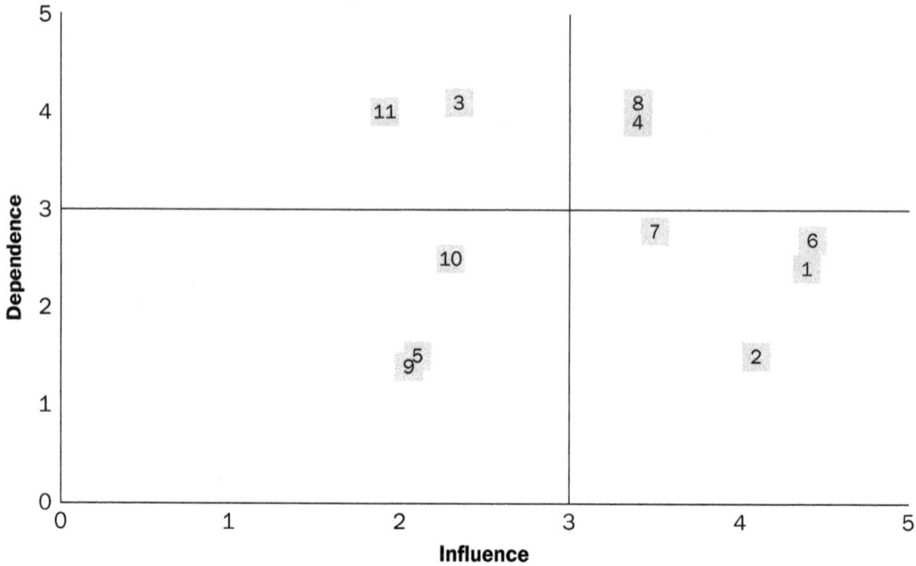

1	Government
2	Regulators
3	Community
4	Shareholders
5	Professional organizations
6	Customers
7	Owners, investors and financiers
8	Employees
9	Competitors
10	Non-governmental organizations
11	Suppliers, subcontractors

Figure 7.9 shows the mean score of various stakeholders who can pose a threat to the company's sustainability issues.

Figure 7.9 **Threat posed by the stakeholders**

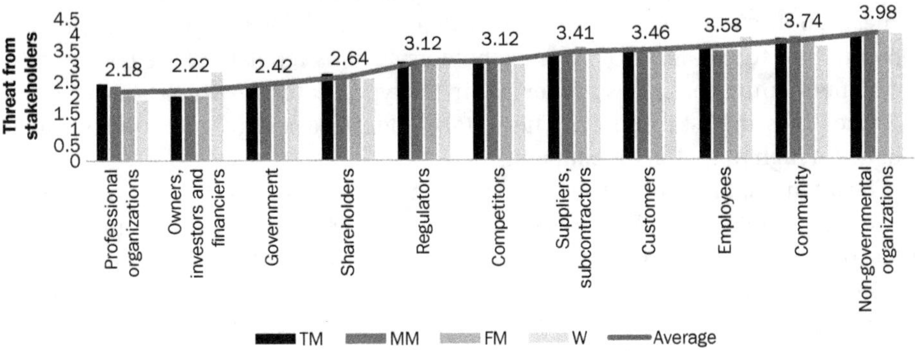

The level of threat was assessed on the scale of 1 (not at all) to 5 (very high). Respondents felt that NGOs (with mean score 3.98), followed by community (3.74) and employees (3.58) can be threats to sustainability issues. The next question was aimed at ascertaining the potential for cooperation with the stakeholders for addressing sustainability issues of the company. The level of cooperation was assessed on the scale of 1 (not at all) to 5 (very high). It is perceived from the responses that the top four important stakeholders who can significantly cooperate with the company are employees (4.36), shareholders (4.02), the community (3.94) and customers (3.92). Figure 7.10 shows the mean score of potential for cooperation with the various stakeholders on the company's sustainability issues

Figure 7.10 **Stakeholders' potential for cooperation**

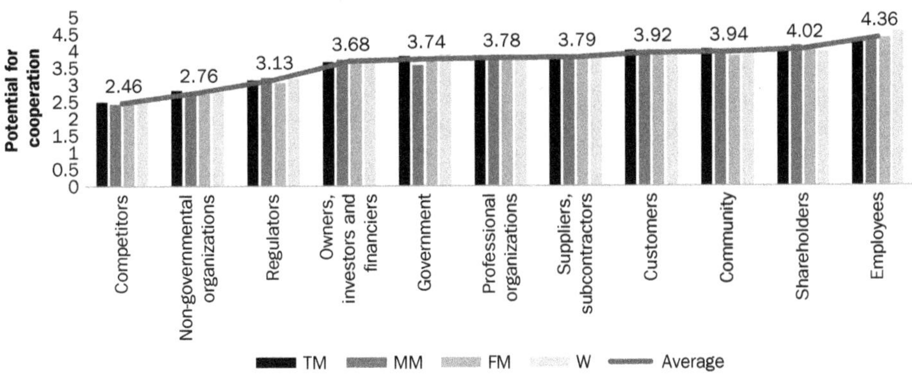

According to Savage *et al.* (1991), stakeholders are categorized based on their potential to threaten or cooperate with the corporation. The categorization helps in developing strategies to manage these stakeholders effectively. Based on the survey results, stakeholders are categorized based on a stakeholder's potential for cooperation and a stakeholder's potential threat to an organization. As shown in Figure 7.11, the government, shareholders, professional organizations and investors fall into the type 1 zone, i.e. supportive stakeholders having a high level of cooperation and a low level of threat. However, competitors and NGOs fall into the type 3 zone, i.e. non-supportive stakeholders with low potential for cooperation and high potential for threat. Most of the stakeholders such as regulators, the community, customers, employees and suppliers fall in the type 4 category which is also termed a "mixed blessing" stakeholder. These stakeholders have high potential for threat but also a high potential for cooperation.

The intention of the next question was to gain some insight into the level of existing engagement with stakeholders. The level of engagement was measured on the scale of 1 (not at all) to 5 (very high level of engagement). The engagement level was further categorized in the various stages as: 1 (Passive and Monitor), 2 (Inform and Educate), 3 (Transact and Consult), 4 (Involve and Collaborate) and 5 (Empower). It is perceived from the responses that the highest level of engagement is with employees (4.26) where employees are working directly to ensure that the company objectives and their goals are fully implemented.

Figure 7.11 **Stakeholder categorization**

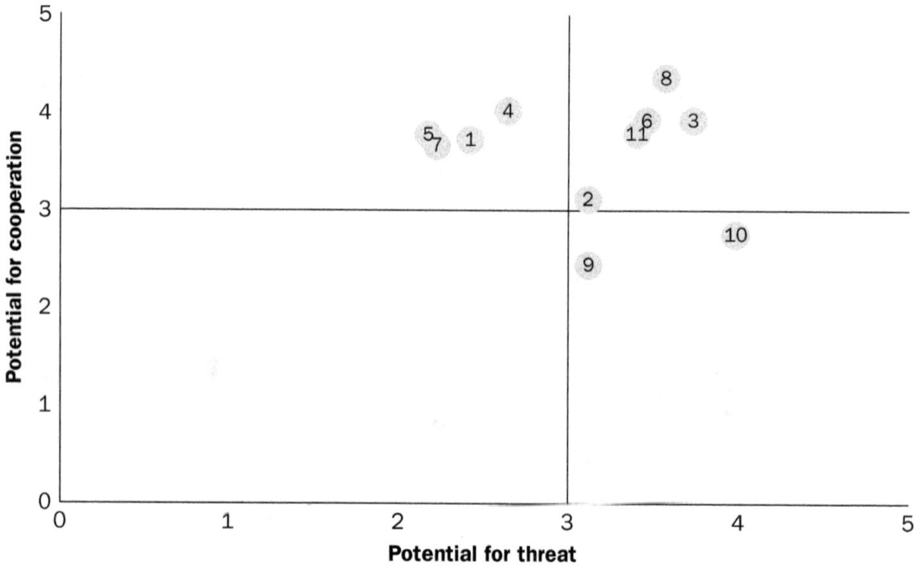

1	Government
2	Regulators
3	Community
4	Shareholders
5	Professional organizations
6	Customers
7	Owners, investors and financiers
8	Employees
9	Competitors
10	Non-governmental organizations
11	Suppliers, subcontractors

The government (with a mean score of 4.1), shareholders (4.03) and customers (3.91), clearly demonstrate that their level of engagement is mostly between the Transact/Consult and Involve/Collaborate stage. Figure 7.12 shows the mean score of levels of engagement for the various stakeholders on the company's sustainability issues.

Figure 7.12 **Levels of engagement**

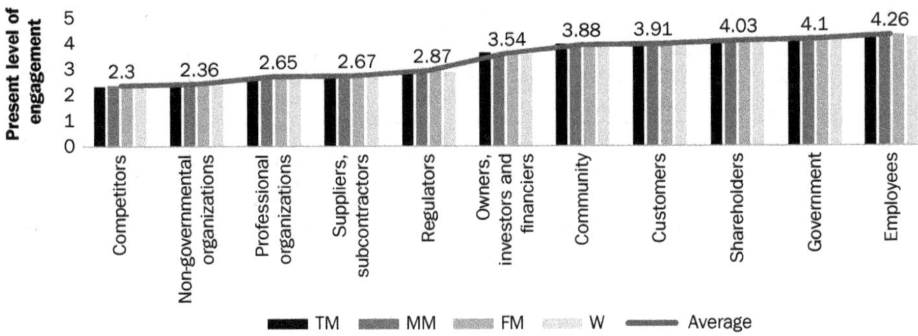

When managers were asked what benefits the stakeholder interaction would create for the company, 67% of respondents stated that the company would significantly benefit from stakeholder interaction.

7.3.1 Stakeholders' perspectives

Expectations of the stakeholders were sought in part B of the questionnaire. When the respondents had completed the questionnaires, a Stakeholder Satisfaction Level (SSL) was calculated for each concern using the following four formulas:

- Performance (P) – Importance (I); (P-I)
- Performance (P) – Expectations (E); (P-E)
- (Performance [P] – Expectations [E]) × Importance (I); ((P-E) × I)
- Performance (P) only; (P)

Data were analysed using SPSS and a Stakeholder Satisfaction Level was calculated. Different instruments such as Importance–Performance analysis (IPA), Service Quality (Servqual) and Service Performance were used to assess the Stakeholder Satisfaction Level. The four most important expectations of stakeholders, with the mean score for Expectations (E), Performance (P), Importance (I) and various indicators such as (P–I), (P–E) and ((P–E) × I) are presented in Table 7.1. Table 3.1 also compares the mean scores for expectations and performance, and the results clearly show a negative satisfaction gap in all dimensions.

Table 7.1 **Stakeholder concern analysis**

Stakeholders	Stakeholder concerns	I	P	E	(P–E)	IPA(P–I)	(P–E) x I
Shareholder	Profitability of the company	4.62	4.01	4.76	-0.75	-0.61	-3.465
	Creation of wealth	4.21	3.98	4.59	-0.61	-0.23	-2.5681
	Stock price	4.12	3.78	4.62	-0.84	-0.34	-3.4608
	Grievances and complaints	3.76	3.44	4.1	-0.66	-0.32	-2.4816
Employees	Safe and healthy working condition	3.92	3.74	4.11	-0.37	-0.18	-1.4504
	Good remuneration packages and professional growth	4.54	3.76	4.28	-0.52	-0.78	-2.3608
	Quality of life and welfare measures	4.37	3.8	4.29	-0.49	-0.57	-2.1413
	Training and career development	3.98	3.67	4.01	-0.34	-0.31	-1.3532
Suppliers	Partnership with value creation	4.21	3.68	4.56	-0.88	-0.53	-3.7048
	Timely payment	4.45	3.92	4.31	-0.39	-0.53	-1.7355
	Percentage of local suppliers	4.12	3.88	4.17	-0.29	-0.24	-1.1948
	Supplier satisfaction	4.06	3.69	4.37	-0.68	-0.37	-2.7608
Customers	Partnership with value creation	4.21	3.92	4.42	-0.5	-0.29	-2.105
	Product quality	4.61	4.01	4.62	-0.61	-0.6	-2.8121
	Delivery compliance and customer satisfaction	4.33	4.06	4.44	-0.38	-0.27	-1.6454
	Complaints	3.92	3.88	4.08	-0.2	-0.04	-0.784
Community	Quality of life	4.26	3.95	4.21	-0.26	-0.31	-1.1076
	Job opportunities	4.68	3.45	4.29	-0.84	-1.23	-3.9312
	Education	3.92	3.67	4.06	-0.39	-0.25	-1.5288
	Welfare measures	4.12	3.68	4.22	-0.54	-0.44	-2.2248
	Medical facilities	3.96	3.21	3.92	-0.71	-0.75	-2.8116
Government	Revenue and tax distribution	4.1	4.12	4.18	-0.06	0.02	-0.246
	Profitability	4.23	3.92	4.04	-0.12	-0.31	-0.5076
	Employment and contribution to GDP	3.89	3.67	4.11	-0.44	-0.22	-1.7116
	Safe working and environmental compliance	3.82	3.87	3.99	-0.12	0.05	-0.4584
Banks and Insurers	Financial risk	4.16	3.98	3.75	0.23	-0.18	0.9568
	Debts and borrowings	3.89	3.52	4.06	-0.54	-0.37	-2.1006
	Potential liabilities	3.98	3.72	3.95	-0.23	-0.26	-0.9154
	Compliance to statutory requirements	3.56	3.67	3.89	-0.22	0.11	-0.7832

Stakeholders	Stakeholder concerns	I	P	E	(P–E)	IPA(P–I)	(P–E) x I
NGOs	Environment quality	4.2	3.88	4.22	-0.34	-0.32	-1.428
	Human rights issues	4.11	3.62	4.09	-0.47	-0.49	-1.9317
	Freedom of association	3.76	3.33	3.87	-0.54	-0.43	-2.0304
	Compliance to child and forced labour	3.69	3.82	4.05	-0.23	0.13	-0.8487
Regulators	Environmental compliance	4.06	3.68	4.1	-0.42	-0.38	-1.7052
	Human rights issues	3.78	3.59	4.21	-0.62	-0.19	-2.3436
	Number of accidents	3.92	3.62	4.31	-0.69	-0.3	-2.7048
	Compliance to ILO conventions	3.45	3.45	4.06	-0.61	0	-2.1045
Professional	Partnership with value creation	3.78	2.92	3.98	-1.06	-0.86	-4.0068
	Employment and contribution to GDP	3.45	3.19	3.67	-0.48	-0.26	-1.656
	Training and development	3.89	2.89	3.92	-1.03	-1	-4.0067
	Ethics violations	3.22	3.12	3.42	-0.3	-0.1	-0.966
Competitors	Knowledge sharing	3.82	2.98	3.78	-0.8	-0.84	-3.056
	Partnership with value creation	3.56	2.78	3.49	-0.71	-0.78	-2.5276
	Anti-competitive behaviour	3.78	3.65	3.92	-0.27	-0.13	-1.0206
	Consumer privacy	3.33	3.45	3.86	-0.41	0.12	-1.3653
Manager	Profitability of the company	4.78	4.72	4.76	-0.04	-0.06	-0.19
	State-of-the-art technology implementation for value added products	4.54	4.01	4.48	-0.47	-0.53	-2.13
	Good remuneration package and professional growth	4.38	3.98	4.5	-0.52	-0.4	-2.28
	Safe and healthy work condition with quality of life	4.24	3.94	4.1	-0.16	-0.3	-0.68

The stakeholder concern analysis clearly shows that the performance score for each sustainability issue is less than the expectation score irrespective of type of stakeholders. The response of various stakeholders on their expectations are very high in comparison to their perceived performance level.

7.4 Conclusions

The key outcome of the survey classifies the expectations of the various stakeholders. Since the organization studied is a public sector unit, 97% of employees identified the government as key stakeholder. The survey results indicated that the customer is the most important stakeholder. The second and third most important stakeholders are the government and shareholders, respectively. The four significant stakeholders with regards to level of power to influence are customers, government, regulators and financial companies. The company can significantly influence employees. The other stakeholders who can be influenced by the company are shareholders, the community, suppliers and subcontractors. The result indicates that customers followed by the government, employees and regulators can have significant levels of legitimacy in influencing the company. According to respondents, the stakeholders, viz. community, employees, NGOs and regulators, have significant levels of urgency in influencing the company's sustainability issues.

While applying typology prosed by Savage *et al.* (1991) the government, shareholders, professional organizations and investors fall into the type 1 zone, i.e. supportive stakeholders with high levels of cooperation and low levels of threat. However, competitors and NGOs fall into the type 3 zone, i.e. non-supportive stakeholders with low potential for cooperation and high potential for threat.

The study shows that the government, customers and regulators can be categorized into high influence and low dependence areas. Employees and shareholders occupy the high influence and high dependence zone. The suppliers and the community fall into the low influence and high dependence area.

The study also shows that NGOs followed by the community and employees can pose a threat to sustainability issues. Here the communication between NGOs, the community and employees needs to be developed in a structured manner to address their expectations. The top four important stakeholders who can significantly cooperate with the company are employees, shareholders, the community and customers.

The outcome of the research is that stakeholder relationships can be improved by categorizing the stakeholders, developing stakeholder-specific strategies and strengthening communication. Considering the Importance–Performance analysis (IPA), the outcome indicates that industry-specific concerns must be addressed in order to fulfil the needs and expectations of stakeholders as well as their managers.

The study also indicates that commitment from top management plays a predominant role in addressing sustainability issues through constructive stakeholder dialogues. Transparency is key to the stakeholder engagement process. Communication with stakeholders can be further strengthened through various dialogue mechanisms. Organizations need to discuss successes and failures with a clear focus on the sustainability issues pertaining to short-term and long-term perspectives. Relationships and trust should be built with stakeholders. Organizations need to remain patient and aim towards inclusive growth in order to enhance the perceptions of stakeholders of performance on various sustainability issues.

References

Clarkson, M.E. (1995). A stakeholder framework for analyzing and evaluating corporate social performance. *Academy of Management Review*, 20(1), 92-117.

Davenport, K. (2000). Corporate citizenship: A stakeholder approach for defining corporate social performance and identifying measures for assessing it. *Business and Society*, 39(2), 210-219.

Dimaggio, P.J., and Powell, W.W. (1986). The iron cage revisited: Institutional isomorphism and collective rationality in organizational fields. *American Sociological Review*, 48, 147-160.

Donaldson, T., and Preston, L.E. (1995). The stakeholder theory of the corporation: Concepts, evidence, and implications. *Academy of Management Review*, 20(1), 65-91.

Freeman, R.E. (1984). *Strategic Management: A Stakeholder Approach*. Boston: Pitman.

Frederick, W.C., Post, J.E., and St Davis, K. (1992). *Business and Society: Corporate Strategy, Public Policy, Ethics* (7th ed.). New York: McGraw-Hill.

Hart, S.L. (1997). Beyond greening: Strategies for a sustainable world. *Harvard Business Review*, 75, 66-76.

Mitchell, R., Agle, B., and Wood, D. (1997). Towards a theory of stakeholder identification and salience: Defining the principle of who and what really counts. *Academy of Management Review*, 22(4), 853-886.

Nunnally, J.C. (1978). *Psychometric Theory* (2nd ed.). New York: McGraw-Hill.

Roberts, R.W. (1992). Determinants of corporate social responsibility disclosure: An application of stakeholder theory. *Accounting, Organizations and Society*, 17(6), 595-612.

Rowley, T.J. (1997). Moving beyond dyadic ties: A network theory of stakeholder influences. *Academy of Management Review*, 22(4), 887-910.

Savage, G.T., Nix, T.W., Whitehead, C.J., and Blair, J.D. (1991). Strategies for assessing and managing stakeholders. *Academy of Management Executive* 5, 61-75.

Tabachnick, B.G., and Fidell, L.S. (1996). *Using Multivariate Statistics* (3rd ed.). New York: HarperCollins.

Ullmann, A. (1985). Data in search of a theory: A critical examination of the relationship among social performance, social disclosure and economic performance. *Academy of Management Review*, 10(3), 540-577.

Wheeler, D., and Sillanpää, M. (1998). Including the stakeholders: The business case. *Long Range Planning*, 31(2), 201-210.

Wood, D.J. (1994). The Toronto conference: Reflections on stakeholder theory. *Business and Society*, 33(1), 101-105.

Appendix: questionnaire for the stakeholder survey

Part A

1) Write under following headings who your company's stakeholders on sustainability issues are and their most important expectations of your company. (*Stakeholders are all the groups and individuals whose actions affect the company or whom the company's actions affect*)

- Government
- Regulators (e.g. Ministry of the Environment)
- Community
- Shareholders
- Professional organizations
- Customers
- Owners, investors and financiers
- Employees
- Competitors
- Non-governmental organizations
- Suppliers, subcontractors
- Other (please specify)

2) Place the following stakeholders in order of importance to your company (1 is the least important, 5 is the most important)

• Government	1	2	3	4	5
• Regulators (e.g. Ministry of the Environment)	1	2	3	4	5
• Shareholders	1	2	3	4	5
• Community	1	2	3	4	5
• Professional organizations	1	2	3	4	5
• Customers	1	2	3	4	5
• Owners, investors and financiers	1	2	3	4	5
• Employees	1	2	3	4	5
• Competitors	1	2	3	4	5
• Non-governmental organizations	1	2	3	4	5
• Suppliers, subcontractors	1	2	3	4	5

3) How significant do you feel are the following stakeholders' powers to influence your company's sustainability issues?

• Government	1	2	3	4	5
• Regulators (e.g. Ministry of the Environment)	1	2	3	4	5
• Shareholders	1	2	3	4	5
• Community	1	2	3	4	5
• Professional organizations	1	2	3	4	5
• Customers	1	2	3	4	5
• Owners, investors and financiers	1	2	3	4	5
• Employees	1	2	3	4	5
• Competitors	1	2	3	4	5
• Non-governmental organizations	1	2	3	4	5
• Suppliers, subcontractors	1	2	3	4	5

4) How significant is your company's influence on the following stakeholders?

• Government	1	2	3	4	5
• Regulators (e.g. Ministry of the Environment)	1	2	3	4	5
• Shareholders	1	2	3	4	5
• Community	1	2	3	4	5
• Professional organizations	1	2	3	4	5
• Customers	1	2	3	4	5
• Owners, investors and financiers	1	2	3	4	5
• Employees	1	2	3	4	5
• Competitors	1	2	3	4	5
• Non-governmental organizations	1	2	3	4	5
• Suppliers, subcontractors	1	2	3	4	5

5) How significant do you feel are the following stakeholders' legitimacy to influence your company's sustainability issues?

• Government	1	2	3	4	5
• Regulators (e.g. Ministry of the Environment)	1	2	3	4	5
• Shareholders	1	2	3	4	5
• Community	1	2	3	4	5
• Professional organizations	1	2	3	4	5
• Customers	1	2	3	4	5
• Owners, investors and financiers	1	2	3	4	5
• Employees	1	2	3	4	5
• Competitors	1	2	3	4	5
• Non-governmental organizations	1	2	3	4	5
• Suppliers, subcontractors	1	2	3	4	5

6) How significant do you feel are the following stakeholders' urgency to influence your company's sustainability issues?

• Government	1	2	3	4	5
• Regulators (e.g. Ministry of the Environment)	1	2	3	4	5
• Shareholders	1	2	3	4	5
• Community	1	2	3	4	5
• Professional organizations	1	2	3	4	5
• Customers	1	2	3	4	5
• Owners, investors and financiers	1	2	3	4	5
• Employees	1	2	3	4	5
• Competitors	1	2	3	4	5
• Non-governmental organizations	1	2	3	4	5
• Suppliers, subcontractors	1	2	3	4	5

7) How big a threat do the following stakeholders pose to your company on sustainability issues?

• Government	1	2	3	4	5
• Regulators (e.g. Ministry of the Environment)	1	2	3	4	5
• Shareholders	1	2	3	4	5
• Community	1	2	3	4	5
• Professional organizations	1	2	3	4	5
• Customers	1	2	3	4	5
• Owners, investors and financiers	1	2	3	4	5
• Employees	1	2	3	4	5
• Competitors	1	2	3	4	5
• Non-governmental organizations	1	2	3	4	5
• Suppliers, subcontractors	1	2	3	4	5

8) How large a potential for cooperation do the following stakeholders have with your company on sustainability issues?

• Government	1	2	3	4	5
• Regulators (e.g. Ministry of the Environment)	1	2	3	4	5
• Shareholders	1	2	3	4	5
• Community	1	2	3	4	5
• Professional organizations	1	2	3	4	5
• Customers	1	2	3	4	5
• Owners, investors and financiers	1	2	3	4	5
• Employees	1	2	3	4	5
• Competitors	1	2	3	4	5
• Non-governmental organizations	1	2	3	4	5
• Suppliers, subcontractors	1	2	3	4	5

9) What is the level of engagement with the stakeholders and your company on sustainability issues?

• Government	1	2	3	4	5
• Regulators (e.g. Ministry of the Environment)	1	2	3	4	5
• Shareholders	1	2	3	4	5
• Community	1	2	3	4	5
• Professional organizations	1	2	3	4	5
• Customers	1	2	3	4	5
• Owners, investors and financiers	1	2	3	4	5
• Employees	1	2	3	4	5
• Competitors	1	2	3	4	5
• Non-governmental organizations	1	2	3	4	5
• Suppliers, subcontractors	1	2	3	4	5

9) What sustainability issues do you feel your company should address with its stakeholders?

10) Do you feel that stakeholder interaction creates benefits for your company?

Part B

I Stakeholders' response on sustainability issues

Name of the Stakeholder:
Group:
Organization:
Address:

Stakeholders from various areas are requested to give a rating, on a 5-point Likert scale, the level of expectations and performance of company as shown below.

Expectations: 1 = no expectation, 5 = very high expectation.
Performance: 1 = very dissatisfied, 5 = very satisfied.
Importance: 1 = No importance, 5 = very high importance

Note: Stakeholders are requested to give their views on their respective stakeholder category. Other area may please be left blank.

Expectation (E), Performance (P) and Importance (I) Matrix rating

Sl No	Stakeholder category	Four key stakeholder concerns	Stakeholder rating		
			Expectations (1 to 5)	Performance (1 to 5)	Importance (1 to 5)
1	Government	1. 2. 3. 4.			
2	Regulators (e.g. Ministry of the Environment)	1. 2. 3. 4.			
3	Shareholders	1. 2. 3. 4.			
4	Community	1. 2. 3. 4.			
5	Professional organizations	1. 2. 3. 4.			
6	Customers	1. 2. 3. 4.			
7	Owners, investors and financiers	1. 2. 3. 4.			
8	Employees	1. 2. 3. 4.			
9	Competitors	1. 2. 3. 4.			
10	Non-governmental organizations	1. 2. 3. 4.			
11	Suppliers, subcontractors	1. 2. 3. 4.			

II Managers' response on sustainability issues

Managers are requested to give a rating, on a 5-point Likert scale, the level of expectations and performance of company as shown below.

Expectations: 1 = no expectation, 5 = very high expectation.
Performance: 1 = very dissatisfied, 5 = very satisfied.
Importance: 1 = No importance, 5 = very high importance

Expectation (E), Performance (P) and Importance (I) Matrix rating

Sl No	Four key sustainability concerns	Managers' response		
		Expectations (1 to 5)	Performance (1 to 5)	Importance (1 to 5)
1	1. 2. 3. 4.			

(Signature)

8

Greening engineering SMEs in India

Gurudas Nulkar
Symbiosis Centre for Management and HRD, India

Environmental sustainability has predominantly been the realm of large businesses. Media and government attention has also focused on this area. With their large manufacturing set-ups, these corporations can have potentially major environmental impacts. What is overlooked is that many engineering corporations now outsource their activities to small and medium enterprises (SMEs), effectively transferring their environmental burdens. India has a phenomenal 7.3 million manufacturing SMEs supporting industry. High diversity in their activities, their fragmented presence and their small sizes pose huge challenges to regulatory bodies. Voluntary efforts going beyond compliance have proved fruitful in large corporations in India and other countries. However, such efforts require investment and managerial capabilities that are scarce in SMEs. Moreover, the efforts do not always yield a business benefit. This chapter discusses findings from a research on environmental performance of SMEs in India and offers recommendations on reducing SMEs' environmental impacts.

8.1 Introduction

The relation between environment and industry has, for a long time, been controversial. However, there is a general agreement that industrial activities, in a short span, have changed the face of the Earth. In India, rapid industrial growth has resulted in a degraded environment and loss of biodiversity. The environment, which played a crucial role in shaping the life of its inhabitants, now stands threatened. Industrialization and consumption-driven growth have caused depletion of non-renewable resources and pollution of the renewable ones.

Following the Brundtland Commission (WCED, 1987) and the various Rio summits, which elevated environmental issues to the "sustainability" initiatives, industries have responded in many ways. Many Indian businesses, like Tata, Mahindra, ITC, Godrej and others, have realized the importance of sustainability goals but some are still driven by regulation. The pursuit of sustainability does not imply business advantages and this hampers extensive acceptance. Many initiatives require significant investments of time, money and managerial resources and may not deliver short-term business benefits. While this may not deter large firms from sustainability, it poses a formidable challenge for the more numerous small businesses. Green practices that save costs are well diffused within small and medium enterprises (SMEs)—reducing energy, material and waste increases productivity while benefitting the environment. But measures that do not promise business benefits are unlikely to be adopted. The potential benefits of improving the environment cannot be assessed without consideration of the small and medium enterprises. Engineering SMEs produce intermediate goods needed by larger companies in their production. Consequently, a significant portion of the environmental impact of large corporations is shifted to SMEs. Their environmental impact due to their sheer number may perhaps equal or exceed that of large companies. As the adoption of sustainable practices by SMEs is critical for national environmental goals, they need to go beyond the usual eco-efficiency practices.

This chapter discusses environmental performance in Indian SMEs and is based on a study conducted with engineering SMEs in Pune industrial region in western India. While a large body of research is available on green SMEs in developed economies, studies in the Indian context are few. The study employed empirical research in engineering SMEs. These units have potential for reducing environmental impacts but have to deal with arcane policy and regulations which offer little encouragement for improvements.

Challenged by limited resources and managerial capabilities, stakeholder support is vital for SMEs in the path of greening. Many countries have acknowledged this and responded with SME-specific measures. In Europe, France, the Netherlands and the United Kingdom have simplified regulatory requirements for SMEs. "Green loans" are available for SMEs in Finland, France and the United States. In Namibia, the SME Bank along with the Environmental Investment Fund of Namibia offers a Green Soft Loan Scheme offering heavily subsidized interest rates for investments in green technology. Korea and Japan have green funds and industry facilitation to diffuse greening within SMEs. The general trend of European Union legal instruments is eco-conscious. The Small Business Act of the European Commission recognizes the importance of SMEs in the EU economy and promotes an SME policy framework. However, Indian regulators seem to overlook specific SME concerns. India has over 44 million SMEs serving customers in various sectors

(Ministry of MSME, 2012). This huge number and diversity in operations poses a daunting challenge for regulators and policy-makers. On the other hand, the numbers themselves present a huge opportunity for India to improve its environment, through greener practices.

8.1.1 Indian SMEs and the environment

Small and medium enterprises are defined in several ways in different countries. However, their characteristics are similar (Deloitte, 2008). They are typified by being owner-driven, serving a limited region or limited customer bases and facing multiple business challenges which are dealt with by limited managerial capabilities. SMEs in India are highly differentiated in their activities. A small family-owned shoe maker is an SME, as is a manufacturer of high-technology electronics for aerospace customers. This makes it impossible to generalize and therefore for this study only engineering SMEs operating in industrial markets were considered. Such firms are technology-oriented, require engineering capabilities and serve industrial customers. This makes them more homogenous. Difference within sectors changes the polluting capacity. Yet the argument that SMEs must contribute to green growth holds good across sectors. In India, SMEs are defined in the MSMED Act of 2006 (Ministry of MSME, GOI, 2012) which defines SMEs based on their investments in plants and machinery and they are classified as micro, small or medium enterprises (Table 8.1).

Table 8.1 **Definition of SMEs in India**

Source: http://www.dcmsme.gov.in/ssiindia/defination_msme.htm

Investments in plant and machinery	Micro	Small	Medium
Manufacturing	up to INR 2.5 million	INR 2.5-50 million	INR 50-100 million
Services	up to INR 1 million	INR 1-20 million	INR 20-50 million

An estimated 7.3 million manufacturing SME units are spread across a country of about 3.2 million km^2, serving nearly 1.2 billion people living in 28 different states. They are significant contributors to employment, export earnings and the GDP. The supply chain that large firms require makes their presence critical for attracting investment. The total SME sector contributes to about 8% of the GDP, 45% of the manufactured output and 40% of exports (Force, 2010).

8.2 Environment and the regulatory framework

The environmental regulatory mechanism in India is led by the Ministry of Environment and Forest (MoEF). This ministry is responsible for framing policies under the various acts of parliament. The Central Pollution Control Board (CPCB), an apex statutory body, is entrusted the powers and functions under the Water and Air Acts. The CPCB provides technical services to the MoEF as well as supporting their state counterparts—the State Pollution Control Boards (SPCB)—in their activities. The SPCBs are responsible for monitoring and controlling industrial pollution at the state levels. The ministry has categorized industries on their potential to pollute into red, orange and green. Firms in the red list are under observation by the SPCBs. A bureaucratic function with complex systems and processes ensures weak enforcement. This was highlighted in a report by the working of the Planning Commission which stated that the SPCBs are financially strained and understaffed (Planning Commission, 2012).

8.3 Previous research on green practices of SMEs

Research from other countries—Taiwan, Italy, Sri Lanka, Malaysia, the UK and Austria (Chen and Lai, 2006; Megacom, 2008; Ortiz Avram and Kühne, 2008; Lee, 2009; Weerasiri and Zhengang, 2012) proved invaluable in this study. This contributed to the understanding of green behaviour in SMEs. Specifically, studies identifying motivators (Smith and Duff, 2000; Moorthy *et al.*, 2012), the enablers (Gadenne, Kennedy and McKeiver, 2009) and barriers (Iraldo, Testa and Frey, 2010) within SMEs, towards green practices, were studied. Hillary (2004) suggests classifying the barriers into internal and external. This was used in this analysis. Awareness and knowledge of SME owners is identified as a major barrier by some researchers (Gibson and Casser, 2005; Iraldo, Testa and Frey, 2010; Ortiz Avram and Kühne, 2008). Others suggest that SME owners may be largely unaware of current environmental standards (Gerrans and Hutchinson, 2000) and it is not clear if they understand relevant legislation (Williamson, Lynch-Wood and Ramsay, 2006). The lack of awareness may keep firms away from realizing the impact of their activities on the environment (Simpson, Taylor and Barker, 2004). Some studies point out that positive attitudes alone are not enough to produce behaviours consistent with the attitudes (Nafziger, Ahmed and Montagno, 2003). Detailed studies involving practices and environmental technologies they employ (Shrivastava, 1995; Hobbs, 2000) have been undertaken too. Porter's essay on competitive advantage (1995) has led to literature on green strategy and competitive advantages in firms.

Reducing costs and meeting regulations are the major influencers for SMEs. This is understandable since economic benefits are important for SMEs (Bansal and Roth, 2000). Similarly, lowering material consumption, energy and waste results in saving costs and also helps the environment. Investments with no such promise may be unattractive (Esty and Winston, 2009). For this reason a clean technology that cannot reduce costs may be overlooked by SMEs.

There is a general agreement within the current literature about the scope for improvement of SMEs' green performances. Green practices of large firms that are well studied may not be appropriate for SMEs due to resource constraints and lack of awareness (Hitchens, 2004) which necessitates an SME-focused approach to achieve greener SMEs.

8.4 Methodology

Published research and studies by government agencies in various countries including India were reviewed. This was followed by exploratory meetings with Confederation of Indian Industries–Sohrabji Godrej Green Business Centre[1] (CII-Godrej GBC) executives. This is a centre of CII, one of India's leading industries associations, which focuses on greening industries. Semi-structured interviews with sustainability managers in five large firms gave insights from the customer's perspective. These firms had SMEs supplying intermediate goods. After this, exploratory interviews with eight SME owners were conducted. By the end of the exploratory phase, a conceptual model was developed and hypotheses, based on findings in the exploratory phase and from previous studies, proposed. A questionnaire for collecting data was framed based on this model. The questionnaire sought data about various aspects of SMEs, including awareness, barriers, drivers and the benefits observed. Further, detailed questions sought out practices within the life-cycle of the firm's products. Surveys were sent out by email to over 700 SMEs drawn from three sampling frames. Twenty-two responses were recorded in person and over 50 were received electronically. From this, 60 valid responses were collated. For the analysis, firms were given scores on the various aspects and several groupings were made from the data. The respondents represented five industries (Table 8.2).

Table 8.2 **Respondents and the industries they represented**

Industry	Percentage of respondents
Engineering	55%
Electrical and electronics	17%
Plastics and packaging	12%
Chemical	8%
Others	8%

1 www.greenbusinesscentre.com

8.5 Theoretical framework

The questionnaire was developed based on a theoretical framework prepared for the study (Figure 8.1).The framework proposes two forces which SMEs are subjected to—the barriers that deter improving environmental performance and the influencers of green practices. The resultant force would determine the level of green performance that the firm undertakes.

Figure 8.1 **Theoretical framework for the study**

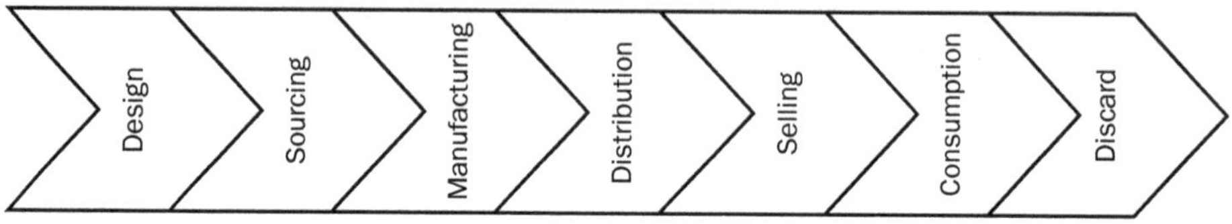

Further, to understand green practices, the questions were grouped by the generic stages in a product life-cycle (Figure 8.2).

Figure 8.2 **Greening within the product life-cycle stages**

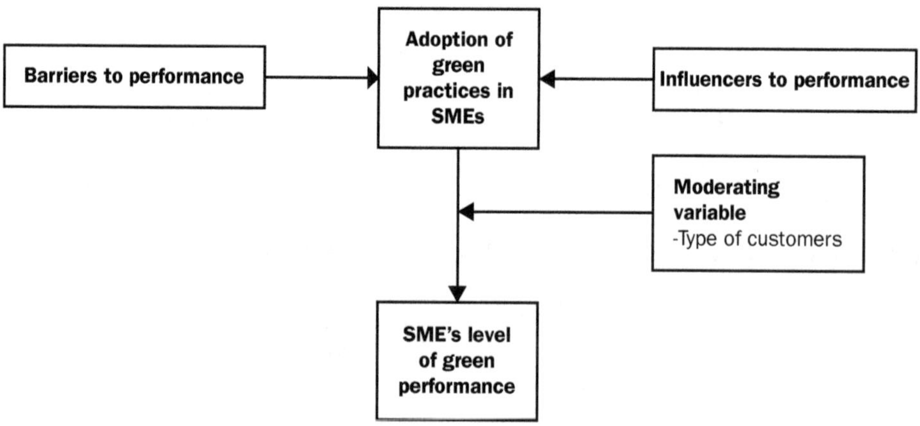

Respondents were scored at each stage and the total green scores were grouped into three levels of green performance (GPL).

8.6 Findings and discussions

8.6.1 Low awareness among owners

To measure the awareness of the respondents, various questions were asked and responses were given marks. An awareness score was computed for each respondent. The scores were grouped into three levels of awareness. In spite of considerable evidence of environmentally beneficial practices of energy, material and waste reduction, 80% of the SMEs display moderate to low awareness about the industry–environment relationship and advances in green management (Table 8.3).

Table 8.3 **Level of awareness among respondents**

Respondents grouped on level of awareness	Description	Percentage of firms
High	Demonstrated a high level of awareness of environment-industry relationship, practices and advances in these	20.0
Moderate	Moderate awareness, may have scored less in environment-industry relationship or practices and advances	51.7
Low	Shows poor awareness about environment and industrial practices	28.3
	Total	**100**

Tools such as the Global Reporting Initiative (GRI) and life-cycle analysis (LCA) were unknown to many. Less than 20% of the respondents had attended any environmental training or workshop in the last year. It was considered important to the study to understand what perceptions owners carry of the industry–environment relationship. These are shown in Table 8.4.

Table 8.4 **Perceptions on the industry–environment relationship**

Measure	Response
Industrial activities are responsible for environmental degradation.	59% of respondents strongly agreed
SMEs do not have a significant impact on the environment.	55% of respondents agreed
Every business should be responsible for improving environmental performance.	83.7% of respondents strongly agreed

Prior research has shown that low awareness can weaken chances of inducing positive behaviour in SMEs. The perceptions suggest that owners can envision their own environmental impacts but cannot visualize the collective impact of 7.3 million units. The diffusion of lean and Six Sigma practices are understandable considering the technical nature of the respondents' businesses. As discussed earlier, business advantages, especially of reducing costs, are sought by SMEs. On the other hand, clean tech may not always be a cost benefit as claimed, with only 14.6% using them. Subsidies could encourage acceptance of clean tech within small firms.

8.6.2 Variance in attitudes towards environmental practices

There were mixed responses on attitude (Table 8.5). A range of questions were asked to assess attitudes in customer, competitor and regulatory contexts.

Table 8.5 **Attitude towards green practices**

Statement	Strongly agree (%)	Somewhat agree (%)	Neither agree nor disagree (%)	Disagree (%)
For SMEs, regulatory bodies have the most important role.	45.8	33.3	8.3	10.4
In our business, most customers are not concerned about our green practices.	35.4	25	12.5	16.7
In our business, most customers would not pay more for green products or practices.	62.5	20.8	-	6.3
In our business, most competitors do not strictly comply with environmental regulations.	50	22.9	8.3	4.9
Undertaking voluntary green practices could negatively affect our costs.	14.6	25	14.6	31.3

Fifty per cent of respondents strongly agreed that their competitors do not strictly comply with regulations, while another 22.9% somewhat agreed with it. This suggests perception of a weak enforcement mechanism which condones non-compliance. In the interviews, some respondents were critical of the enforcement mechanism. To quote one respondent from the electroplating industry:

> The PCB officials, who visit us for routine checks or audits, have very low awareness about environmental technologies and practices. In one visit, we were asked to reuse 100% of our process water. This is impossible in the electroplating industry. They themselves are unsure of what is required.

A relatively high number of respondents (31.3%) disagreed that voluntary green practices may leave the firm weak. This is a positive attitude and one that can be leveraged. A low awareness of environmental technologies and practices coupled with weak enforcement and business pressures jointly act against this attitude manifesting in positive behaviour.

8.6.3 Customers' influence on the firm's practices

As proposed by the theoretical model, the type of customers that SMEs served would affect green behaviour. This is based on the finding from exploratory studies that large customers demand quality and environmental compliance from their vendors. Health, safety and environment audits are required by many customers from vendors. Three groups could be made from the responses, based on the type of customers that the firm served (CUSTTYPE). Table 8.6 shows the grouping of respondents on CUSTTYPE. The level of green performance was tested within the three groups.

Table 8.6 **Grouping respondents on type of customers they served**

CUSTTYPE	Description
Type 1	Large Indian customers, MNCs or foreign customers in top two positions.
Type 2	Have any two of large Indian customers, MNCs or foreign customers in top three positions.
Type 3	All others. They may serve SMEs, traders, micro-firms or others in their top three ranks.

8.6.4 Levels of green performance in SMEs

The responses were scored on environmental performance in each stage of the value chain. A total score was computed for the firm. The scores ranged from 42 to 99 and were grouped into three levels called Green Performance Levels (GPL). Table 8.7 shows how the respondents fared on GPL.

Table 8.7 **Green Performance Levels of respondents**

GPL (Green Performance Level)	Description	Percentage of firms
L1	Low level of green performance, reflected only in cost saving practices and some metrics being used.	45.8
L2	Medium level typified by practices in manufacturing and sourcing. Also some considerations in design stage too.	47.9
L3	High level, reflected by practices in multiple stages of value chain from vision statement and environmental targets to product design and discard.	6.3

Statistical tests supported the hypothesis—the type of customers and level of green performance are related. Interview responses corroborated this. One manufacturer of electrical transformers said:

> Our customers have such stringent norms of soldering that we have to use clean technologies. This means that we always perform higher than PCB norms. Also, we must procure RoHS certified components, because our clients' products are sold in European countries.

Another respondent making solenoid valves for the refrigeration and air-conditioning industry was on the opposite side of the scale. His customers did not demand anything other than lower price and credit. He said:

> We have a hard time competing with importers of Chinese valves. I can't even think of green practices right now. Our products are sold to traders in Mumbai selling refrigeration and air-conditioning spares. I doubt they have ever heard of any green manufacturing. Certainly they won't pay any more for them.

In spite of this attitude, this respondent recycled every bit of silver brazing rods. They have a technique to use up even small bits which were previously scrapped.

This demonstrates how environmentally beneficial practices that lower costs are employed by SMEs.

A manufacturer of membrane keyboards for GE Healthcare said

> Some years back, GE audit team had questions which seemed irrelevant to us—what is the colour of leaves around your factory, etc. But now we realize their significance, when we are undergoing ISO 14000 certification... We have to use RoHS certified components for GE. ...We are pursuing an enquiry from Germany that wants REACH compliance. Most of our competitors have not even heard these names before; thus we are uniquely positioned to target this business.

The study suggested that large customers can demand environmental management from their suppliers. Large organizations have a growing awareness towards the environment and many have sustainability goals in place. In a 2012 study of sustainability in large firms it was seen that over 54% of US firms have sustainability goals and practices. In such cases, firms must work with greener supply chains and impose environmental performance on their suppliers.

8.6.5 Barriers to adopting green practices

Among SMEs, the diversity in size, age and type of industry make it challenging to identify common barriers. Prior research and exploratory interviews helped identify eight barriers (Table 8.8). Of these, four are internal to the firm where the firm has some control over them while the external barriers are independent.

Table 8.8 **Barriers to greening**

		Barriers
Internal	1	Financial barriers
	2	Knowledge and awareness
	3	Lack of skills
	4	Lack of time
External	1	Lack of government support mechanism
	2	Low return on investments
	3	Lack of industry support (associations)
	4	Competitive pressures

8.6.6 Financial barriers

This was the leading barrier among the respondents. Previous research has shown that small firms are often financially constrained, operate with longer working capital cycles and have limited access to funds. Research in India highlights weak financial management in SMEs (Thampy, 2010; InfoDev, 2012). A report by the

Prime Minister's task force (2010) flags it as a major issue in Indian SMEs. This suggests that SMEs with financial constraints are not likely to invest in voluntary green activities. Environmental certifications are not scarce among SMEs. The ISO 14001 certification is now an integral part of the European Union's Eco-Management and Audit Scheme (EMAS, 2013). Such requirements will be increasingly sought by clients in EU and North America. SMEs stand to miss out on these opportunities if underprepared.

A manufacturer of plastic injection moulded components said:

> In our industry, customers pay us after three months. This is considered standard practice. Many pay even later. This increases working capital costs and lowers our profitability. Managing cash flow for wages and monthly expenses is not easy and we really cannot think of spending for voluntary green activities.

The manufacturer of air pollution equipment lamented that they had already lost an opportunity because they considered environmental certification as an unnecessary investment.

> We had a good chance of a signing a joint venture agreement with a Swedish firm. They were keen on investing and buying back our products to be sold in Europe. But they would not budge about their ISO 14000 requirements from their partner. We offered to get the certification within 12 months, but they couldn't wait.

8.6.7 Lack of knowledge and skills

This is perceived as a major barrier by owners. In India, SMEs do not have any sources to reach out to for gaining knowledge or skills in green practices. ISO 14000 certification workshops are aimed at large firms and none exist for SMEs. Only 23% of the respondents had attended some form of environmental training or seminar in the last year, all of which were offered by their own clients. In another question, 53.1% respondents strongly agreed that SMEs do not quite understand the benefits of green management.

Among the external barriers, lack of government support and low return on investments were the leading ones. In the exploratory interviews, respondents felt that there is no encouragement or support from government agencies to propagate greening in SMEs. Some respondents recalled how a government subsidy of INR 75,000 offered for ISO 9000 certification in SMEs, popularized the certification. This encouraged taking up what was perceived as a disruptive process for small firms.

A manufacturer of air pollution control equipment explained:

> EMS should be incentivized by the government. Some years back, there was a subsidy on ISO 9000 certification for SMEs. This should be offered for EMS certifications too, because the nation would benefit from it. It will also help SMEs be competitive in the international markets.

Poor returns on voluntary green investments discouraged some respondents. One manufacturer of chemical filter screens said:

> Clean electroplating process plants are available in the world. Even though they are expensive, we are ready to import. But with present interest rates and dollar price the ROI is not attractive. Full import duties don't encourage us either.

8.6.8 The influencers to adoption of green practices

Various factors are suggested in studies conducted in other countries. Based on this and on insights gained in the exploratory stage, ten influencers were listed and respondents were asked to rate them (Table 8.9).

Table 8.9 **Influencers of green performance**

Rank	Influencers of green performance improvement
1	Personal awareness
2	Customers
3	Employees
4	Society/community
5	Technical/joint venture partners
6	Suppliers
7	Bankers
8	Investors
9	Insurers

The potential to reduce costs is a major influencer, as suggested in earlier studies. As saving energy, reducing waste and preventing pollution help lower costs, these practices are well accepted.

One SME producing painted automobile components for a car manufacturer said:

> Any clean tech must have the potential to reduce costs. Only then would SMEs be interested. We cannot switch over to water-based paints because of higher costs. Nor can we do away with paint stripper even though it is a strong solvent. Green solutions should have the potential to save money.

8.6.9 Influence of personal awareness

At the top of the list is personal awareness. One respondent making brake shoe assemblies for a motorcycle manufacturer said:

> In the last few years my environmental sensitivity has been growing. I am closely associated with an NGO involved in greening Pune's hills. My

> family enjoys weekends in nature and vacations in India's wildlife reserves. I find that this is also pushing me in to green practices in my business. We display environment posters and make targets for each department and encourage employees to take up innovative green projects. We are already performing much beyond compliance.

However, as noted in earlier studies, a high awareness may not result in positive behaviour, due to presence of other barriers. Yet it is important to note that the perception among SME owners is that personal awareness can influence their green performance.

8.6.10 Customers as influencers

Customers influence green behaviour, as suggested in the previous section. Many large corporations now run sustainability programmes and these practices trace back to the supply chain. Vendors are assessed on quality, environment, health and safety measures. One owner supplying electronic assemblies to GE Healthcare said:

> Environmental measures now touch every aspect of our business. This was possible only because the GE team failed to qualify us as a vendor. We cleared every aspect except environmental performance. To qualify, we went all out in understanding and complying with their EHS standards. Our target was to qualify within next 12 months, and achieved it in a little less than that. All of us are proud and now our employees make suggestions on green practices.

8.6.11 Other influencers

It is interesting to note that insurers have no influence on their customers. It would be reasonable to assume that a firm with lower environmental risks should have lower insurance premiums. Either this is not communicated by insurance firms or Indian SMEs may not be insuring themselves against environmental risks. There is no information available currently on this, and this could be the basis for further research. The Insurance Regulatory and Development Authority (IRDA), a body constituted by an act of parliament, can mandate charging lower differential insurance premiums for different levels of environmental performance.

In countries like the Netherlands, ABN AMRO (now acquired by RBS) asks for environmental impacts assessments for large project funding. This can be strongly influential in encouraging small firms to choose clean technologies over older, more detrimental processes.

8.6.12 Green practices within the product life-cycle

The questionnaire sought out green activities within each stage of the product life-cycle. SMEs strive for sustainable competitive advantage which drives practices of continuous improvement. Lean management practices that help save costs are noticeable in many SMEs. Similarly, energy efficiency initiatives, reducing process waste and recycling materials are all ubiquitous within SMEs. However, these are the low-hanging fruits which are easy to observe and initiate. The majority of such practices are within the ambit of manufacturing and are relatively late in the product life-cycle. They are observable, measurable and offer something "to act on". However, greening the other stages is not as apparent and may require capabilities not common in all SMEs. They are further obscured because they may not lead to savings. The respondents recorded the green practices in the five generic stages of a product life-cycle—planning, design, sourcing, manufacturing and sales. The percentage of respondents with practices in each stage are shown in Table 8.10.

Table 8.10 **Incidence of firms having green practices in product life-cycle**

Stage in the value chain	Percentage of respondents
Planning	42
Design	73
Sourcing	62
Manufacturing	98
Sales and distribution	50

The planning stage has the least incidence. Earlier studies in SMEs have shown that SMEs confine their focus to business issues and short-run outcomes. Choices are guided by business outcomes without regard to the environment. In the design stage, a high incidence is explained by the potential to save money. Designing products for lower material costs, lower energy consumption, increased recycled content, or increased product life reduces costs. However, there is a perception that environmental considerations in the design stage compromise functionality. While this seems to be the barrier, the real issue would be of lack of awareness, which creates the perception. The sales and distribution stage has low incidences of green practices. Some owners who had high green performance levels admitted that they did not realize the importance of communicating with customers. The communication gap between what firms do and what buyers know may put off better choices. SMEs with greener product life-cycles may suggest a high level of maturity in the firm.

These findings suggest that low awareness within SME owners may prevent them from recognizing the less obvious areas in the product life-cycle.

8.7 Conclusions and recommendations

Indian SMEs face multiple challenges, and environmental considerations do not top their priorities. By their sheer number, they offer huge potential for improving

India's environment. Much of this potential is not yet realized due to weak regulation and lack of a facilitative industrial structure. Regulatory compliance, energy saving, waste and material reduction are practices that are diffused already within Indian SMEs. While necessary, they are not enough to improve the environmental conditions in India. This study has revealed a singular aspect, an understanding of which is vital to performance improvement—the environmental performance of an SME is highly dependent on the owner's environmental awareness. Statistical testing shows a highly significant dependence between the two variables. The other key to improving green performance is the greening within the product life-cycle beyond the manufacturing stage. To create a facilitative atmosphere for greening Indian SMEs, each stakeholder has a role to play. Based on the findings, recommendations are proposed for each. These are specific to India and are discussed in detail below.

8.7.1 Role of government ministry

In India, the apex body for the formulation and administration of rules, regulations and laws relating to SMEs is the Ministry of Micro, Small and Medium Enterprises. The ministry offers several programmes to assist SMEs. However, the ministry does not seem to have any strategic environmental focus in the programmes. The Prime Minister had set up a task force to offer recommendations for improving the SME business environment, which was a response to industry representation. Surprisingly, the task force report (2010) ignores any environmental considerations or even the potential for environmental improvement that Indian SMEs offer.

Some time ago, Indian SMEs had a poor track record of safety with accident rates higher than in other countries. The National Safety Council (NSC) of India was set up in 1966 to initiate a preventive culture of safety in industry. The NSC played a vital role in spreading awareness in industries and SMEs in particular. A similar agency could be considered aimed at improving environmental awareness in industry. This council could work with local bodies, trade associations or chambers of commerce, to spread awareness within SMEs.

Similarly, ISO 9000 certifications were considered an unnecessary expense by SMEs. A subsidy was offered to certified SMEs which helped diffuse this. This certification helped SMEs gain business when ISO certification became almost mandatory in international business. Presently, environmental management systems are perceived as "good to have" activities. Already some European customers demand certifications such as EMAS, REACH or RoHS. Offering subsidies or low-interest loans would benefit its acceptance within SMEs. The Ministry needs to set up such environmental initiatives.

The Reserve Bank of India has mandated banks to treat SMEs as a priority sector in lending. Extending this further, offering lower interest for green investments can further stimulate green practices. Successful initiatives in other countries need to be considered in the Indian context. The Environment and Energy Management Agency (ADEME) in France offers financial assistance to projects going beyond compliance. The German public bank Kreditanstalt für Wiederaufbau has a special fund for energy efficiency in SMEs. This allows SMEs to cover costs of professional advice on energy efficiency improvements. The Korean Ministry of Environment extends financial support to SMEs in the priority areas of air pollution reduction and increased recycling. The Ministry operates a Resource Recycling Promotion Fund to provide grants to eligible small businesses (Mazur, 2012).

It is now inevitable that the Ministry of MSME incorporates the environment in its strategic goals. Only a top-down approach will provide the impetus for other stakeholders in their own roles.

8.7.2 Role of the regulatory agencies

The general industry perception is that Indian standards are on a par with developed countries. However, they are at the end of pipe. There is no mechanism to control inputs. Indian regulators must consider regulations like Restriction of the Use of Certain Hazardous Substances (RoHS) and Registration, Evaluation, Authorization and Restriction of Chemicals (REACH). These are already in place in the European Union.

SMEs feel that the regulators have failed to set up a just and uniform enforcement mechanism. This is detrimental to adoption of regulatory and voluntary practices. The SPCBs must respond with increased staff, offices and capabilities, and additionally to the recommendations of the Working Group initiated by the Planning Commission (2012).

8.7.3 Role of industry

SMEs perceive environmental practices to be technically complex and resource-intensive. Despite widespread awareness of cost benefits of eco-efficient practices, SMEs and entrepreneurs are less aware of practices in other areas. Thus, business benefits from greening may be unclear. The findings suggest that Indian SMEs lack the capability of identifying economic or business benefits of green efforts. In many stages, the benefits cannot be directly related to business activities. A study with European SMEs by OECD supports this finding (2010). Further, training and assistance in greening are not available for SMEs. Low awareness is a major internal barrier which needs to be corrected.

To facilitate the change, creation of an agency is a proposed solution. The leading industry associations of India—Federation of Indian Chambers of Commerce and Industry (FICCI), Confederation of Indian Industry (CII) and the National Association of Software and Services Companies (NASSCOM) have played important roles in industrial development in India. They can initiate such facilitation. Here, too, lessons from other countries provide a direction. In France, for example, 21 Technical Industrial Centres[2] covering 32 SME-dominated industry sectors, act as facilita-

2 www.reseau-cti.com

tion centres. They work with support from different business organizations and are funded through fees paid by businesses. In the UK, the National Industrial Symbiosis Programme[3] provides information, networking and matching service for firms, with a strong focus on sustainable businesses.

In conclusion, the growing Indian population places ever-increasing demands on human economic activities. Depletion of natural resources and generation of industrial and consumptive waste is already peaking. Increasingly, large corporations outsource manufacturing activities to smaller, low-cost producers which transfers their environmental burdens to the SMEs in their supply chain. Even as this offers a huge opportunity for environmental improvement, it can only be realized with a strategic approach which is lacking in India today. It is already becoming too late for the environment. Without immediate actions, humankind will face the consequences of a degraded environment.

References

Bansal, P., and Roth, K. (2000). Why companies go green: A model of ecological responsiveness. *The Academy of Management Journal*, 43(4), 717-736.

Chen, Y.-S., and Lai, S.-B. (2006). The influence of green innovation performance on corporate advantage in Taiwan. *Journal of Business Ethics*, 67(4), 331-339.

Deloitte. (2008). *Growth Opportunities for Indian SMEs.* Delhi: Deloitte Touche Tohmatsu India Pvt. Ltd.

EMAS (2013). Environment, EMAS. Retrieved from www.ec.europa.eu/environment/emas.

Esty, D.C., and Winston, A.S. (2009). *Green to Gold.* New York: John Wiley.

Force, S.T. (2010). *Report of Prime Minister's Task Force on MSME.* New Delhi: Planning Commission.

Gadenne, D., Kennedy, J., and McKeiver, C. (2009). An empirical study of environmental awareness and practices in SMEs. *Journal of Business Ethics*, 84(1), 45-63.

Gerrans, P.A., and Hutchinson, W. (2000). Sustainable development and small and medium-sized enterprises: A long way to go. In R. Hillary (Ed.), *Small and Medium Sized-Enterprises and the Environment* (pp. 75-81). Sheffield, UK: Greenleaf Publishing.

Gibson, B., and Casser, G. (2005). Longitudinal analysis of relationships between planning and performance in small Firms. *Small Business Economics*, 25(3), 207-222.

Godrej, J., and Forbes, N. (2012). *Report of the Working Group "Effectively integrating industrial growth and environmental sustainability".* New Delhi: Planning Commission.

Hillary, R. (2004). Environmental management systems and the smaller enterprise. *Journal of Cleaner Production*, 12(6), 561-569.

Hitchens, D.C. (2004). Competitiveness, environmental performance and management of SMEs. *Greener Management International*, 44, 45-57.

Hobbs, J. (2000). Promoting cleaner production in SMEs. In R. Hillary (Ed.). *SMEs and the Environment* (pp. 149-157). Sheffield, UK: Greenleaf Publishing.

InfoDev (2012). *Issues in SME financing.* InfoDev.

3 www.nispnetwork.com

Iraldo, F., Testa, F., and Frey, M. (2010). Environmental management system and SMEs: EU experience, barriers and perspectives. In S.K. Sarkar (Ed.). *Environmental Management* (p. 258). Scivo: Rijeka.

Lee, K.-H. (2009). Why and how to adopt green management into business organizations?: The case study of Korean SMEs in manufacturing industry. *Management Decision*, 47(7), 1,101-1,121.

Megacom (2008). *A Study on Environment as an Aspect of MSME Policy development in Egypt.* Cairo: International Development Research Centre and CIDA.

Ministry of MSME (2012). *MSME Annual Report 2012–13.* New Delhi: GOI.

Ministry of MSME, GOI (2012). *Annual Report 2011–12.* New Delhi: Government of India.

Moorthy, M.K., Yacob, P., Chelliah, M.K., and Arokiasay, L. (2012). Drivers for Malaysian SMEs to go green. *International Journal of Academic Research in Business and Social Sciences*, 2(9), 74-86.

Nafziger, D., Ahmed, N., and Montagno, R. (2003). Perceptions of environmental consciousness in US small businesses: An empirical study. *Advanced Management Journal*, 68(2).

OECD (2010). *SMEs and Green Growth: Promoting Sustainable Manufacturing and Eco-innovation in Small Firms.* Bologna: OECD.

Ortiz Avram, D., and Kühne, S. (2008). Implementing responsible business behavior from a strategic management perspective: Developing a framework for Austrian SMEs. *Journal of Business Ethics*, 82(2), 463-475.

Planning Commission (2012). *Effectively Integrating Industrial Growth and Environment Sustainability.* New Delhi: Planning Commission.

Porter, M.E., and van der Linde, C. (1995). Toward a new conception of the environment–competitiveness relationship. *Journal of Economic Perspectives*, 9(4), 97-118.

Shrivastava, P. (1995). Environmental technologies and competitive advantage. *Strategic Management Journal*, 16(1), 183-200.

Simpson, M., Taylor, N., and Barker, K. (2004). Environmental responsibility in SMEs: Does it deliver competitive advantage? *Business Strategy and the Environment*, 13(3), 156–171.

Smith, A., and Duff, C. (2000). Small firms and the environment: factors that influence SMEs' environmental behaviour. In R. Hillary (Ed.), *SMEs and the Environment* (pp. 24-34). Sheffield, UK: Greenleaf Publishing.

Thampy, A. (2010). Financing of SMEs in India. *IIMB Management Review.*

WCED (1987). *Our Common Future.* Oxford, UK: Oxford University Press.

Weerasiri, S., and Zhengang, Z. (2012). Attitudes and awareness towards environmental management and its impact on environmental management practices (EMPs) of SMEs in Sri Lanka. *Journal of Social and Development Sciences*, 3(1), 16-23.

Williamson, D., Lynch-Wood, G., and Ramsay, J. (2006). Drivers of environmental behaviour in manufacturing SMEs and the implications for CSR. *Journal of Business Ethics*, 67(3), 317-330.

9

Rethinking CSR

The case of the oil and gas sector in India

R.K. Mishra, Punam Singh and Shulagna Sarkar
Institute of Public Enterprise, India

Oil and gas companies have contributed to India's growth immensely. Considering the nature of the operations of these companies, there is a growing need for research into the CSR initiatives of these companies to compensate the damages caused by them to the environment, people and other stakeholders. This chapter highlights the implications of Sec. 135 of the Companies Act, 2013 pertaining to CSR and intends to elaborate the need for CSR practices by the oil and gas sector. The chapter discusses the need for collaborative approach to CSR. The study uses exploratory research based on secondary data collected from seven major oil and gas sector companies in India to identify the various social and environmental interventions undertaken as CSR. The chapter acts as a framework for further research on assessment of the CSR impact of oil and gas companies in India for environmental sustainability and social progress.

9.1 Introduction

There is a growing realization that long-term business success can only be achieved by companies that recognize corporate social responsibility (CSR) as part of the process of wealth creation and as providing a competitive advantage. Advocates of the concept of CSR believe that organizations receive a social sanction from society that requires that they, in return, contribute to the growth and development of the society. Despite differences of opinion about the efficacy of CSR, there is a general consensus among academicians, policy-makers, and practitioners that corporations should operate within the norms and mores of the societies in which they exist.

The Commission of the European Communities (2003), has explained CSR as the concept that an enterprise is accountable for its impact on all relevant stakeholders. It is the continuing commitment by business to behave fairly and responsibly and contribute to economic development while improving the quality of life of the workforce and their families, as well as of the local community and society at large. The World Business Council for Sustainable Development (2002) defined CSR as the commitment of business to contribute to sustainable economic development, working with employees, their families, the local community and society at large to improve their quality of life. Being part of the society, business has numerous stakeholders. Carroll and Buchholtz (2003) classify some major stakeholder groups into primary and secondary categories. Primary stakeholders include shareholders, employees, customers, business partners, communities, future generations and the natural environment. The secondary stakeholders include the state, local and federal government, regulatory bodies, civic institutions and groups, special interest groups, trade and industry groups, media and competitors.

Years after independence, India has seen the growth of giant oil and gas companies. The contribution of oil and gas companies to the growth of the nation is immense yet, due to the nature of its operations, the sector has tremendous negative impacts on environment and society. The various impacts can be categorized as human, socioeconomic and cultural impacts, atmospheric impacts, aquatic impacts, and terrestrial and ecosystem impacts. In view of the tremendous damages caused to society and environment, there is a lot of hue and cry by social activists, NGOs, government and other stakeholders in recent times questioning the social responsibility of this sector.

Realizing the importance of CSR as a strategic tool for sustainable development, oil and gas sector companies across the globe have initiated focused efforts for championing CSR to gain social sanction and goodwill. Oil companies have successfully implemented various CSR initiatives to mitigate environmental risks, yet their absolute impact on the industry's environmental footprint remains questionable. Blowfield and Murray (2008) questioned the importance of "indirect" impact in determining the role played by the oil companies in sustainable development. Companies contemplating the triple-bottom-line approach have also initiated interventions for social inclusiveness. It has been observed that organizations have been using CSR as a tool for brand building rather than as it should be used as a tool to engage with stakeholders using the triple-bottom-line approach.

The province of corporate social responsibility with an aim to bring India's geographically remote and low-income groups into the mainstream of economic life now has the potential to become the most valuable business opportunity of the next decade. The time is perfect for companies to aggressively pursue the agenda of inclusive growth. The 11th Plan defines inclusive growth to be "a growth process which yields broad-based benefits and ensures equality of opportunity for all". Inclusive growth for India needs to be assessed from every perspective: personal, societal, cultural and economic. Inclusiveness is benchmarked against achievement of monitorable targets related to (i) income and poverty, (ii) education, (iii) health, (iv) women and children, (v) infrastructure and (vi) environment.

In the backdrop of the above discussion highlighting the significance of CSR in the oil and gas sector, there exists significant scope for studying CSR interventions for environmental sustainability and socio-economic progress. The chapter aims to discuss CSR interventions in the oil and gas sectors in India with special reference to Central Public Sector Enterprises (CPSEs). The chapter shares a metric that can be utilized for the assessment of companies' CSR initiatives. The chapter also highlights the need for collaborative approaches to implementation of CSR activities.

9.2 The need for CSR in oil and gas sectors: a global perspective

Global companies the primary operations of which consist mainly of extraction and refining of oil and gas resources—British Petroleum, Shell, ExxonMobil and Total—display similarities that characterize the industry. IEA (2002) has highlighted the importance of the oil and gas industry in managing the global energy consumption. SFT (2005) and Olje- og energidepartementet, (2005) have explained that oil and gas have immense environmental impacts, both when produced and used. An IGPCC (2001) report has raised concern with regards to the release of greenhouse gases causing climate change. Crude oil is constituted of substances with high toxicity and eco-toxicity (EPA, 2004). Thus, the oil and gas industry is a high-risk industry, both in societal and environmental terms.

Tebebba (2003) has talked about the geographical limitations of oil and gas resources and has discussed the large scale of environmental and social challenges related to new extraction fields. The classical utilitarianism concept justifies a higher need for implementation of CSR practices by organizations as it is expressed that an action is right if and only if it produces the greatest balance of pleasure over pain for everyone. Utilitarianism is a concept with a view that actions and policies should be evaluated on the basis of the benefits and the costs they will impose on society. Ismail (2009) explains that utilitarianism suggests that the corporation needs to accept social duties and rights to participate in social cooperation.

Numerous issues such as the volume of hazardous materials and chemicals contaminating water bodies, long-term impact on marine environments, waste disposal, impact on wetland, greenhouse gas emissions, soil degradation, health impacts, depletion of natural resources and decreases in forest area are disturbing the ecosystem. Increases in the surrounding temperature also occur due to flare, release of dust fumes, gas, mist, odour, smoke and vapours causing harm to the natural environment. These issues are closely connected to the outputs of the production process. Some of these issues are also associated with unexpected incidents, e.g. oil spills. Managing spills has much in common with safety management; failure in this carries the consequence of impacting upon the environment.

Based on the research by Frynas (2009), it is identified that Shell, BP, Exxon and Chevron support policies such as CO_2 emission reductions, community development projects and transparency of revenues paid to governments. All four companies support broad initiatives such as the voluntary principles on security, human rights and the Extractive Industries Transparency Initiative (see Table 9.1.) Every initiative involves numerous implementation issues. Similarly, the implementation of CSR involves numerous broad constraints such as:

- Country- and context-specific issues
- Failure to involve the beneficiaries of CSR
- Lack of experts in implementation of projects
- Social attitudes of oil company staff/focus on technical and managerial solutions
- No integration into a larger development plan

Table 9.1 **Summary of CSR policies and initiatives by company**

Source: J.G. Frynas (2009). *Beyond Corporate Social Responsibility: Oil Multinationals and Social Challenges.* Cambridge, UK: Cambridge University Press, p. 25.

	CSR policies			CSR multi-stakeholder initiatives			
	Reductions in CO_2 emissions	Community development projects	Government revenue transparency	United Nations Global Compact	Voluntary Principles on Security and Human Rights	Extractive Industries Transparency Initiative	World Business Council for Sustainable Development
Shell	✓	✓	✓	✓	✓	✓	✓
BP	✓	✓	✓	✓	✓	✓	✓
Exxon	✓	✓	✓	×	✓	✓	×
Chevron	✓	✓	✓	×	✓	✓	✓
Petrobras	✓	✓	✓	✓	×	×	✓

	CSR policies			CSR multi-stakeholder initiatives			
	Reductions in CO_2 emissions	Community development projects	Government revenue transparency	United Nations Global Compact	Voluntary Principles on Security and Human Rights	Extractive Industries Transparency Initiative	World Business Council for Sustainable Development
Indian Oil	×	✓	×	✓	×	×	×
PDVSA	×	✓	×	×	×	×	×
Kuwait Petroleum	×	✓	×	×	×	×	×

9.3 CPSEs in India: the role of the oil and gas sector

The Indian public sector has always played a dominant role in shaping the path of the country's economic development. Over the years, PSU operations have extended to include a wide range of activities such as manufacturing, engineering, steel, heavy machinery, machine tools, fertilizers, drugs, textiles, pharmaceuticals, petrochemicals, extraction and refining of crude oil; services such as telecommunication, trading, tourism and warehousing; and a range of consultancy services.

Crude oil and natural gas is another industry within the mining sector characterized by significant presence of CPSEs. However, with the introduction of New Exploration Licensing Policy in 1999, the industry has witnessed significant change with private players gradually gaining a foothold in the industry. Among the non CPSEs, the key players include private majors such as Reliance Industries Limited, Gujarat State Petroleum Corporation, Cairn Energy India Ltd, Essar Oil Ltd, etc. In 2011–12, India was the fourth largest consumer in the world of crude oil and natural gas. The availability of crude oil in the country increased from 18.51 MT during 1970–71 to 106.52 MT during 2000–01, and then to 209.82 MT during 2011–12 (MOSPI, 2013). It has also been estimated that consumption of crude oil has a seen steady increase, from 18.38 MT during 1970–71 to 211.42 MT during 2011–12 with CAGR of 5.99%. It increased from 206.15 MT in 2010–11 to 211.42 MT in 2011–12 (MOSPI, 2013). This data reveals that this sector has been constantly growing.

Over the years, oil and gas companies in India have been forced into more challenging operating environments. Cost–benefit language has often been used to excuse the damage caused in one place because it is outweighed by the overall financial benefits (Jenkins *et al.*, 2006). However, the global oil and gas industry has addressed its social and environmental responsibilities. Numerous factors have contributed to this, such as government regulation, international norms and stakeholder activism. Many corporate policies of the global oil and gas industry now explicitly address broader social justice objectives, local and indigenous employment, security and human rights, sustainable livelihoods, culture and heritage, the need for undertaking social impact assessments, ethical procurement, and stakeholder and/or community consultation (Kemp *et al.*, 2006).

The oil and gas sector in India has contributed to the development of the nation, yet simultaneously caused hazards both socially and environmentally. Oil and gas production imposes significant costs on society, including air pollution, oil spills, injuries and deaths. It is also sometimes associated with second-order costs including social dislocation and conflict. Thus, societies look to oil and gas companies to self-regulate: to do more to guard against risks to societies than merely comply with the law. Perhaps more so than in any other industry, people demand CSR from oil and gas companies (Spense, 2011).

9.4 CSR guidelines with special reference to Central Public Sector Enterprises (CPSE)

The Department of Public Enterprises (DPE) in India came up with comprehensive guidelines on CSR in March, 2010 (namely F.No.15 (3)/2007-DPE (GM) GL 99 dt: 9th April 2010) for the Central Public Sector Enterprises in India with respect to the concept, planning, research, documentation, advocacy, promotion, funding aspects, documentation and monitoring of the CSR activities. *The concept of CSR as per the guidelines emphasized sustainable development and clearly stated that CSR is a company's commitment to operate in an economically, socially and environmentally sustainable manner, while recognizing the interests of its stakeholders.* This commitment is beyond statutory requirements. CSR is, therefore, closely linked with the practice of sustainable development.

The provisions of the Companies Act 2013 relating to CSR makes CSR mandatory to not only Indian CPSEs but also to private sector enterprises. Section 135 (under Chapter IX: Accounts of companies) of the Companies Act 2013 deals with CSR provisions. Section 135 has 5 sub-sections. Schedule VII of the Act lists out the CSR activities.

Section 135 (1): CSR Committee

Every company having a net worth of rupees five hundred crore or more, or a turnover of rupees one thousand crore or more, or a net profit of rupees five crore or more during any financial year shall constitute a Corporate Social Responsibility Committee of the Board consisting of three or more directors, out of which at least one director shall be an independent director.

Section 135(2): Disclosure of CSR committee constitution in the Boards Report

The Board's report under sub-section (3) of section 134 (o) shall disclose the composition of the Corporate Social Responsibility Committee

Section 135(3): The Corporate Social Responsibility Committee shall,

1. formulate and recommend to the Board, a Corporate Social Responsibility Policy which shall indicate the activities to be undertaken by the company as specified in Schedule VII;
2. recommend the amount of expenditure to be incurred on the activities referred to in clause (a); and
3. monitor the Corporate Social Responsibility Policy of the company from time to time.

Section 135 (4): The Board of every company referred to in sub-section (1) shall,

1. After taking into account the recommendations made by the Corporate Social Responsibility Committee, approve the Corporate Social Responsibility Policy for the company and disclose the contents of such Policy in its report and also place it on the company's website, if any, in such manner as may be prescribed; and
2. ensure that the activities as are included in Corporate Social Responsibility Policy of the company are undertaken by the company.

Section 135 (5): CSR expenditure/Mandatory CSR spending.

The Board of every company referred to in sub-section (1), shall ensure that the company spends, in every financial year, at least two per cent of the average net profits of the company made during the three immediately preceding financial years, in pursuance of its Corporate Social Responsibility Policy: Provided that the company shall give preference to the local area and areas around it where it operates, for spending the amount earmarked for Corporate Social Responsibility activities: Provided further that if the company fails to spend such amount, the Board shall, in its report made under clause (o) of sub-section (3) of section 134, specify the reasons for not spending the amount. "Average net profit" shall be calculated in accordance with the provisions of section 198.

Under Clause (o) of Sub-Section (3) of Section 134

There shall be attached to statements laid before a company in a general meeting, a report by its Board of Directors, which shall include:
(o) The details about the policy developed and implemented by the company on corporate social responsibility initiatives taken during the year.

SCHEDULE VII

1. Eradicating hunger, poverty and malnutrition, promoting preventive health care and sanitation and making available safe drinking water:
2. Promoting education, including special education and employment enhancing vocation skills especially among children, women, elderly, and the differently able and livelihood enhancement projects;
3. Promoting gender equality, empowering women, setting up homes and hostels for women and orphans; setting up old age homes, day care centers and such other facilities for senior citizens and measures for reducing inequalities faced by socially and economically backward groups;
4. Ensuring environmental sustainability, ecological balance, protection of flora and fauna, animal welfare, agro forestry, conservation of natural resources and maintaining quality of soil, air and water;
5. Protection of national heritage, alt and culture including restoration of buildings and sites of historical importance and works of art; setting up public libraries; promotion and development of traditional arts and handicrafts:
6. Measures for the benefit of armed forces veterans, war widows and their dependents;
7. Training to promote rural sports, nationally recognized sports, Paralympics sports and Olympic sports;
8. Contribution to the Prime Minister's National Relief Fund or any other fund set up by the Central Government for socio-economic development and relief and welfare of the Scheduled Caste and the Scheduled Tribes, other backward classes, minorities and women;
9. Contributions or funds provided to technology incubators located within academic institutions which are approved by the Central Government.
10. Rural development projects.

9.5 Implications of Section 135 of Companies Act 2013

The Ministry of Corporate Affairs (MCA) has estimated that 14,358 companies fall into this **"mandatory" CSR-reporting category.** CSR activities in the first year (14–15) would amount to over rupees 20,000 crore spent in social welfare.

Section 135 of Companies Act pertaining to CSR seeks to create an enabling environment by promoting and facilitating better connections between businesses and communities. It will facilitate deeper consideration and longer-term strategies for addressing some of our most persistent social, economic and environmental problems; it will assist in synergizing partnerships between corporations, governments, civil society organizations, academic institutions and social entrepreneurs.

Business resources can be channelled into a diverse array of programmes to address social, economic and environmental problems and to bring about a sustainable future for all. The array of activities mentioned in Schedule VII holds the potential to create an all-inclusive society; but this requires an integrated and defined role to be undertaken by corporations, civil society organizations, government at central and local level, and also by the community itself. The interpretation and implementation of Sec. 135 of Companies Act, 2013 is as given in Table 9.2.

Table 9.2 **Decoding Sec. 135 of Companies Act 2013**

Challenges: interpretation and implementation of the section 135 of the Act.	Opportunities: the way ahead
Framing of a CSR policy	A reference document to guide structured CSR implementation in an organization, linking CSR with business strategy
Board-level CSR committee	Strategic focus to CSR by incorporating CSR as a part of the structure
Defining the responsibility of the board	Top management accountability for CSR implementation
Schedule VII	Activities in line with societal and environmental needs=
Mandatory reporting	Informing the stakeholders of the reasons for not spending an assigned amount on CSR; a way to ensure responsible and continuous CSR spending
Sustainability reporting	A way to showcase responsible business practices to stakeholders, transparency in spending, knowing the impact of the company's activities
Implementing partners	Need for capacity-building initiatives at all levels: corporations, NGOs, government and academic institutions
Political interferences and misuse of funds	CSR policy document disclosed in public domain will help to reduce political interferences; CSR audit takes care that the fund is spent responsibly

9.6 Addressing the social sector gap: a collaborative approach to CSR

There are various existing schemes and flagship programmes of government in the areas of health, sanitation, education, sustainability, skill development and capacity building. In spite of numerous development efforts by both central and state government, a gap still exists. This gap in the development of the nation can be dealt with using a collaborative approach from government, business and civil society. A collaborative effort from both government and business will pool large amounts of funding and effort to channel easy access to all facilities for all the citizens of India. A simultaneous effort will ensure that companies' CSR vision will integrate with that of the government (see Figure 9.1).

Figure 9.1 **A collaborative approach to CSR**

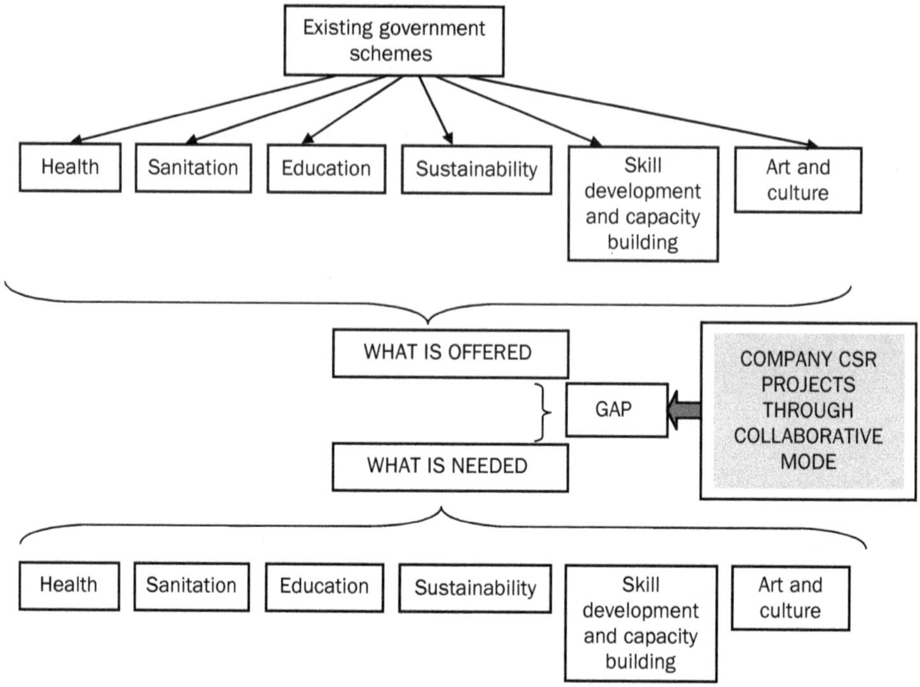

9.7 The role of government, corporate and civil societies

The international prominence of the initiatives for development can be traced to the objectives of Millennium Development Goals (MDGs) which established businesses as partners of development (WBCSD, 2010). However, realizing the corporate sector's constraints in playing a role as an agent of development, CSR initiatives need to be implemented with the involvement of civil society and government agencies to promote community development. There are critics that argue that the corporation alone is unable to promote community development through a CSR project (Frynas, 2005; Fox, 2004). The crisis at the ground level has encouraged people to look for new ways to develop collective action to deal with social demands that cannot be met by the government alone. This has led to the appearance of partnership projects, with governments, companies and civil society organizations working together. CSR has oiled the wheels of these new partnerships, and the CSR literature reflects the clear link between CSR and social partnership (Nelson and Zadek, 2000; Gribben *et al.*, 2001; Kjaergaard and Westphalen, 2001). The challenge for governments is to find a way to design and implement public policy that will generate leadership- and partnership-based innovation, seeking to maximize the benefits of these innovations by ensuring their systematic acceptance and application among the wider business community.

Figure 9.2 **The role of government, corporate and civil societies**

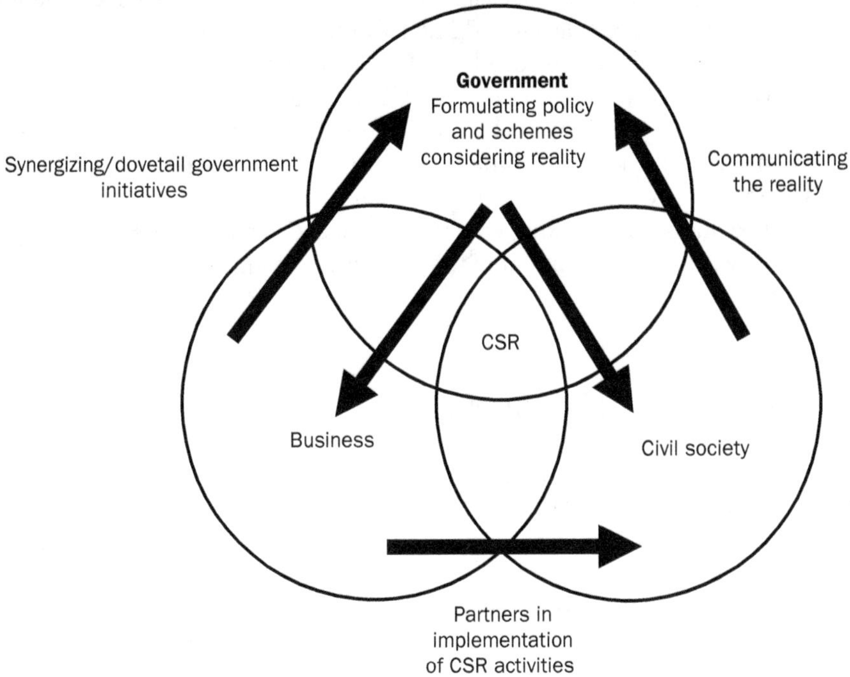

9.8 The role of government

At the macro level, the government sector is expected to play the role of driver of CSR initiatives by the corporation for the benefit of society (Moon, 2004; Fox, Ward and Howard, 2002). However, at the micro level this role is reflected in the implementation strategy which is known among other things as a public–private partnership CSR strategy. The aims of the partnership are to share resources, knowledge and capability between business corporations and the government agency. The government sectors are expected to provide an enabling environment to assist and encourage business corporations to undertake CSR efforts as part of their business strategy in the country. The enabling role played by the government sector would consist of mandating, facilitating, partnering and endorsing (Fox *et al.*, 2002).

9.9 The role of corporations

With the prolific number of both public and private sector companies in India, there is a huge volume of funds which needs to be channelled appropriately in order to reach the grassroots level. The role of corporations is to ensure support to civil society organizations (CSOs) and also extend an arm to the government for fulfilment of the vision of a developed India. Corporations are required to envision CSR as a tool for an inclusive society and for a sustainable future. This requires them to formulate a CSR policy in line with their organizational strategy. Corporations need to design CSR projects by understanding the real need of the community and synergize/dovetail the initiatives of the government towards sustainable inclusive growth. They have to partner with civil society organizations to understand realities on the ground and, with their help, develop a successful implementation model with the involvement of the local government.

9.10 The role of civil society

The term civil society organization (CSO) may be wide in scope and include an array of organizations, including NGOs and not-for-profit organizations. Among others, CSOs include trade unions, religious institutions, academic institutions and ethnic tribal groups as well as different charitable organizations and foundations. Civil society has a crucial role to play in the strengthening of local institutions and in bringing innovation into government programmes. The role of CSOs includes the awareness-raising of stakeholders. CSOs have played a critical role in pushing for CSR globally. Campaigning groups have been key drivers of inter-governmental negotiations, ranging from the regulation of hazardous wastes to a global ban on child labour and the elimination of slavery. CSOs are also expected to be implementers of companies' CSR initiatives in different spheres, particularly related to community issues. CSOs have a critical role in influencing public policy and opinion, and corporate CSR decisions through advocacy, networking, lobbying and public campaigns, and shaping and delivering CSR programmes. Grassroots CSOs usually are required to have detailed knowledge of communities and their needs to enable stakeholder engagement and dialogue.

9.11 Methodology

The initiative taken by the Indian government to constitute CSR as a provision of the Companies Act, 2013 has forced companies to rethink their CSR initiatives. Thus there is a huge scope for sector-specific research on CSR initiatives. The chapter is based on exploratory research where the CSR initiatives of the seven oil and gas CPSEs in India have been studied to identify the areas of concern that need more focus. Considering the fact that the oil and gas sector in India is dominated by public sector organizations, the CSR initiatives of the following seven companies have been studied: Oil and Natural Gas Corporation Ltd (ONGC), Indian Oil Corporation Ltd (IOCL), Oil India Ltd (OIL), Bharat Petroleum Corporation Ltd (BPCL), Hindustan Petroleum Corporation Ltd (HPCL), Gas Authority of India Ltd (GAIL) and Numaligarh Refinery Ltd (NRL). Documents such as annual reports, CSR initiatives of the company, sustainability reports, CSR policy documents and sustainability policy documents were studied to gain a complete insight of the CSR practices of oil and gas CPSEs in India.

The metric used to study the CSR initiatives of the oil and gas sector is based on the concept of a triple-bottom-line approach using economic, social and environmental parameters. Table 9.3 elaborates parameters used for measuring the CSR initiatives.

Table 9.3 **Metric for sustainability**

Social metric	**Labour and employment issues**	Health and safety, education, training, industrial relations, wages, benefits, employee retention
	Community initiatives	Involvement in local community, contribution to the local economy, ensuring local wealth and skills
	Corporate philanthropy	Donations, pre-tax profits and grant programmes
Environmental metric	**Pollution prevention**	Water pollution and waste disposal, greenhouse gas emissions
	Environmental safety	Oil spills, aftermath effect handling
	Climate change	Energy conservation, emissions, flaring, global warming
Economic metric	**Impact on government**	Corporate governance, tax payments, subsidies, policies and regulations
	Financial performance indicator	Net profit/earning, total revenue, investment in R&D
	Impact on communities	Job creation, infrastructure and technology development, social and economic inclusion, women's empowerment

Table 9.4 **Comparative view of social, environmental initiatives of oil and gas CPSEs in India**

Name of organization understudy	Reduction in CO_2 emissions	Community development projects	United Nations Global Compact	SA8000 (Social Accountability)	ISO 14001 (environmental management system)	Any other international reporting standards
ONGC	✓	✓	✓	✓	✓	×
IOCL	✓	✓	✓	✓	✓	×
OIL	✓	✓	✓	✓	✓	×
BPCL	✓	✓	✓	✓	✓	×
HPCL	✓	✓	×	✓	✓	×
GAIL	✓	✓	✓	✓	✓	×
NFL	✓	✓	×	✓	✓	×

Table 9.4 reflects the various social and environmental initiatives of oil and gas CPSEs in India. It is by and large clear that organizations are aware of the social and environmental impact of their operations and are taking initiatives to make their operations sustainable. All the companies are engaged in community development because they realize the fact that the negative impact is mostly borne by the community surrounding the area of operation. Organizations are taking initiatives in terms of reduction of CO_2 and other greenhouse gases. Organizations with the exception of a few such as HPCL, BRPCL and NFL are members of the United Nations Global Compact, India chapter. All the companies studied are certified to SA8000 and ISO 14001.

Table 9.5 **Comparative study of CSR interventions of oil and gas CPSEs in India**

Name of organization studied	H	E	RID	L/SD	WE	ES	DM	A&C	WM
ONGC	✓	✓	✓	✓	✓	✓	✓	×	✓
IOCL	✓	✓	✓	✓	✓	×	×	✓	×
OIL	✓	✓	✓	✓	✓	×	×	×	×
BPCL	✓	✓	✓	✓	✓	✓	×	×	×
HPCL	✓	✓	×	✓	✓	✓	×	×	×
GAIL	✓	✓	✓	✓	✓	✓	✓	×	×
NFL	✓	✓	✓	✓	✓	✓	✓	✓	×

H = Health
E = Education
RID = Rural infrastructure development
L/SD = Livelihood/skill development
WE = Women's empowerment
ES = Environmental sustainability
DM = Disaster management
A&C = Promoting threatened art and culture
WM = Water management

Table 9.5 elaborates the prominent areas of CSR initiatives of the organizations studied, which includes health, education, rural infrastructure development, livelihood/skill development, women's empowerment, environmental sustainability, disaster management, promoting threatened art and culture, and water management. It is observed that organizations are required to take up more initiatives in the area of water management with a view to reshaping the future of global water scarcity. It was found in the present study that a number of organizations are not taking the necessary initiatives in the area of disaster management. The study also highlights that the companies have taken numerous initiatives in the area of health, education, women's empowerment and livelihood generation. It is noteworthy that the above thrust in areas of CSR, and the level of dedication displayed by companies, if synchronized, could bring about the desired outcome of inclusive growth through a collaborative approach to CSR. In the backdrop to Schedule VII of the Companies Act, 2013, it has been observed that organizations are not spending adequately on R&D, grassroots technology innovation, technology incubation, protection of national heritage, and threatened art and culture. Organizations can play a crucial role through a collaborative CSR model in the area of food security and improvement of nutrition among children in India. It is important to identify the required area of CSR intervention, but it is equally important to develop an appropriate model for the implementation of companies' CSR initiatives.

9.12 Conclusion

There are clear rules associated with measuring the economic pulse of a company at any given point in time. The sustainability performance of a company is generally measured by assessing three aspects of sustainability: economic, social and environmental performance. Assessment of environmental performance is still very limited since it is primarily based on environmental impacts such as natural resource depletion, land degradation, pollution emissions, energy consumption and waste generation. What really needs to be done and is missing is a long-term perspective: organizations should study the impact assessment of their business and work to mitigate the negative impact of the business on the environment.

The study identified that the oil and gas sector is undertaking a number of activities within a social sustainability parameter. Yet what needs to be addressed is the impact of such activities on societal development. In this regard, the concept of CSR audit needs to be implemented and it is recommended that this is conducted by a reliable external third party. CSR activities also need to be well documented and disclosed in the public domain to ensure transparency.

It is observed that most of the organizations have incorporated community development or peripheral development as a thrust area of their CSR. In this regard, organizations have focused on providing facilities such as schools or hospitals for the community around the vicinity of the organization. The real issue lies in providing a sustainable source of income generation for the community at the same time as basic infrastructure such as roads, electricity, safe drinking water, health, and education. In the case of tribal communities, organizations should work to bring these communities into the mainstream by the way of a private–public partnership or public–public partnership model.

The business of exploring for and producing oil and gas entails environmental and social challenges. Therefore, governments, NGOs and the public will continue to pressure oil and gas companies to respond to evolving social and regulatory norms. The oil and gas CPSEs require "will and passion" to serve the society through their CSR activities. Earlier emphasis on the MoU system and the requirement of abiding by the DPE guidelines has led the oil and gas CPSEs in India to make great strides towards doing business in a more sustainable and socially responsible way. Sec. 135 of the Companies Act, 2013 has emphasized that the path to sustained business is through strategic approaches to CSR.

9.12.1 Suggestions

To ensure success of CSR activities, the following points need to be considered:

- Leadership and vision. Key top managerial staff must be committed to the CSR objectives and companies must ensure that sustainability values and missions are not only integrated into the business strategy, policies and culture, but also communicated to all stakeholders.
- Stakeholder engagement. Engagement with internal and external stakeholders as well as with sectoral and multi-stakeholder initiatives enhances credibility, commitment and innovation. Reporting and communicating CSR investments and achievements helps demonstrate transparency and seriousness of intent and rewards staff and partners for their inputs into such initiatives.
- There is a significant need to train employees on areas of planning, funding, implementing, documenting, monitoring and evaluating CSR by the employees of CSR departments.
- Companies need to appreciate the need to initiate more appropriate and relevant CSR projects.
- There is a need to establish clear and user-friendly methodologies and tools to measure the progress that companies are making towards sustainability.
- The oil and gas companies should work together as a joint sector approach to CSR in a holistic and systematic manner which will mobilize greater funding and viable CSR projects with greater impact.

References

Bharat Petroleum Corp. Ltd (2005–06, 2006–07, 2010–11, 2011–12). *Annual Report. CSR Report.* Mumbai: Sustainability Report.

Blowfield, M., and Murray, A. (2008). *Corporate Responsibility: A Critical Introduction.* Oxford, UK: Oxford University Press.

Carroll, A.B., and A.K. Buchholtz. (2003). *Business and Society: Ethics and Stakeholder Management.* 5th ed. Australia: Thomson South-Western.

Commission of the European Communities (2003). What is Corporate Social Responsibility (CSR)? Retrieved from www.europarl.europa.eu/meetdocs/committees/deve/20020122/com(2001)366_en.pdf.

DPE (Department of Public Enterprises) (2010). CSR Guidelines. Retrieved from www.dpe.nic.in.

DPE (Department of Public Enterprises) (2013). CSR Guidelines. Retrieved from www.dpe.nic.in.

DPE MoU (Department of Public Enterprises Memorandum of Understanding) (2013). Guidelines. Retrieved from www.dpemou.nic.in.

Economic Times (2012). CPSEs required to double minimum CSR contribution. Retrieved from www.articles.economictimes.indiatimes.com/2012-12-31/news/36079566_1_crore-on-csr-activities-net-profit-cpses.

EPA (Environmental Protection Agency) (2004). EPA guidelines. Retrieved from https://ofmpub.epa.gov/sor_internet/registry/substreg/home/overview/home.do.

Francisco, S., and Marianna, K. (2005). Responsible leadership and corporate social responsibility: Metrics for sustainable performance. *European Management*, 23(6), 628-647.

Fox, T., Ward, H., and Howard, B. (2002). Public sector roles in strengthening corporate social responsibility: A baseline study. Washington, DC: World Bank.

Frynas J.G. (2009). *Beyond Corporate Social Responsibility: Oil Multinationals and Social Challenges.* Cambridge, UK: Cambridge University Press.

Gas Authority of India Ltd (2005–06, 2006–07, 2010–11, 2011–12). *Annual Report, CSR Report, Sustainability Report.* New Delhi: Gas Authority of India Ltd.

Gribben, C., Pinnington, K. and Wilson, A. (2001). Governments as partners: the role of the central government in developing new social partnerships. Copenhagen: The Copenhagen Centre.

Hindustan Petroleum Corporation Ltd (2005–06, 2006–07, 2010–11, 2011–12). *Annual Report, CSR Report, Sustainability Report.* Mumbai: Hindustan Petroleum Corporation Ltd.

Hindustan Prefab Ltd (2011). Report on Corporate Social Responsibility (2010–2011) New Delhi.

IEA (International Energy Agency) (2002). *World Energy Outlook 2002.* Paris: OECD/IEA.

IPCC (Intergovernmental Panel on Climate Change) (2001). *Climate Change 2001: Synthesis Report—Summary for Policymakers.* Intergovernmental Panel on Climate Change. Retrieved from https://www.ipcc.ch/pdf/climate-changes-2001/synthesis-syr/english/front.pdf.

Indian Oil Corporation Ltd (2005–06, 2006–07, 2010–11, 2011–12). *Annual Report, CSR Report, Sustainability Report.* New Delhi: Indian Oil Corporation Ltd.

Ismail, M. (2009). Corporate social responsibility and its role in community development: An international perspective. *Journal of International Social Research*, 2(9), 199-209.

Jenkins, H., and Yakovleva, N. (2006). Corporate social responsibility in the mining industry: Exploring trends in social and environmental disclosure. *Journal of Cleaner Production*, 14(1), 271-284.

Kjaergaard, C., and Westphalen, S. (2001). *From Collective Bargaining to Social Partnerships: New Roles of the Social Partners in Europe.* Copenhagen: The Copenhagen Centre.

MCA (Ministry of Corporate Affairs) (2013). MCA CSR Guidelines. Retrieved from www.mca.gov.in.

Moon, J. (2004). Government as a driver of corporate social responsibility. *ICCSR Research Paper Series*, 20, 6-7.

MOSPI (Ministry of Statistics and Programme Implementation) (2013). Energy statistics. Retrieved from www.mospi.nic.in/mospi_new/upload/Energy_Statistics_2013.pdf.

Nelson, J., and Zadek, S. (2000). *Partnership Alchemy: New Social Partnerships in Europe*. Copenhagen: The Copenhagen Centre.

Numaligarh Refinery Ltd (2005–06, 2006–07, 2010–11, 2011–12). Annual Report, CSR Report, Sustainability Report. Guwahati: Numaligarh Refinery Ltd.

Oil India Ltd (2005–06, 2006–07, 2010–11, 2011–12). *Annual Report, CSR Report, Sustainability Report*. New Delhi: Oil India Ltd.

Oil and Natural Gas Corporation Ltd (2005–06, 2006–07, 2010–11, 2011–12). *Annual Report, CSR Report, Sustainability Report*. New Delhi: Oil and Natural Gas Corporation Ltd.

Olje- og energidepartementet (2005). *Miljø—Xrsk petroleumvirksomhet—2005*. Oslo: Olje- ogenergidepartementet.

Spense, D. (2011). Corporate Social Responsibility in the oil and gas industry: The importance of reputational risk. *Chicago: Kent Law Review*, 86(1), 59-85.

World Business Council for Sustainable Development (2002). Business case for sustainable development. Retrieved from www.wbcsd.com.

10

Intellectual property and business enablers for transfer of carbon capture and storage technologies in Asia

A. Damodaran
Indian Institute of Management, Bangalore

One of the policy prescriptions advanced in international forums to address the issue of climate change is to go for mitigation strategies that prevent the adverse CO_2 impacts of conventional fossil fuels. For coal-dependent developing countries such as India and China, Carbon Capture and Storage offers an attractive solution as it overcomes the problems of CO_2 associated with coal. This chapter focuses on Intellectual Property Rights (IPRs) related to Carbon Capture and Storage technologies, and explores financing and other enabling conditions for the commercialization of Carbon Capture and Storage (CCS) technologies in the Indian context with reference to the coal sector. It is argued that, despite policy concerns, sound technology transfer regimes can provide viable solutions to issues arising from IPRs, and CCS could be a commercial reality in coal- and oil-dependent countries of Asia in general and India in particular.

Carbon Capture and Storage Technologies (CCS) have been advocated as a feasible alternative for both coal- and oil-dependent economies of the world, since they capture CO_2 emissions from coal-/oil-fired power plants and store it underground, thus avoiding CO_2 emissions into the atmosphere. CCS has been criticized, however, as a step backwards in developing a low-carbon future since it legitimizes the continued use of fossil fuels, and halts the development of renewable energy sources. In addition to this, in countries in south Asia such as India, there are serious concerns about societal risks arising from underground storage of sequestered CO_2 in aquifers and oil wells. The more fundamental issue is that of "CCS-readiness" in developing countries. CCS technologies, especially carbon capture technologies, are yet to be commercially tested (IPCC, 2005; Johnstone, 2009; IEA-GHG, 2007; Anonymous 2009a, 2009c). They call for large incremental capital investments in research and development and testing in actual field conditions (Anonymous, 2009b, 2009c). The risk of technology failure in carbon capture is as high as the risks of environmental accidents from storage systems (Watson, 2012; Anonymous, 2009a). As a result, power plants employing carbon capture technologies are saddled with the prospect of high unit costs of power generation. Moreover, CCS technologies are shackled by patents over key quality technologies. Nevertheless, with sound technology transfer regimes that provide viable solutions to issues arising from Intellectual Property Rights (IPRs), CCS could be a commercial reality in coal- and oil-dependent countries. However, as of today, CCS has not met with policy approval in India both for testing and commercial applications. The Carbon Sequestration Leadership Forum (CSLF), which is the apex ministerial-level international climate change initiative focused on the development of improved cost-effective technologies for the separation and capture of carbon dioxide (CO_2) for its transport and long-term safe storage, has admitted that the first-generation CO_2 capture technology has a high energy penalty and is expensive to implement (Anonymous, 2013). The CSLF also states the importance of gaining experience from large demonstration projects (Anonymous, 2008b) and for developing second-generation and third-generation technologies that are cost-effective and commercially viable (Ibid). It is obvious that for such frontier technologies to be deployed, a variety of enabling technology transfer and financing regimes are called for, which protect IPRs through sound business models.

This chapter focuses on Intellectual Property Rights related to Carbon Capture and Storage Technologies, and explores financing and other enabling conditions for the commercialization of Carbon Capture and Storage Technologies (CCS) in the Indian context with reference to the coal sector. As in the case of China, India's power sector and its massive expansion plans are largely based on coal as the energy source (67% of total electricity production in India is based on coal-fired power plants while the figure is 79% for China). China has CCS demonstration plants, tied to its coal-fired power utilities. India has none to date. Nevertheless, CCS is an important technological option for India, given the preponderant dependence of the country's power sector on coal as the energy source and the importance acquired in its climate policy to reduce CO_2 emission intensity as part of its commitments to the Climate Change Convention in the wake of the developments following the 15th Session of the Conference of Parties. India has to therefore look keenly at the various clean coal technological options connected to CO_2 capture, assess the potential of CO_2 storage and create enabling conditions by way of appropriate business models that can ensure that CCS technologies are transferred on terms that are desirable form the viewpoint of the country's economic interests. Since CCS technologies are in their nascent stage, it becomes important to assess how they have functioned in controlled or non-commercial conditions in other countries. The issue of IPRs assumes significance to India as technology transfer can be inhibited by patents obtaining over CCS technologies. This can be obviated by business partnership models that promise enabling conditions for technology transfer. This chapter thus looks at CCS from the point of view of its possible application to India.

The menu of carbon capture and sequestration technologies is varied. Technological diversity compounds decision-making (Watson, 2012). Carbon capture technologies can be categorized into "pre" and "post" coal combustion technologies. Pre combustion technologies include Integrated Gasification Combined Cycle (IGCC), while post combustion technologies include amine adsorption, sorbents, oxyfuel combustion and membrane technologies. There are an array of technologies from carbon storage that are also patented.

The chapter is divided into the following sections. The first section surveys patterns of research and development, innovations and patents obtaining over key CCS technologies. The second part deals with the precursor conditions for CCS technologies to be pushed to commercialization phase. The third part deals with structures of possible public and private partnerships that can lead to commercialization of CCS technologies while the fourth section deals with business models that can render CCS feasible. The fifth section outlines the contours of a global multilateral financing mechanism for implementing CCS. The concluding section outlines the prospects of CCS in India in the light of the issues discussed in the first five sections.

10.1 Research and development and patents on CCS technologies

Almost all frontier innovations related to CCS technologies are patented. The largest number of patents during 2000–08 is in the area of membrane technology, followed by carbon sequestration, IGCC, oxyfuel combustion and amine adsorption (Dechezleprêtre *et al.*, 2008). In the majority of cases, the assignees of patents have been companies rather than individual vendors. There is reason to infer that in the realm of membrane technologies the situation is likely to be a patent thicket that may enhance the probability of Intellectual Property (IP) infringement litigation

(Lemley, 2002). All the same, such a patent thicket creates conditions for smoother transfer of technologies by lowering the supply price of technologies on the part of vendors or alternatively creating conditions for lower licence fees and royalties (Damodaran, 2000; Schwartz *et al.*, 2007).

Most of the patents that are filed in the area of oxyfuel combustion deal in the main with process improvements. The major thrust of the inventions is to reduce the use of carbon-based fuel as compared to conventional combustion systems without loss of energy output. Other pursuits in the area include efforts to improve effectiveness of CO_2 sequestration, and improve the purity of oxygen streams to ensure better combustion. The inventions underlying the patents' applications, if technically and economically sound, have the effect of reducing variable costs in the operation of CCS-fitted plants. Patent applications for sequestering CO_2 also are process-based. The emphasis is on strengthening oxidation processes that capture CO_2 effectively.

Regarding amine adsorption, the focus of most of the patent applications are on new sorbents and systems that separate CO_2 from other gas mixtures more efficiently.

In the case of IGCC and combined-cycle power plants, the focus is on processes and methods that increase the energy and cost efficiency through improvements in the design of gas turbine plants and compressor units and turbines. The other set of patent applications relate to improvements in gasifiers and incorporation of production enhancement processes in IGCC plants.

Carbon storage is the area where demonstration and test sites provide the impetus for technology evolution. Here technological progress needs to be evaluated in terms of risks addressed and potentially mitigated. Robustness of storage facilities cannot be assessed in a short timespan. Nevertheless, simulations and controlled conditions experiments, coupled with multi-test sites, can obviate to a large extent the problem of indeterminacy.

The results emanating from transport and storage systems developed at the Altmark gas field in Germany and the AEP test project storage in deep saline aquifers can be crucial to developing countries, in order to facilitate their understanding of the risks involved in CCS projects (Johnston, 2009).

A survey of the patents data indicates the following trends in international research on pre-combustion and post-combustion CCS technologies.

10.1.1 Pre-combustion: IGCC

As far as IGCC is concerned, there have been four broad strands of research. The basic focus of research is on improvements in gasification and gas clean-up systems that lower operations and maintenance (O&M) and capital costs of the technology. Improving gasification technology by allowing it to be adapted to a variety of fuels (from hard coal to lignite and from biomass to petroleum residues) is a major research focus. Scaling up coal gasification to meet the need of higher-capacity power plants has been the second challenge. Gasifier and gas turbine output enhancement has been another focus of research in this area. Another stream of ongoing research is on enhancing overall efficiency by recovering heat from gasification process and the gas turbine exhaust. This is used to improve steam production that could be employed to generate auxiliary power. In all these cases demonstration plants are critical to test the new technologies.

The second strand of research has been on fine-tuning operational "availability" for IGCC plants. Currently, the 90% efficiency level is stated to have been exceeded for IGCC-equipped power plants.

The third strand of research is on bringing down the high capital cost of IGCC. Currently, because CCS-based IGCC is higher in capital costs, this will be economical only when all thermal power plants go for CCS incorporation. Until then, the costs of power generated from CCS-fitted pulverized coal plants will exceed that of the IGCC plants.

The fourth strand of research is on optimized system of integrating gasifiers and combined cycle by companies such as Siemens. A sub-strand is research into novel power generation systems, more specifically integrated power generation and air separation systems. The aim of the innovation is to maximize cycle efficiency, and contribute to additional power as well as reducing energy costs for IGCC operations. In a more specific sense this is achieved by optimizing the turbine configuration that drives air compressors.

10.1.2 Post-combustion

10.1.2.1 Amine absorption and solvents

The major research focus is on developing customized renewable solvents that enable chemical scrubbing (adsorption) processes for off-gas which facilitates post-combustion capture and also desorbs CO_2 at high temperature. A closely related development is complementary research into ways of enhancing steam output from the power plant cycle. This is to enable heating of the CO_2-laden absorbent prior to the CO_2 stripping process and the heating of the stripper itself. Savings from reduced energy use in adsorption is another area of research. The process improvements need constant evaluation and pilot-testing. The critical need is for large-scale pilot plant demonstrations to test CO_2 concentration in flue gas. Present costs range from \$30–40/ton CO_2. The target of ongoing research is to reduce it to \$20/ton CO_2.

Developing capture-ready plants that build in steam plants that can be easily converted for CO_2 capture has been another major research pursuit for major companies.

10.1.2.2 Oxyfuel combustion

Production of oxygen-enriched gas streams lies at the core of oxyfuel combustion process. The major thrust of research and patents has been on novel processes and methods that enhance oxygen enhancement in air streams.

Steam-generating combustion system and methods for emission control using oxygen enhancement have also engaged innovators. The unique nature of oxyfuel combustion patents is that is that they aim at enhancing the scope of joint benefits. A case in point is the removal of SO_2 and/or NO_x from carbon dioxide flue gas produced through an oxyfuel combustion process in a pulverized coal-fired power station.

10.1.2.3 Membrane technologies

The latest trend is towards membrane-based separation methods. Many patents have been filed in this area as discussed above. The economic and technical feasibility of the use of membrane technologies in CO_2 capture is yet to be proven. A study of membrane-related patents filed in Japan, USA, Europe and Australia indicates that the focus is on membranes that enhance adsorption by minimizing leakages. Reducing energy costs in the adsorption process has been another focus of research. Among the process patent applications are those that deal with manufacturing methods of membranes. The research is still ongoing.

10.1.2.4 Carbon sequestration

Some of the ongoing work and patents in the field of sequestration has fundamental implications for preventing risks arising from carbon storage in various aquifers, both offshore and onshore. For instance, there is an Australian patent (No AU 761848 B2), granted for "a method of sequestering carbon dioxide (CO_2) in oceans", which involved "testing an area of the surface of a deep open ocean in order to determine both the nutrients that are missing and the diffusion coefficient by applying to the area a first fertilizer that comprises a missing nutrient, and measuring the amount of carbon dioxide that has been sequestered"; this is of fundamental relevance to CO_2 sequestration in offshore oil fields.

Notwithstanding the phenomenal increase in the number of patent applications in various patent and trade offices on CCS technologies, there are many imbalances. The thrust of present research is on capture technologies, mainly from the viewpoint of technical efficiencies (Damodaran, 2010). Transport and storage have not attracted research and patent applications as much as one would have desired. Even these inventions are not conclusive as evident from the continuing streams of patents applications.

Even in capture technologies there is need for major attention on economic efficiencies that reduce capital and operational costs and are focused on customization to local conditions. The following areas call for systematic joint research:

1. Developing cost-effective processes and methods of various pre-combustion and post-combustion technologies in the actual operational situations of various power plants in developing countries
2. Cost-effective and safe CO_2 transport systems that have faster mobility and low risk of accidental or fugitive leakages

3. Carbon sequestration and storage in various type of aquifers at lower costs and low risks of leakages and collateral ecosystem damages

The focus of joint research should be in the areas mentioned above. The joint research programmes that seek to focus on the above areas should concentrate on technical and risk assessments and study of operational functioning of the technologies through demonstration plants. The need is for a financing mechanism that supports these activities in an optimal manner.

10.2 Enabling the financing of CCS technologies

Since financial resources are limited in comparison to potential investment avenues, the challenge of allocating financial resources to CCS projects needs to be presaged upon technical, economic and environmental assessment exercises. The three main categories of risks that can affect the performance of project-based emissions crediting are: (i) technological risks that are tied to the process of production and refer to uncertain output quantities; (ii) economic risks that refer to uncertain input and output prices; and (iii) political risks.

A risk assessment exercise also needs to be added to the repertoire for technologies that are perceived as likely to carry societal and environmental risks. At present these exercises take place in independent layers in developing countries.

Assessments provide the basis for technology ranking particularly for a new genre of technology such as CCS which is yet to be fully proven, research is still progressing and intricate patent thickets characterize the IPR spectrum. Patent thickets normally result when the degree of distinction between successive inventions is low, and the newer products only fulfil the requirements of novelty, non-obviousness and "industrial application". As mentioned, patent thickets raise the probability levels of IP infringement due to the "close cluster" nature of existing patents and the high propensity of newer inventions to encroach on existing patents. The second problem created by such patent clusters is that of an "embarrassment of riches" which create problems of making informed technology choices for potential customers. The transaction costs of making judgements is high for developing countries and their fossil-fuel-fired power sector firms that may desire to take up CCS projects. Further "information asymmetry" in the IP markets adds to the problems of making judgements on technologies such as CCS which developing countries are generally reluctant to accept due to their "mandatory" and non-proven nature. The fact that safety issues associated with CCS are also a major concern to developing countries adds to the problem of technology choice.

Finally, what is considered to be a disadvantage for low-carbon, renewable energy technologies may be an advantage in the case of CCS which can be coupled to coal combustion technologies. It is stated that multilateral development institutions spend large amounts of money on large-scale, capital-intensive fossil fuel projects with predictable rates of return.

10.3 Public–private partnership in CCS technologies

Amey (2008) mentions the following specific factors as forming the rationale for public–private partnerships (PPPs) in the testing, development and commercial applications of CCS technologies:

- The need for a long-term, and transformational, investment to effectively implement a CCS system
- The focus on common delivery and storage elements (storage and transport) in which the role of government is critical in navigating through regulations by adopting appropriate safeguards, and in the conduct of proper and rigorous environment impact and risk assessments and issues relating to site identification of CCS projects
- Ensuring participation by multiple levels of government and industry
- Putting in place a clear policy framework for regulation of CCS
- The need for risk sharing in the early implementation of CCS technologies and the development of markets
- Ensuring the overall "public good" nature of CO_2 reduction opportunities
- Overcoming lack of public understanding about CCS and the ultimate need for well-managed stakeholder inputs to install capture and pipeline facilities
- Ensuring the establishment of a focal point for all important partners and stakeholders in CCS to debate, formulate and manage CCS development
- The need to provide an arm's-length vehicle for governments to manage and monitor CCS development, while appropriately managing direct government involvement and risk
- To develop short-, medium- and long-term plans for the staged development of CCS to maximize both economic and environmental efficiencies
- To provide a bridge to concerned countries and projects to achieve a better understanding of developments on international CCS technology and policy developments
- To provide the potential for an investment vehicle to effectively manage the funding of CCS and emission reduction costs fairly across the key stakeholders

There are different models of PPPs for CCS depending on the depth and scope of the partnerships. These are:

1. Life-cycle PPPs which encompass the entire chain of a new product or technology development commencing from RD and proceeding to the phases of generation of new technology, its protection, testing and assessment, demonstration, customization, scale-up and commercialization,

awareness and capacity building, and continual improvement. A variant of the life-cycle approach is the approach of the Alberta Development Council in Canada that has provided an enabling policy environment for the setting-up of new large-scale industrial facilities for capture of CO_2, enabled formulation of plans for large-scale facilities to be "capture-ready". It is also undertaking steps to meet emissions reduction milestones through "firm-specific" CCS plans and policy approaches to secure finances to build CO_2 infrastructure and set up R&D and demonstration projects.

2. Segmented PPPs where a segment of the life-cycle is taken up for partnerships. Segmented PPPs include the following variants:
   - PPPs in R&D through joint R&D efforts to develop new technologies at the "lab" or "bench scale" or conduct R&D for adaptation or customization of technologies that have been developed. Joint R&D involves joint sharing of IPRs and share in commercial development or customization of the products.
   - Post Innovation Partnerships involving commercial scale-up of technologies by the proprietor firm (which holds IP on the technology) with the support of the government or special-purpose vehicles set up by the government.
   - Post Innovation Partnerships, whereby a consortium of firms join hands with the government agency or its special-purpose vehicles, to source the appropriate technology from the vendors, customize it, demonstrate its working and upgrade it for commercial scale-up.
   - PPPs that exist to carry out enabling activities of capacity building, technology assessment, risk assessment, demonstration, and awareness building (MacFarland *et al.*, 2006)

The choice of a PPP model will determine the choice of the business model and the structure of financial mechanisms that are designed to provide financial support for the technology or the product.

In the light of the lessons learnt from existing cases of CCS PPPs, the following challenges emerge:

1. The challenge of developing joint products is still to be addressed in a systematic manner. As CCS is a costly option, revenue streams need to be broader and more diverse to cover costs. Apart from the possibility of CCS–CER linkages, one has to see how CO_2 that is captured can have a secondary reuse such as "enhanced gas recovery" in oil fields that face reserve drawdown as was noted in the case of the Altmark gas field.

2. The second challenge is to utilize public CCS funding and programmes to facilitate transfer of technology and enable risk assessments and capacity building.

3. The third challenge is to integrate programme-based approaches to project development in CCS or facilitate programme–project Linkage for sounder PPPs in pre-innovation and post-innovation R&D.
4. Further R&D work is required to develop cost-effective technologies in capture, transport and storage of CO_2 involving inter-agency approaches taking a cue from Australia's cooperative research centre for greenhouse gas technologies (CO2CRC).
5. PPP-based R&D work to support non-incremental breakthrough in research needs to be taken up to improve the economic viability and safety of CCS technologies; this involves international agencies such as CSLF and national public R&D centres and private industry.
6. Setting up a "Technology Exchange" for disseminating information on CCS technologies, their safety features and results of demonstration exercises on CCS in various parts of the world. As technology choice is a tricky issue for CCS-seeking entities, there is need for information on these technologies. The idea of the exchange is to match the buyer with the best seller. For instance, Norway has developed a system of seeking bidding for CCS technologies to enable pick-up of the best technologies. A global system of bidding for CCS technologies is essential in order for CCS technologies to find a successful application.
7. An IPR facilitation system that promotes joint patents for inventions that arise from PPPs and also informs stakeholders of the type and range of rights over CCS technologies over which patents have been obtained.

10.4 Business models and cost–benefit analysis

It is reckoned that investments in R&D on clean energy technologies are of the order of \$16.3 billion. Of this, private funding of clean energy technologies is estimated to be \$10.5 billion. This is only a fraction of the funds devoted to conventional energy sources and just 2% of overall energy R&D (IPCC, 2008; McKinsey and Company, 2008). A good business model should be able to leverage more financial resources that can raise the scale of resources available to spend on clean energy technologies (McKinsey and Company, 2008). More significantly, it is important to raise the level of public funding in CCS technologies on account of the fact that private investors are not willing to crowd in due to the technology not yet being proven.

There are three business models that promote transfer of technologies.

1. Purchase of technologies by dedicated financing mechanisms for transfer to end users

2. Licensing in of technologies through dedicated financing mechanisms for transfer to end-users
3. Joint ventures that promote transfer and commercialization of technologies

The typology of technology transfer varies. The early phase of technology transfer involves transfer of know-how and prototypes developed initially and tested out through pilot demonstration exercises. In "later phase technology transfer", the technology transferred can be one that has crossed pilot and post-pilot phase (or pre-commercial demonstration that needs fine-tuning and customization at the end-user level, before commercial running).

The early-phase transfer may be in the form of transfer of designs in the form of drawings of processes, equipment and material specifications. In the case of CCS, transfer entails process description and specifications of equipment configuration and material specifications. In some cases, while knowledge is transferred in this manner, the know-how about critical components is withheld and sold separately in an embodied form. As has been the experience with non-CCS-enabled IGCC technology in India, the general tendency was for designs, core processes and components to be protected with IPRs. The same situation may occur for CCS-enabled IGCC as well.

Either way, the supply price at which technologies belonging to the first and later phases are transferred can be high, the latter being higher than the former on account of more advanced demo plant installation and running.

There are three models for effecting transfer of CCS technologies. These are outright purchase, licensing of technologies, and formation of joint ventures between donor and recipient (Damodaran, 2010).

In the **purchase model**, the CCS technology and its associated IPRs are purchased or imported upfront by making a down-payment that covers the supply price of the technology (Ibid). In this system, what matters is the supply price of CCS technologies, which is as below:

- Supply price = Sunk costs + Patent-related expenses + Return on capital + Premium

Thus the supply price of technology is the cumulative value of sunk costs that firms/vendors spend on R&D, costs of filing and obtaining a patent (along with costs on redressing infringement challenges), if any, and a margin or premium for the quality of the invention, apart from profits.

Some calculations based on data provided by IEA on demo plant costs provide the following estimates of supply prices for pre-combustion CCS technologies:

- Supply price of early-stage technologies = Demo expenses + Pure R&D expenses + IP-related expenses = \$1.25 billion + \$ 0.25 billion = \$1.5 billion
- Supply price of late-stage technologies = Demo expenses + Pure R&D expenses + IP-related expenses = \$1.5 billion per later pre-commercial demo + Rs 0.75 billion = \$2.25 billion

It goes without saying that the supply price of commercial technologies will be more than the levels indicated above.

The above prices are on the high side and beyond the reach of normal utilities that desire to carry further customization and research prior to commercialization. Revenue streams are likely to be delayed for some years while sunk costs are to be incurred, resulting in negative cost–benefit ratios (Damodaran, 2008, 2010).

From the point of view of the supplier, there are two options vis-à-vis taking the technology through its evolution stage from pre-commercial to commercial phase (something that majors like Siemens will attempt to do), selling the technology at its early phase, or seeking a partner to take it to through the pre-commercial and commercial phases. In the latter case, the mode is taking up joint research projects which will transform to a JV that carries out future "commercial production" based on share capital pooling and profit sharing. A major company like Siemens will go through both processes alone.

The advantage of selling an early-phase technology upfront is that it transfers risks of technology and market failure to the buyer. At the same time, the downside for the supplier is the loss of the option of tapping future commercial benefits that exceed expectations.

Licensing is the alternative many innovators prefer as it enables the inventor to retain ownership rights, while assuring them a royalty (variable rate normally linked to sales or turnover) or licence fee (fixed or specific in nature) which can cover a share in equity of the recipient company, absorb patent costs (including costs of transfer of patents and technical know-how), the cost or a share in future revenues besides ensuring commercial development in terms of a viable business plan. Licensing transactions may include upfront payments, milestone payments and royalties on sales.

Licence systems can be broadly categorized into two groups: "exclusive" and "non-exclusive". By nature, non-exclusive licences are low-cost and are preferred by innovators who would like to enter an important market where IPR laws are less tight either in terms of legal rights or enforcement. This limitation is more than offset by increased market size and penetration.

An exclusive licence operates in a market where IPRs are well protected. Much depends on how licence agreements are worked out. For a technology like CCS which is expected to contribute to the conservation of a global public good like climate, it is important to ensure that licence agreements are based on fair and concessional terms. (Damodaran, 2010).

In the model of centralized technology transfer—an Indian company such as BHEL acquiring CCS technology from tech provider—instead of payment of a huge upfront amount, a licensing model can be followed for payment. In this model, a certain percentage of revenue garnered from carbon credits can be given as royalty to the technology provider (Alam, 1999). The royalty payments, hence, would depend on value of carbon credits generated.

A **joint venture** (JV) is a business entity that is premised on partnership between partners, either private or public–private, to pursue a business agenda involving a technology, product or service (Alam, 1999). A JV can partake of a consortium of players including host-company institutions and power utilities which collaborate with overseas technology vendor entities or firms to form a company that researches, develops and sells CCS technologies. The financial resources of a JV are mobilized by the partners and denominated in shareholdings, while the task of managing the entity is jointly undertaken by partners through staff members designated or appointed by them. JVs tap complementary knowledge and information and capture learning value. The ability of a technology receiving firm to utilize the resource depends not just on learning but its ability to conduct research on the features of the technology from the point of view of its application. It may happen that, in this process of research, the recipient firm may alter or reconfigure the technology to suit its application environment. To this extent it is important for a JV to have its own R&D set-up. The second advantage of a JV is that, by contributing to the development of complementary skills, it can tap into economies of scale. This, in effect, ensures that more than one product can be created by a JV at costs that are competitive. Thus while pre- or post-combustion capture can be ensured by a transferred technology, the competencies in transport and storage can be best achieved by the recipient partner, which may have scope to achieve economies in the latter segments. Economies of scope enhance cost competitiveness and ensure faster acceptability of a complex technology that has multiple processes and outcomes. Finally a JV has the ability to smooth the process of technology internalization by the recipient firm or country by creating conditions for local learning and adsorption. All the same it helps the donor to get around the charge of not being helpful in transferring the technology to the recipient by sacrificing the privileges that it enjoys as a patent holder.

JVs also enable market creation through leverage of favourable policy environment and regulations for CCS. A JV in CCS that is focused on R&D, technology development and sale in the form of services and equipment in CCS enables sharing of sunk costs and capital investment on demonstration plants (both pre-commercial or commercial), sharing of risks of failure, shared revenue streams from joint patents, besides enabling better conditions of realization of benefits from patents and their working. However, in the case of CCS technologies, it is important that JVs that focus on applied R&D are taken up as the critical challenge is in demonstration, customization and fine-tuning of technologies from an integrated life-cycle perspective which encompasses capture, transport and storage. The critical issue is for such a JV to have competencies in mapping its commercialization options and broker buy-in to the R&D programme.

JVs have proved to be contentious in the development of pre-commercial technologies through scale-up plants. The experience of BHEL India with NTPC indicates that sharing of IPRs on joint research has been an issue. But parcelling of risks is a great incentive and overcomes all other hurdles. Either way, CCS technologies cannot gravitate to commercial levels unless power utilities come forward to test them and agree to do joint research on customization. Large power utility conglomerates will be happy to enter into joint R&D deals provided these technologies offer the maximum likelihood of success. A multilateral facility that assesses technologies in a robust manner and absorbs part of pure R&D costs and costs on demos besides patent and non-patent royalties can promote joint R&D on mature technologies.

10.5 The structure and operations of dedicated financing mechanisms for CCS

A dedicated financial mechanism for financing CCS technologies is called for on account of the following factors: (a) CCS technologies are evolving and yet to reach the stage where they are due for deployment in multi-locational applications. They need to be tested comprehensively and demonstrated conclusively at the centres where they have evolved and been commercially deployed before they are considered for transfer and commercial application in countries that have lower levels of financial and technological capabilities and do not mitigate obligations under the Kyoto Protocol on Climate Change. (b) The risks of technological and economic failure can be costly in terms of investment resources. This raises the probability of high "sunk" costs that are to be made and forgotten (Damodaran, 2010). This also raises the burden of costs on developed countries who plan to invest in these technologies. (c) The need for customization and adaptation of CCS is high as it is plant-specific, energy-feedstock-specific when it comes to capture, and "eco-system-specific" when it comes to transport and storage. (d) The implication of (c) is that CCS technologies call for a variety of multi-sectoral and multi-locational demonstration plants in developing countries even when they pass muster in the developed world.

All the same, unlike the Multilateral Funding Mechanism of the Montreal Protocol (Kelly, 2004; Luken *et al.*, 2006), the challenge of a dedicated fund for CCS is more daunting. The issue here is transforming the production system of large numbers of power, oil and chemical utilities which form the infrastructure backbone of developing economies. Any change in production process that has increased cost implications can have macro multiplier impacts on the economy as a whole. This is a tall order when compared to the narrow scope of the Montreal Protocol financial mechanism (Damodaran, 2010; Porter *et al.*, 2007). The need is for collective approaches to ensure operationalization of CCS technologies (Amey, 2008).

For the reasons mentioned, a dedicated CCS financing mechanism calls for leveraging funding sources and commitments that are "new" and "additional" to existing global environmental funding facilities like dedicated climate funds of multilateral agencies such as the EBRD, the World Bank and the GEF which focus mainly on incremental cost financing and related capacity building programmes. The priority for the industry end-users of CCS technologies is to have a stockpile of technologies that are technically sound, smoothly scalable and financially viable

(Scott, 2008). The end-users also need to be enabled to map technology options based on the inventory, and to make informed choices of technologies that pass the technology and risk assessment tests. In order to ensure that the supply price and technology configurations are optimal, a process of matching the best buyer with the best seller (vendor) is essential. The transaction costs associated with transfer of technology and related IPRs need to be absorbed by a dedicated financial mechanism considering the fact that CCS technologies do not operate in a seller's market. Development of customized technologies that are suited to the finer needs of the user facility is a basic requirement. This means that support for redesign of technologies is necessary. Pre-commercial demonstration plants are essential to achieve this result and these call for financial support preferably on concessional basis. Post-commercial demos are also important to test commercial scale technologies from the technical, financial and risk assessment perspectives. Finally, the business models associated with technology transfer require careful negotiations of contracts, whatever be the model—licensing, purchase or joint ventures. A financial mechanism that facilitates pre-project enabling activities, project financing and post-project activities and also brokers technology transfer is the requirement from the point of view of a user facility.

The priority insofar as CCS goes is to develop and put in place a financial mechanism that has three dimensions or windows: (1) Innovation Financing that supports development and demonstration of new technologies (2) a Technical Assistance Window that funds information dissemination about the results arising from the functioning of demonstration plants, capacity building, technical assessments and demonstration plants and (3) a Project Financing window that is based on incremental cost financing. While the first two windows need to be funded by grants, the latter window can involve grants and soft loans, since the project financing scheme is premised on the principle of leveraging private finances.

By nature, being multilateral, the financing facility should operate within the framework of the FCCC objectives and seek guidance from the Conference of Parties on investment policies, criteria and key assessment issues. As is the case with the Montreal Protocol Multilateral Financing Facility, an Executive Committee needs to be constituted to run the fund in terms of operational policies, guidelines and administrative arrangements, including the disbursement of resources for the purpose of achieving the objectives of the Multilateral Fund. The Executive Committee could involve members of the CSLF and donors and representatives of Multilateral Development Financing Institutes. The Executive Committee will be assisted by a Secretariat.

The Multilateral Fund shall be financed by contributions from Annexure 1 countries, bilateral and multilateral agencies. Contributions by other Parties including private sector and private foundations need to be welcomed. Finances will be "new" and "additional" to existing flows that exist for redressing multilateral environmental agreements and climate change.

A trust fund approach may be adopted as is the case with the GEF and the Montreal Protocol MLF insofar as management of finances is concerned. The systems of governance of the trust fund need to be transparent and accountable with periodic reporting to the executive committee. The facility should have freedom to raise revenues by way of fee for services provided. This may include management fees, etc.

An umbrella grant agreement approach as has been adopted for the Montreal Protocol MLF is important for the proposed CCS financing facility as it reduces the duration of the total project cycle and is less cumbersome, yields greater outcomes and is effective. In the case of the CCS financing facility a similar umbrella grant facility is also desirable. This is because it permits greater integration with national priorities and guarantees greater likelihood of success for the projects. Indeed, the adoption of the umbrella grant approach is premised on acceptance of CCS as a desirable technology under the FCCC and the Kyoto Protocol.

Demonstration projects can provide critical data and guidelines for CO_2 storage monitoring and verification practices. Both pre-commercial and commercial demonstration CCS projects need to be funded. These projects need to be carried out in diverse storage sites.

The flow chart of the facility in terms of its processes is presented in Figure 10.1. The activities of the facility can be categorized into three: "Pre-project", "Project" and "Post-project" activities. Pre-project activities include operating innovation funds to co-finance joint inter-country and inter-institutional joint research on new and promising CCS technologies, fund pre-commercial demonstration plants to test lab-generated technologies, disseminate information of the functioning of plants in developing countries, provide technical assistance to enable risk assessment, technical assessment and regulatory regimes over new CCS technologies, disseminate information on operations of demonstration plants and capacity building for operating technologies at the plant level and carrying out technical and risk assessments. The commercial phase activities of the mechanism will include project financing by way of incremental costs financing and facilitating contracts for transfer of technology through purchase, licensing or promoting joint ventures. The post-project activities of the fund will include monitoring and evaluation of projects from the point of view of CO_2 leakages from storage points, laying down thresholds of standards on leakage and non-leakage-related emissions, and operation of a clearinghouse mechanism for disseminating information on various technologies that are available and operational, including their successes and failures. Figure 10.2 details the operational flows of the facility in terms of its governance structure. As may be seen from this figure, the UNFCCC is positioned as the apex body for the purposes of the facility in terms of its policy and guidance functions. A similar position on the functioning of the Trust Fund will be submitted by the fiduciary agency to the Executive Committee for their approval. Finally, as can be inferred from Figure 10.2, the financing facility should facilitate intermediation between commercial entities by enabling business-to-business interactions for exchange of technologies and know-how.

Figure 10.1 **Governance structure for the proposed financing mechanism for CCS**

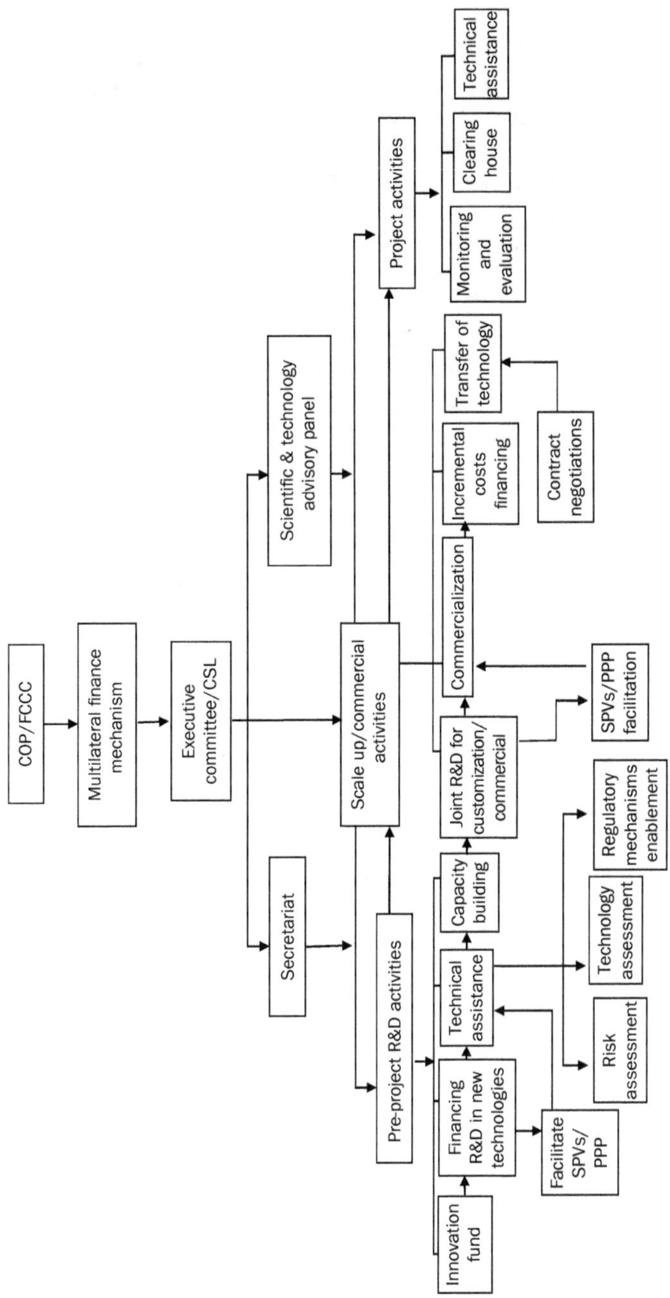

Figure 10.2 **Processes connected with the proposed CCS financial mechanism**

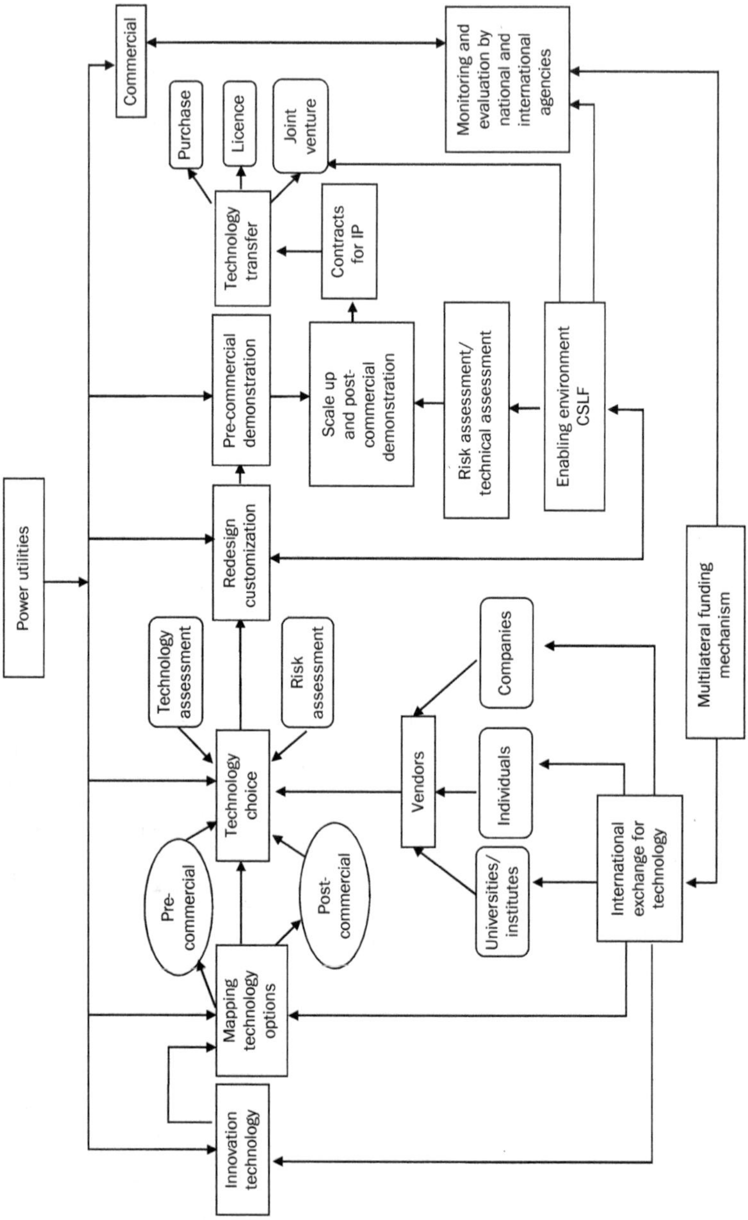

10.6 Conclusion: implications for India

Despite emphasis on renewables, the world continues to use coal in a major way. India is short in power generation and counts on coal as the chief energy source. This is also the case with China. Unlike India, China has used CCS demonstration plants in Tianjin and in Inner Mongolia to capture and store CO_2. However, unless these demonstration plants are replicated on a large scale, it is doubtful as to whether CCS technologies will be tested and commercially upscaled on a wider basis. The main argument developed in this chapter is that, through enabling business models and global financing systems for these technologies that respect legitimate Intellectual Property Rights over these technologies, it is possible to cushion technological and financial risks associated with CCS technologies and create an evolutionary process from first-generation to third-generation CCS technologies. India can take the first steps towards "CCS-readiness" by developing and testing viable protocols and techniques of risk assessment before technologies are pretested for their economic and technological sustainability. In the ultimate analysis, joint R&D and testing holds promise for CCS technologies to be tried out in Asia. Such approaches raise the stake of developing countries in the evolution and development of the technology. This could then be the basis for CCS technologies to take both social and economic roots in India.

References

Alam, G. (1999, October). A study of the transfer of environmentally sound technologies to India, Seminar on Accessing environmental friendly technologies within the within the context of MEAs, UNCTAD-IIPM, Bangalore.

Amey, A. (2008). Carbon capture and storage: The need for a longer-term collective approach to implementation. Retrieved from www.climatechangecentral.com/files/attachments/DiscussionPapers/C3_CCS_DiscussionPaper.pdf.

Anonymous (2013). Carbon Sequestration Leadership Forum Technology Roadmap 2013. Retrieved from www.cslforum.org/publications/documents/CSLF_Technology_Roadmap_2013.pdf.

Anonymous (2009a, 5 March). Carbon capture and storage: Trouble in store. *The Economist*. Retrieved from, www.economist.com/displaystory.cfm?STORY_ID=13226661.

Anonymous (2009b). Position paper of the EU power plant suppliers on knowledge sharing in the framework of CCS demonstration. Retrieved from www.eppsa.org/fileadmin/user_upload/EPPSA_Publications/ZEP_Knowledge_Sharing_28_April_-_final.pdf.

Anonymous (2009c). What are the costs and benefits of Carbon Capture and Sequestration? Retrieved from www.netl.doe.gov/technologies/carbon_seq/FAQs/benefits.html.

Anonymous (2008a). Climate change: Technology development and technology transfer. Prepared for the Beijing High-level Conference on Climate Change: Technology Development and Technology Transfer Beijing, China, 7–8 November 2008. Retrieved from www.ccchina.gov.cn/WebSite/CCChina/UpFile/File370.pdf.

Anonymous (2008b). EU demonstration programme for CO_2 capture and storage, ZEP's proposal, European technology platform for zero emission fossil fuel power plants (ZEP), November.

Anonymous (2003). Transfer of environmentally sound technologies from developed countries to developing countries, Background Document for the Ad Hoc Expert Group on Finance and Environmentally Sound Technologies, The Secretariat of the United Nations Forum on Forests. Retrieved from www.un.org/esa/forests/pdf/aheg/finance-tests/f-tests_background-indufor.pdf.

Damodaran, A (2010). Carbon dioxide capture and storage: Intellectual Property Rights, business models and multilateral financing mechanisms for transfer of technology: An exploratory analysis. Technical Report -1/EFGPG/2010, IIMB.

Damodaran, A. (2008). Carbon Capture and Storage: India's Concerns. CSLF Financial Issues Task Force Meeting, New Delhi, India, 2–3 December 2008.

Damodaran, A. (2000). Implications of international conventions and opportunities for transfer of environmentally sound technologies to developing countries. Proceedings of Ad-hoc Expert Group Meeting on Promotion of New Forms of Financing for Transfer, Development and Application Environmentally Sound Technologies, United Nations Economic and Social Commission for Asia and the Pacific/UNAPCTT, New Delhi, 15–17 November 2000.

Dechezleprêtre, A., Glachant, M., Hascic, I., Johnstone, N., and Ménière, Y. (2008). Invention and transfer of climate change mitigation technologies on a global scale: A Study drawing on patent data. Retrieved from www.cerna.ensmp.fr/index.php?option=com_content&task=view&id=192&Itemid=288.

IEA (International Energy Agency) (2006a) Global energy technology perspectives. Retrieved from www.iea.org.

IEA GHG (International Energy Agency Greenhouse Gas Research and Development Programme) (2007). Expert workshop on Carbon Capture and Storage: Barriers and solutions. Technical Study, 2007/9, July and 2007, UK.

IPCC (Intergovernmental Panel on Climate Change) (2005). *IPCC Special Report on Carbon Dioxide Capture and Storage.* Prepared by Working Group III of the Intergovernmental Panel on Climate. Cambridge: Cambridge University Press.

Johnstone, H. (2009). The time is now: Carbon capture and storage. *Power Engineering International.* Retrieved from pepei.pennnet.com/display_article /362123/17/ARTCL/none/none/1/The-time-is-now:-carbon-capture-and-storage.

Kelly, L. (2004). *The Multilateral Fund for the Implementation of the Montreal Protocol: Addressing Challenges of Globalization: An Independent Evaluation of the World Bank's Approach to Global Programs.* Washington, DC: The World Bank Operations Evaluation Department.

Lemley, M.A. (2002). Intellectual Property Rights and standard-setting organizations. *California Law Review,* 90, 1889.

Luken, R., and Grof, T. (2006). Montreal Protocol's multilateral fund and sustainable development. *Ecological Economics,* 56(2), 241-255.

McFarland, J.R., and Herzog, H.J. (2006). Incorporating Carbon Capture and Storage technologies in integrated assessment models. *Energy Economics,* 28(5–6), 632-652.

McKinsey and Company (2008). Carbon Capture and Storage: Assessing the economics. Retrieved from www.mckinsey.com/clientservice/ccsi/pdf/ccs_assessing_the_economics.pdf.

Scott, M. (2008). Clean Energy R&D: The returns on investment. Retrieved from www.climatechangecorp.com.

Porter, G., Bird, N., Kaur, N., and Peskett, L. (2008). *New Finance for Climate Change and the Environment.* Washington, DC: WWF and the Böll Foundation.

Schwartz, R.G., and Bollmann, F.G.E. (2007). Choose wisely: How IP value depends on R&D strategy. Retrieved from www.buildingipvalue.com/07KTI/p.67-71%20Duff%20&%20Phelps.pdf.

Watson, J. (2012). Carbon Capture and Storage: Realising the potential? Retrieved from www.ukerc.ac.uk.

About the authors

Venkatachalam Anbumozhi is a Senior Economist at the Economic Research Institute for ASEAN and East Asia (ERIA), Indonesia. His previous positions include Capacity Building Specialist at Asian Development Bank Institute, Assistant Professor at the University of Tokyo, Senior Policy Researcher at the Institute for Global Environmental Strategies and Assistant Manager in Pacific Consultants International, Tokyo. He has published several books, authored numerous research articles and produced many project reports on natural resource management, climate-friendly infrastructure design, and private sector participation in Green Growth. Anbumozhi was invited as a member of the APEC Expert Panel on Green Climate Finance and the ASEAN Panel for promoting climate-resilient growth. He has taught Resource Management, International Cooperation and Development Finance at the University of Tokyo and has speaking engagements at some of the leading international organizations. He obtained his PhD from the University of Tokyo.

Indranil Chakraborty is the Director in the office of the Directorate General of Civil Aviation (DGCA), Ministry of Civil Aviation. He has more than 20 years of aviation experience, including aircraft design and aviation environment.

A. Damodaran is Professor of Economics and Social Sciences at the Indian Institute of Management, Bangalore. He also holds the Ministry of Human Resources Development Chair on IPRs. As well as consulting for multilateral development banks, he has extensively published on climate and biodiversity financing and on the economics of IPRs in relation to technology transfer of environmentally sound technologies.

Somnath Debnath received a BSc with Honours in Physics from the University of Calcutta, India, an MBA from Walden University, USA, and an MTech in Business Systems from Swinburne University of Technology, Australia. He earned a PhD in the field of Management from Birla Institute of Technology, India, with a dissertation exploring the need for environmental accounting systems and their role in improving corporate decision-making processes. He is also a Certified Management Accountant (CMA) and a Fellow (FCMA) of the Institute of Cost Accountants of India. He has extensive service and consulting experience in the fields of cost management, process automations and ERP implementations. His research interests include the areas of management accounting, green accounting, green IS/IT, and decision sciences. He can be reached at sndebnath@yahoo.co.in.

Anil Kumar Dikshit is Professor in the Centre for Environmental Science and Engineering at the Indian Institute of Technology, Bombay, India. He completed his graduation and master's in civil engineering in 1985 and 1987, respectively and a PhD in civil and environmental engineering from Cornell University, USA in 1994. The areas of his interest in teaching are environmental systems planning and management; environmental impact assessment; water supply and wastewater engineering; environmental engineering; and solid and biomedical waste management, and areas of research interest include environmental infrastructure and clean technology; urban solid waste management, environmental modeling, optimization and sustainability; and GIS applications to water and environment related problems. He has more than 25 years of experience in teaching, research and consultancy at IIT Kanpur, Cornell University, IIT Kharagpur and IIT Bombay.

Lalit Gupta is the Joint Director General of the Directorate General of Civil Aviation (DGCA), Ministry of Civil Aviation. He has more than 30 years of aviation experience varying from aircraft design and development, flight safety, flight operations, air transportation and aviation environment. He is also a member on various Committees of the Bureau of Indian Standards assisting in development of standards pertaining to aviation-related products.

P.D. Jose is Professor of Corporate Strategy and Policy at the Indian Institute of Management Bangalore. His research interests include sustainability, corporate social responsibility and governance issues, strategy formulation and implementation, change management, crisis management and organizational renewal. Jose is a Fellow of the Indian Institute of Management, Ahmedabad. He is a visiting faculty at University of Goteborg's Business School. He has also consulted with several government agencies, state governments, international agencies and private sector organizations on issues related to corporate strategy as well as sustainability.

Panagiotis Karamanos served in the framework of the European Union–India Civil Aviation Cooperation Project, as the Senior Environmental Expert to the DGCA on noise, climate change and other environmental issues. For more than a decade he managed the Environmental Services Department at Athens International Airport, while he chaired the Task Force of Airports Council International (ACI)-Europe which developed *Airport Carbon Accreditation*, the only global standard for carbon management for airports. He currently leads the EU Technical Cooperation for Environment in India project.

R.K. Mishra, Senior Professor and Director, Institute of Public Enterprise, India is a graduate of International Management Programme, SDA Bocconi, Milan, Italy. He was a fellow of the British Council and Commonwealth Secretariat and a member of the UN International Task Force on Standards of Excellence in Public Administration.

Gurudas Nulkar is an entrepreneur turned academician by profession and ecologist by choice. He is an adjunct faculty at the Symbiosis Center for Management & HRD in India. His research interests include environmental sustainability and eco-entrepreneurship. He is a trustee of the Ecological Society, an NGO involved in ecological education and research in socio-economic conservation practices.

Michael O'Connor is the Manager of the Environmental Services Department of Athens International Airport in Greece where he has accrued more than 10 years of experience in climate change and local air quality issues. He also served as a Senior Environmental Expert to the European Union–India Civil Aviation Cooperation Project on environmental issues on a part-time basis.

Prem Pangotra is a Professor at the Indian Institute of Management, Ahmedabad. He specializes in urban management, urban economics, environment management and public finance. He has done research on urban development strategies, urban quality of life comparisons and urban infrastructure planning. He has served on expert committees of the Government of India and the Government of Gujarat in the urban sector. He has also been a consultant to several local governments and international organizations involved in urban development. He holds a PhD from University of Wisconsin, USA.

Saurabh Saraf is a consultant with Bioplus, and has extensive experience in the Indian environment and energy sector. He founded and assisted start-ups in the cleantech domain. Currently he is leading the development of integrated resource management solution for high-density urban slums. He has also been involved in independent consulting assignments with the Swedish Energy Agency, Asian Development Bank and other agencies concerning development and implementation of cleantech innovations. He is an Erasmus Mundus scholar and graduated with a MS in Environmental Sciences, Policy and Management (MESPOM) from Lund University, Sweden and Central European University, Hungary, for which he was awarded full scholarship.

Shulagna Sarkar is Assistant Professor, Institute of Public Enterprise, India. She has worked in the areas of Corporate Social Responsibility, baseline surveys, impact assessment and green HRM in India. Her areas of interest include CSR, green HRM, and environmental competencies.

Shabari Shaily is an Indian Architect based in Johannesburg, South Africa, and a certified IGBC Accredited Professional and GRIHA Evaluator and Trainer. She is an independent Sustainability Consultant and previously worked as Senior Environmental Analyst at *VK:e environmental*, Pune. Her specialization relates to Sustainable Master Planning and Architecture Design, Green Building Certification Facilitation, Affordable Housing Developments, Environmental Impact Assessment and Management Planning, Building Energy and Thermal Comfort Modelling, Natural Resource Management and Renewable Energy Systems. She holds an MSc in Advanced Sustainability of Built Environment from the University of Dundee (UK), and is a regular author on eco-neighbourhood development, and on cost-effective and sustainable vernacular architecture.

Priyadarshi R. Shukla is a Professor at the Indian Institute of Management, Ahmedabad. He has been lead author of several international reports on energy, environment, climate change and development. He was a member of the Indian delegation to the UNFCCC COP8 and COP9. He is currently the Co-chair of Working Group III of the IPCC. He has co-authored 14 books and numerous publications in reputed international journals. He holds a PhD from Stanford University, USA.

Punam Singh, Assistant Professor, Institute of Public Enterprise, India, is a Management graduate from the Indian School of Mines, Dhanbad. Her area of research includes Corporate Social Responsibility, baseline studies, impact assessment studies and environmental management. She has published books and papers in the area of CSR.

Rajesh Kumar Singh is Managing Director of thinkstep Sustainability Solutions Pvt Ltd, a subsidiary of thinkstep (formerly PE INTERNATIONAL), Germany. He has over 23 years' experience in the areas of environmental management, life-cycle assessment, corporate sustainability management and reporting, policy and strategy formulation and carbon footprinting. He holds a bachelor's degree in Civil Engineering and master's in Environment Engineering from IIT, Kharagpur and a doctorate in Sustainability Management from IIT Bombay. Before starting the Indian subsidiary of thinkstep, for 18 years Dr Rajesh was part of SAIL, the largest steel company in India. In the area of sustainability, he has multi-sector expertise and exposure including steel, aluminum, glass, energy, textile, agriculture, packaging, automobile, chemicals, buildings, and FMCG sectors.

Rohit Thakur is the Assistant Director in the office of the Directorate General of Civil Aviation (DGCA), Ministry of Civil Aviation. He has more than eight years of aviation experience in various fields, including aircraft design, aircraft production, air transportation and aviation environment.

For Product Safety Concerns and Information please contact our EU
representative GPSR@taylorandfrancis.com
Taylor & Francis Verlag GmbH, Kaufingerstraße 24, 80331 München, Germany

www.ingramcontent.com/pod-product-compliance
Lightning Source LLC
LaVergne TN
LVHW022314150926
848178LV00003B/64

* 9 7 8 1 7 8 3 5 3 0 8 4 7 *